NATURAL CHILD CARE

NATURAL CHILD CARE

A Complete Guide to Safe and Effective
Herbal Remedies and Holistic Health
Strategies for Infants and Children

by Maribeth Riggs

Foreword by Elson M. Haas, M.D.

Herb Illustrations by Elizabeth Garsonnin

HARMONY BOOKS/NEW YORK

Publisher's Note: This book contains recipes of herbal remedies for minor childhood disorders to be used in the context of a children's holistic health program. However, certain of the ingredients may cause an allergic reaction in some individuals, so reasonable care in the preparations is advised. The recipes in this book are not intended as a substitute for professional medical advice.

Published by Harmony Books, a division of Crown Publishers, Inc., 225 Park Avenue South, New York, New York 10003

HARMONY and colophon are trademarks of Crown Publishers, Inc. Manufactured in the United States of America

Library of Congress Cataloging-in-Publication Data

Riggs, Maribeth
Natural child care

Includes Index.
1. Herbs — Therapeutic use. 2. Medicine — Formulae, receipts, prescriptions. 3. Children — Diseases — Treatment. 4. Child care. 5. Holistic medicine. I. Title.
RM222.2.R53 1989   649'.4   88-24694
ISBN 0-517-56831-4

10 9 8 7 6 5 4 3 2 1

FIRST EDITION

F Y
PRODUCTIONS

This book is dedicated to the memory of

Georgene Alexander Sinclair Riggs

"Give her of the fruit of her hands;
and let her own works praise her in the gates."
Proverbs 31:31

ACKNOWLEDGEMENTS

I would like to express my sincere thanks and appreciation to Stephanie Rick, Esther Mitgang, Grace Ricco-Pena, and Melissa Schwarz for their help and guidance throughout the preparation of this book; and to my friend Rita Aero, who encouraged me with foresight, sensitivity, and skill.

CONTENTS

FOREWORD
by Elson M. Haas, M.D.

Author of *Staying Healthy With The Seasons* and
Staying Healthy: The Complete Guide to Diet and Nutritional Medicine.
Medical Director, Marin Clinic of Preventive Medicine and Health Education,
San Rafael, California.

I am very impressed with *Natural Child Care*. It provides clear, informative, and responsible reviews of most common pediatric problems, many of which, I believe, are applicable to adults as well. *Natural Child Care* then offers safe, inexpensive, and historically-proven herbal remedies for these problems.

This commonsense book is filled with practical, educational health information and is a valuable contribution to the health of the entire family. It brings the primary healing force and responsibility back into the home, and empowers parents and children to use a true healing system available since mankind's early beginnings — herbal medicine. The medical philosophy, "let the plants be your medicine," offers all people and countries of the world an effective way to care for themselves.

I have been interested in herbal medicine therapy for two decades. Many current pharmaceutical drugs are based primarily on the research and knowledge gained from the original healing use of plants. *Natural Child Care* offers us the chance to use nature's own remedies to maintain health and treat the most common problems that arise within families and among friends. At the same time, readers are clearly guided as to when to contact a doctor and how to obtain important medical care.

This responsible approach allows me to feel very good about recommending *Natural Child Care* to parents. I believe it is a valuable contribution to the self-care field and brings the knowledge and application of herbal medicine back into the family unit. This is clearly a book I want available for my patients, and at my fingertips on my home bookshelf. I am sure that my family and I will use it throughout the coming years.

INTRODUCTION

My longtime interest in medicinal herbs took a new direction with the birth of my first child in 1977. Like any parent, I was concerned with keeping my daughter healthy, and I decided to investigate herbal remedies that could be used to enhance her health and well-being. I combined my independent study with university classes to explore further the historical and modern uses of medicinal herbs. Over the years, and with the birth of two more children, my use of herbs has become a way of life for me and my family.

I have found herbal medicine to be a fascinating and rewarding tool for maintaining my children's emotional and physical health. Herbs are natural medicines from the earth that have been cultivated and tested for tens of thousands of years. Throughout the world, and especially in the East, medical herbology is used as a regular part of health care, right along with the the most recent surgical and pharmaceutical techniques. I have found that the medicinal use of herbs can provide gentle and safe relief from childhood illness and injuries, and can help promote a child's overall health. Preparing herbal remedies at home has also allowed me to teach my children important fundamentals about caring for their bodies and learning to heal themselves.

Using herbal remedies can be a very positive emotional experience for the entire family. The genuine gratitude children express when a homemade medicine makes them feel good again will fill you with relief and pride. Together, you and your children can learn about self-health care and discover how to work with the body's natural defenses to overcome minor illnesses. After all, providing a child with a healthy and positive attitude toward life, along with a strong, uncompromised immune system, must be a parent's greatest achievement.

The preparation of homemade herbal medicines can be a lot of fun for the whole family. I have discovered that this process is sometimes the only "cure" a child needs. No special equipment is required, and many remedies can be assembled from cooking herbs and other ingredients already found in most kitchens. Most of the herbal remedies here take less than twenty minutes to prepare and many of them taste delicious (except, of course, for the ones that taste awful). My children have accompanied me eagerly on adventures to health food stores and herb shops, and on herb-foraging trips in the wilderness, and they always look forward to impromptu lessons in herbology.

Using safe and effective homemade medicines to soothe the symptoms of childhood illnesses is a priceless opportunity for you to participate in your child's healing process. When you take the time to get actively involved in your child's health care, you will soon discover, as I have, that you are able to work more effectively with health professionals. And should the need arise, you will feel far more confident about making important medical decisions for your children.

GETTING STARTED

When you decide to use herbal remedies for your children, discuss it with your pediatrician beforehand. Many doctors understand the efficacy of herbs (especially since most prescription medications were originally derived from herbal sources) and will appreciate parents who are willing to take the time to prepare herbal remedies. Doctors also take pleasure in working with a parent who knows which illnesses can be dealt with at home and which ones require a professional's care.

Herbal medicine is a natural complement to modern medicine. Herbs are generally used to relieve symptoms, while drugs are used to cure underlying disorders. Sometimes only herbal remedies are needed (as in treating the symptoms of colds) and sometimes only pharmaceuticals are effective (as in the case of serious infections). Whatever the case, one thing that is always required for healing is a positive attitude. Spend as little time as possible dealing with the negative aspects of your child's illness. For best results, maintain an attitude of strength, happiness, and zest for life.

An important part of home medicinal care is explaining the preparation process to the child who will be taking the remedy. Children need to have their thoughts, opinions, and fears carefully considered by their parents. They are naturally curious and enjoy being included in herbal projects and preparations. Before administering an herbal remedy, explain what is in the medicine, how it is made, and what it will taste or feel like. Trust and confidence play a major role in developing a child's positive attitude toward health and can even play a part in the healing process itself.

There are a dozen herbs that

LICORICE
(Glycyrrhiza glabra)

15

should be kept on hand in the medicine chest or kitchen. These are comfrey root, garlic, peppermint, raspberry leaf, slippery elm, camomile, ginger, cinnamon, agar, white willow bark, goldenseal, and licorice. These herbs can be used individually or in combination for just about any illness or condition a child (or an adult) is likely to experience. Other substances to keep in supply are spring water, beeswax, olive oil, cocoa butter, and petroleum jelly. All of these ingredients should be labeled, dated, and stored in airtight, lightproof containers, away from heat. Dark glass jars, with tight-fitting lids are ideal. *Always discard medicinal herbs after six months, unless otherwise specified.*

PEPPERMINT
(*Mentha piperita*)

The tools required for herbal medicine-making are a stainless-steel sieve, cotton cheesecloth, a wooden spoon, stainless-steel or enamel pots ranging in size from two to four quarts, a medium-size cast-iron frying pan with a lid, a kitchen scale, a blender, a coffee grinder or food mill, a good stainless-steel paring knife, and a few stainless-steel bowls of varying sizes. Never use plastic implements for preparing or storing herbal medicines. If you use enamel-lined pots, make sure the inner surface of the pot is intact.

Each of the chapters in *Natural Child Care* deals with minor illness, injuries, and behavior problems that any normal, healthy child might have. Within each chapter, infants (newborn up to ten months) and children are discussed separately. Then a selection of herbal treatments that relieve specific symptoms is recommended, accompanied by the detailed recipes for preparing them. Read each recipe all the way through before you begin. At the back of the book, you will find descriptions of the herbs and other ingredients used in the recipes, along with tips on where to buy them.

THE HERBAL MEDICINE CHEST

The herbs listed below should be kept on hand in the medicine chest. Most of them keep best in dark glass jars with tight-fitting lids. Some herbs, such as garlic or ginger root, may be kept in the kitchen and used along with your other culinary herbs and spices.

AGAR — Agar is an excellent mild laxative that bulks out and tones the lower bowel. It can also be used as a healthy, nutritious substitute for gelatin in pies and homemade gelatin desserts, and as a thickener in sauces and gravies. Keep two packages of agar sticks on hand for both medicinal and culinary use. Agar keeps well in a tightly lidded jar for up to a year, but be sure to replenish your supply after this time.

CAMOMILE — These pretty dried flower buds make an excellent beverage tea, either alone or in combination with other herbs. Camomile can also be used in poultices and washes for many different skin disorders. A strong brew of camomile tea can calm a nervous or frightened child and can also help relieve sleeplessness. Keep eight ounces of camomile buds on hand in a dark glass jar with a tight-fitting lid. Camomile flowers are very delicate, so make sure they are stored properly.

CINNAMON — Curled cinnamon sticks or chopped pieces are a good addition to cold remedies, especially hot toddies. Cinnamon bark pieces fried in oil are also very good for a chest or muscle rub. Keep a few cinnamon sticks or pieces in your medicine chest.

COMFREY ROOT — Keep about a pound of chopped, dried comfrey root pieces on hand. Comfrey is the the herb I use the most, since it is effective alone and also works well in

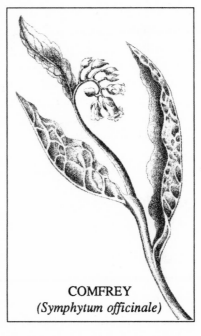

COMFREY
(*Symphytum officinale*)

combination with other herbs. Comfrey root is an excellent herb for children because it is very mild.

GARLIC — Garlic has many applications, but its primary use for children is in ear drops. Garlic oil ear drops are the most effective remedy I have discovered for ear infections. Garlic can also be used in syrups to fight off colds and prevent allergic reactions. Keep at least two or three heads of garlic in the kitchen. Use garlic in cooking as often as possible, too — it's very good for the whole family. Keep the garlic as fresh as possible, and discard it when it looks spotty or dried out.

GINGER — Ginger root is excellent in all cough and cold preparations, and can be fried in oil to make a warming chest or kidney rub. It can be used as a powder, in dried pieces, or fresh. I keep a quarter-pound of fresh root in my kitchen and about four ounces of powdered ginger root in my medicine chest. Store the powdered ginger root in a dark glass jar with a tight-fitting lid. Smell and taste the herb for its characteristic sharpness before using to be certain it is still fresh. Discard fresh ginger root when it is dried out and no longer has a strong smell.

GOLDENSEAL — Goldenseal is astringent and antiseptic, and is excellent for relieving infections and inflammations, both internally and externally. I use it as a gargle, a mouthwash for sore gums, a body detoxifier, as snuff for a runny nose, to relieve diarrhea, and to draw out boils. If there was ever an herb for all the ills that flesh is heir to, this is it. Keep four ounces of powdered goldenseal root on hand.

LICORICE — Licorice is very sweet, mildly laxative and stimulating — warming to the internal organs and soothing to the throat. As such, it is a very useful herb to have in a home with children. It can be added to yucky-tasting teas to make them more palatable and is delicious. Keep about ten six-inch-long licorice root sticks and four ounces of chopped licorice root pieces on hand. Store them separately in dark, tightly lidded jars.

PEPPERMINT — Dried peppermint leaf makes a delicious beverage tea and is an excellent bath herb, so you should keep at least a pound on hand. This herb can also be added to many different tea formulas to improve their taste, or it can be fried in oil to make a chest or muscle rub. Since I use so much of it, I keep my peppermint leaves in a cookie tin with a tight-fitting lid. Peppermint has a long shelf life if it is properly stored, so you may keep it for up to eight months. Discard any unused peppermint after that time.

RASPBERRY LEAF — Raspberry leaf is a staple in my household. I use it for upset stomachs, sore throats, nervousness, and almost all my cold remedies. Raspberry leaves are very delicate and should be stored properly in a dark glass jar with a tight-fitting lid. Keep eight ounces on hand.

SLIPPERY ELM — Slippery elm is my favorite herb for infants since it is the most gentle and benign, yet effective, herb I know. I also use slippery elm in combination with many other herbs, with good results every time. It is excellent for all gastrointestinal disorders and for minor skin wounds. Keep eight ounces of powdered slippery elm root in your herbal medicine chest. You can store it in a large dark jar with a tight-fitting lid or an airtight cookie tin.

WHITE WILLOW BARK — White willow bark is a renowned painkiller and anti-inflammatory agent. It can be added to liniments and tinctures for relieving muscle soreness, and can be brewed into a drink for almost any internal pain. White willow tea is also very good for reducing fever. Keep four ounces of white willow bark pieces in your medicine chest. If you prefer, you may also use commercially prepared willow bark tablets, which are widely available in health food stores. Make sure your child is not aspirin allergic or sensitive before administering this herb in tea or tablet form.

WHITE WILLOW
(Salix alba)

THE GLOSSARY

Alterative — A substance that gradually produces a beneficial change in the body, usually by improving the body's ability to absorb nutrients from food.

Analgesic — An orally administered medication that relieves or lessens pain.

Anodyne — A pain reliever that is usually applied externally.

Anesthetic — A substance that deadens sensation.

Anthelmintic — A substance that destroys intestinal parasites.

Antibiotic — A medication that destroys or retards the growth of microorganisms such as fungi or bacteria.

Antipyretic — A substance that reduces fever.

Antiseptic — A substance that destroys or controls the growth of microorganisms.

Antispasmodic — A substance that relaxes or prevents involuntary muscle contractions or cramps.

Aromatic — A substance that is combined with other medicines to make them more palatable. Also, an agent that helps expel intestinal gas.

Astringent — A substance that can be used internally or externally to contract tissue and reduce secretions and discharges.

Bitter — A substance that stimulates the stomach in order to increase appetite and promote digestion.

Calmative — A substance that produces a mild tranquilizing effect on the body.

Carminative — A substance that stimulates peristalsis, a muscular contraction of the intestines, and expels gas from the gastrointestinal tract.

Decoction — An extraction of mineral salts and bitter principles from roots, wood, bark, or seeds. The herb is usually boiled ten minutes or longer to extract the desired ingredients.

Demulcent — A substance with mucilaginous properties that coats and soothes irritated internal tissues, especially mucous membranes.

Diaphoretic — A substance that increases perspiration and aids the elimination of toxins through the skin.

Disinfectant — A substance that helps combat infection and prevent its spread to other individuals by destroying or arresting the growth of microorganisms in the body.

Emetic — A substance that induces vomiting.

Emollient — A substance with oily or mucilaginous qualities that softens and soothes the skin.

Expectorant — A medication that promotes the discharge of mucus from the respiratory passages.

Fomentation — A process in which a folded cloth is immersed in an infusion or decoction, and then held against the affected area. A fomentation is similar to a poultice, but is milder in its effect.

Herbal Bath — A bath to which herbal decoctions or infusions have been added. Herbal baths include full tub baths, sitz baths, and foot baths. Herbal baths should be comfortably warm, just as a normal bath would be.

Immunoglobulin — Any of a number of serum proteins produced in the human body that act as antibodies to fight infection and disease.

Infusion — A tea made by steeping herbs, rather than boiling them. This method is applied to stems, leaves, and flowers of plants in order to extract their active ingredients.

Juice — A method of extracting nutrients from plants and plant parts. This process is also good for extracting highly volatile ingredients that are usually destroyed by heat.

Laxative — A substance that stimulates evacuation of the bowels.

Nervine — A medication that produces a mildly calming and relaxing effect on the body.

Oil — A preparation made by mixing herbs with a natural oil, such as olive oil, and warming it over a low heat. This extracts the plant oils contained within the roots, leaves, and bark of many different herbs. Not to be confused with essential oils, which require chemical or alcohol solvents in processing.

Ointment — An herbal substance mixed in a base, such as petroleum jelly, cocoa butter, or beeswax, that is solid at room temperature.

Poison — A substance that is harmful or destructive when it comes in contact with living tissue.

Poultice — Bruised or crushed herbs that are applied directly to the skin. A poultice may be applied warm or cold, and can be tied in place with a cloth.

Powder — Plant parts that are ground in a coffee grinder or mortar and pestle to a fine consistency. Powders can be sprinkled or patted on externally or taken internally in capsules.

Sedative — A medication that allays irritability, distress, or nervousness in the body.

Stimulant — A medication that energizes the body by increasing the activity of physiological processes.

Sweetener — A substance added to herbal preparations to make them more palatable. Sweeteners include honey, sugar, corn syrup, molasses, and maple syrup. Sweeteners are especially useful for administering medicine to children. Infants under six months of age should be given corn syrup rather than honey to prevent exposure to bacteria that may be present in honey.

Syrup — An herbal infusion or decoction boiled with enough sugar to produce a thick, sticky base. Herbal syrups can also be made by boiling herbs in honey or maple syrup.

Tea — The general term for a fluid prepared from herbs. A tea may be boiled (a decoction) or steeped in boiled water (an infusion).

Tincture — An herbal extract made by soaking herbs in a solution of approximately 50 percent alcohol for two weeks.

Tonic — An herbal preparation that increases assimilation of nutrients and permanently invigorates specific organs or the entire body.

Vermifuge — An herbal preparation that causes intestinal parasites to be expelled. (See Anthelmintic)

Wash — A process in which a washcloth is immersed in an infusion or decoction, and while still very moist, held against the affected area. A wash is similar to a fomentation, but the cloth is wetter and more thoroughly soaks the skin.

CHAPTER ONE

COLDS

INFANTS

Sleeplessness

Head Congestion

CHILDREN

Head Congestion

Aches, Pains, and Fevers

Coughs and Lung Congestion

Sore Throats

Sleeplessness

S ooner or later your child will catch a cold. If you are fortunate, this will not happen before your child is six months old, since an infant with a cold can cause you a great deal of anxiety. Most of the time, a cold is merely an inconvenience, with few complications, and lasts only a few days. If a cold's symptoms seem to be severe or prolonged, consult and work closely with a physician or pediatric clinic to determine the best way to care for your child.

INFANTS

It is uncommon for infants under the age of three months to catch a cold, perhaps as a result of the protective immunoglobulins acquired from their mothers. Infants catch colds by becoming chilled or coming in contact with an infected person. Occasionally, an infant's immune resistance can be weakened by the stress of cutting first teeth and/or a change in diet such as weaning or the introduction of different solid foods. You will know if your infant has a cold by such symptoms as irritability, sleeplessness, restlessness during feedings, and a clear watery discharge from the nose.

It is important to keep your infant from becoming chilled. Usually, parents are aware of weather conditions and dress their infant appropriately. At night, however, infants have a way of throwing off their blankets and sleeping uncovered. When this happens they may become chilled and, in the morning, a runny nose and sour disposition will greet you.

One-piece blanket sleepers with feet make certain that infants and toddlers stay covered. Choose sleepers made of cotton or flannel, fabrics that are healthy for infants to have next to their skin at night. When infants sleep, their bodies try to sweat out the normal daily buildup of toxins. Cotton and flannel absorb and evaporate these wastes instead of recycling them back through the skin or holding their dampness next to the infant's body.

SLEEPLESS-NESS Sleep aids the body's normal healing processes. Infants normally breathe through their noses while they sleep, so if the nose is stuffy and congested, they will wake and cry during the night. If your infant

24

has a cold and will not sleep, there is a mixture you can try to help induce drowsiness.

Brandy Drops
To help put a restless baby to sleep

Preparation Time: 10 minutes
Yield: 20 treatments
Children's Enjoyment: ☺

Brandy has amazing warming and expectorant powers. In small doses, it helps relieve cold symptoms in infants and makes them feel comfortable enough to sleep. This mixture is best given just before bedtime, since it induces a restful, lengthy sleep. I've also used this recipe for treating colic with success.

> 2 tablespoons brandy
> 1/4 cup water
> 1 teaspoon light corn syrup

1. Mix the brandy, water, and corn syrup in a small pot.
2. Warm the mixture on the stove until it is tepid.
3. Remove the mixture from the stove and stir. It is now ready to use.

APPLICATION: Use a sterile dropper to put 5 drops of the slightly warm liquid under your infant's tongue whenever it is time for sleep. Hum and croon to keep the infant calm while administering the hot toddy. Don't worry if some of the mixture dribbles down the infant's chin; enough will be swallowed to make a difference. Refrigerate any unused brandy drops and reheat with each use. Discard the mixture after 1 week, or when the infant's cold is gone.

If the infant develops a fever or is listless and pale, consult with a physician.

HEAD CONGES-TION

Infants with colds are restless at feeding time. This is usually due to the difficulty they have in breathing through a clogged nose while sucking on a breast or bottle. The best way to make congested infants comfortable is to use an infant bulb aspirator to suction out as much mucus as possible from the infant's nose and throat. A vaporizer is also very effective for breaking up congestion, especially in sleeping infants. Try to get a vaporizer that has a well for oils and preparations, since the steam it produces is much more effective. A combination of oils such as eucalyptus and clove is very good, and commercial mixtures combining these and other ingredients are available in many drugstores. Room humidifiers are also good for helping relieve head congestion.

Another way to relieve infant head congestion is to use saline nose drops. Salty water will help shrink the nasal membranes and assist the drainage of mucus from the nose. If your infant's nose is so stuffy that he or she is having a lot of difficulty breathing, you can use the following recipe to help relieve the condition.

Nose Drops
To make it easier for an infant to breathe

Preparation Time: 5 minutes
Yield: 30 treatments
Children's Enjoyment: ☺

Saltwater is very good at thinning mucus in the nose, making it easier to discharge or suction out. It also helps shrink the nasal membranes so that normal breathing can be resumed. This simple remedy is excellent for infants with stuffy, runny noses owing to a cold. While this is probably enough to keep your household supplied for an entire winter, it is better to make a fresh solution with each cold.

    1 teaspoon salt
    1 cup tepid water

1. Dissolve the salt in the warm water by stirring it with a clean stainless-steel spoon.
2. When the salt is completely dissolved, the solution is ready for use.

APPLICATION: Apply 2 drops of the solution in each nostril, wait a moment, and then suction out the nostrils with the infant bulb aspirator. Do this just before feeding time and before bedtime until the cold clears up.

If the infant develops a fever or is listless and pale, consult with a physician.

CHILDREN

Cold symptoms in older children are usually accompanied by a fever of 100 to 101 degrees, cough, sore throat, poor appetite, irritability, and a clear, watery discharge from the nose. Bacteria and other microorganisms will sometimes create complications, including middle-ear infections, sinusitis, and pneumonia. These illnesses should be suspected in a child with a prolonged, high fever (103 degrees and above) or in one whose symptoms do not disappear in a few days. (See also WHEN TO SEE THE DOCTOR: SINUSITIS, page 43; PNEUMONIA, page 44; and PROLONGED OR HIGH FEVERS, page 100.)

Young children, like infants, can catch a cold by becoming chilled while they sleep. Children in the eight-month to two-year age range, and even those who are older, are highly active as they sleep. A child's sleeping bag will make sure that an active sleeper stays covered during the night. Flameproof sleeping bags with cotton inner linings are best and are available in many department stores. Cotton-flannel nightgowns and pajamas are also excellent for keeping your child warm and snuggly all night long. Long johns made of 100 percent cotton keep the body's heat close to the skin. They can be dyed to any color of the rainbow to meet the high standards of pajama fashion.

The most insidious (and unavoidable) way children catch colds is from other children. If your kid goes to daycare, be prepared: contact with many other children in eating, sleeping, and playing situations will produce a number of colds. You should not be overly concerned, since the immune system gets good and hearty as it gains a little experience fighting off infections. To keep contagiousness to a minimum, teach your child to wash his or her hands during the day and before meals, and to expect a daily bath. This should keep most infections at bay.

A common cause of frequent colds in young children is improper diet and elimination. If your child has frequent colds, about one every other month, look at the diet first. Temporarily reduce the amount of milk and milk products, then closely inspect other foods in the diet. Does your child frequently eat pizza, pop-tarts, and TV dinners? Even the most health-conscious among us resort to fast food every now and then, but the younger a child is, the more plain and unprocessed the diet should be. Young children simply cannot digest processed foods, and the buildup of undigested wastes can compromise their immune systems. Try to feed your child plenty of cooked grain; there are many ways to prepare it so that it's tasty and fun. Also good are fresh fruits and vegetables, juices, and herb teas such as peppermint and rosehip. If you eat more of these foods yourself, your child will too, and you will both feel better. (See also DIETARY GUIDELINES, page 229.)

HEAD CONGES-TION

Head congestion is probably the most uncomfortable symptom of a cold. Many parents are tempted to buy prepared nose drops and decongestants from drugstores so that their children will not have to suffer the discomfort of a stuffed head and a runny nose. Yet a child's nose should not be prevented from running by administering decongestants, because it is the body's only way to drain mucus from the sinuses. The best way to soothe the irritated and swollen mucous membranes, as well as to trigger drainage of the sinuses, is to use head-clearing herbal aromas mixed with steam.

Head Congestion Facial
To relieve mucous congestion in the sinuses

Preparation Time: 20 minutes
Yield: 1 treatment
Children's Enjoyment: ☺

The inhalation of steam that is mixed with the head-clearing aromas of pennyroyal, wintergreen, and rosemary make this treatment excellent for head congestion from colds. The essential oils of these herbs have powerful decongestant properties and reduce inflammation of the mucous membrane lining the nose. Children enjoy this facial, but must be familiarized with the strong smell of the oils before the treatment.

    2 quarts water
    2 drops oil of wintergreen
    2 drops oil of pennyroyal
    2 drops oil of rosemary
    Large bath towel

1. Put the water in a large pot and bring it to a boil.
2. Take the pot off the heat, let the water cool for 10 minutes, and add the essential oils. The oils will naturally remain on the top of the water.
3. Stir with a stainless-steel ladle to combine them as fully as possible.
4. Place the pot on a table or workbench that is comfortable for a child to sit or stand at, and bend his or her head over the pot.

APPLICATION: Perform this treatment once each day, with adult supervision, until head congestion is gone (up to 1 week). Explain to the child that the steam will make the face feel a little hot, and it's all right to come up for a cooling breath of air. Drape the towel over the head and shoulders to form a tent over the pot as the child bends over to inhale the steam. Have the child inhale the steam for 2 or 3 minutes, then take a break. During the break, cover the pot so that the water stays hot and no steam escapes. Jumping around temporarily unblocks the sinus cavities and passages, and renders the facial far more effective. If the child feels up to it, have him or her do 20 jumping jacks during breaks. Repeat the process of facial and jumping jacks at least 3 times within 30 minutes, then discard the water and oil. This treatment clears a child's head for several hours.

If the child's head congestion shows no sign of improvement after 1 week, if the child is feverish or fatigued, or if a sinus infection is suspected, consult a physician.

Eucalyptus and Wintergreen Bath
To invigorate the child and decongest the head and lungs

Preparation Time: 25 minutes
Yield: 1 treatment
Children's Enjoyment: ☺

A Eucalyptus and Wintergreen Bath is excellent for relieving head congestion. Eucalyptus helps expel mucus and has a mild antiseptic action. It is refreshing and invigorating to the skin when used in a bath. Inhalation of the aroma of wintergreen mixed with steam reduces swelling of the mucous membranes and alleviates congestion. If you live near an area where eucalyptus trees grow, it's easy to collect the eucalyptus leaves to boil for the bath, but you must be sure the leaves have not been sprayed with insecticides. In fact, when your child is healthy again you can both have fun on an outing to collect a supply of leaves to store.

2 ounces dried eucalyptus leaves
2 ounces dried wintergreen leaves
2 quarts water

1. Combine the herbs with the water in a covered pot, bring to a boil, and simmer slowly for 20 minutes.
2. Strain out and discard the herbs.
3. Pour this tea into the bathtub while running the bath so that it will be well combined. The tea turns the bathwater a light greenish brown, with a refreshing eucalyptus smell. An herbal bath should be run as hot as the child's usual bath, but make sure the temperature of the bath is not too hot after adding the brewed tea.

APPLICATION: This bath may make the skin tingle slightly, so explain this to the child before the bath. Have the child soak in the bath for 20 minutes, or longer if he or she enjoys it. Encourage deep inhalation through the nose and the mouth to enhance the decongestant and anti-inflammatory effect of the herbs. You can put some of the dried eucalyptus and wintergreen leaves into the bath water for the child to play with, but make sure you have something over the drain of the bathtub to catch them when you drain the bath water. The bath can be repeated once each day until head congestion is relieved (2 days to 1 week). Always use this bath in the morning or early afternoon, since it is slightly stimulating.

If the child's head congestion persists or gets worse after 1 week of treatment, if high fever (over 103 degrees) is present, or if you suspect a sinus infection, consult a physician.

Aches, Pains, and Fevers

The main methods a child's body uses during a cold to discharge toxins are draining sinuses (runny nose), coughing, sweating, and diarrhea. As toxins and wastes are processed to leave the body, joint aches, stomachaches, headaches, and backaches may occur. For these minor aches and pains, the following teas provide excellent relief:

Elder Flower and Mint Tea
To relieve mild fevers from colds

Preparation Time: 20 minutes
Yield: 4 treatments
Children's Enjoyment: ☺

Elder flower tea is a substance that promotes sweating. It has been used for centuries in Europe and America to treat children's colds, muscle aches and pains, upset stomachs, and fevers. Mint, which cools down a fever and reduces pain, combines with elder flowers to make a good-tasting, excellent tonic.

> 1/2 ounce dried peppermint
> 1/2 ounce dried elder flower blossoms
> 2 cups water
> Honey or maple syrup (optional)

1. Combine the herbs with the water in a covered pot, bring to a boil, and simmer for 5 minutes.
2. Remove the pot from the heat and steep the herbs for 15 minutes.
3. Strain out the herbs and discard them. The tea is a dark yellow-green color and smells mostly of mint.
4. Cool the tea to room temperature before serving. Store the leftover tea in the refrigerator between servings and warm it slightly for each use. Discard any unused portion after 2 days.

APPLICATION: Give a child suffering from aches, pains, and fever of a cold 1/2 cup of tea 3 times each day, between meals, for 5 days. This tea can be sweetened with honey or maple syrup, but your child will probably like the taste without it.

If the child seems to be in severe discomfort, if there is no improvement after 3 days, or if the fever climbs above 103 degrees at any time, consult a physician.

Pennyroyal Tea
To bring on an imminent cold

Preparation Time: 20 minutes
Yield: 4 treatments
Children's Enjoyment: ☺

This tea has effective diaphoretic (sweat-producing) and relaxing qualities, as well as a good minty smell. Pennyroyal was used in nineteenth-century medicine to promote perspiration at the beginning of a cold, accelerating the symptoms and helping the body to heal more quickly. Pennyroyal Tea is a good body cleanser and mild sedative. It is excellent for colds that hover for several days before finally coming on. Symptoms of imminent colds in children include inability to sleep, redness around the eyes, no appetite, and irritability. Pennyroyal Tea also relieves the achiness and fever of colds once they are established. It starts the body on the road to recovery by promoting a sweat, increasing the appetite, and stimulating the circulation in the internal organs.

> 1/2 ounce dried pennyroyal
> 2 cups water

1. Place the pennyroyal and the water in a covered pot, bring to a boil, and simmer for 20 minutes.
2. Strain out the herb and discard it. The tea is gray-green in color and smells strongly of mint and camphor.
3. Cool the tea to a comfortable temperature for drinking before serving it to a child. Refrigerate the tea between servings, and reheat it each time you use it. Discard any unused tea after 2 days.

APPLICATION: Give a child with early cold symptoms, or with aches, pains, and fever, 1/2 cup of the tea twice each day, between meals, for 2 days. Serve the tea as warm as the child can comfortably take it, since its heat helps promote a sweat. Wrap the child warmly in a bathrobe while he or she consumes the tea. Pennyroyal tea has a very unusual taste, but it should not be sweetened. You may need to have a chaser such as golden raisins for the child.

If cold symptoms suddenly become severe, consult a physician.

Rosemary and Mint Bath
To reduce a mild fever and relieve muscular aches and pains

Preparation Time: 20 minutes
Yield: 1 treatment
Children's Enjoyment: ☺

This is the most delightful herbal bath tea I can think of for the aches and pains of a cold. Your bathroom — and probably half your house — will smell like heaven. This bath is excellent for reducing fever, relaxing tense muscles, and refreshing the skin and body after exposure to sun and wind. It is also great for a parent after a hard day's work. Rosemary soothes sore muscles and refreshes the skin, while peppermint gives the skin a pleasant tingling sensation and helps lower fevers. Both herbs disinfect the skin surface and help the pores to open and discharge wastes.

> 2 ounces dried or fresh rosemary
> 2 ounces dried or fresh peppermint
> 2 quarts cold water

1. Combine the herbs with the water in a large pot.
2. Cover the pot and simmer the herbs slowly for 20 minutes.
3. Strain out and discard the herbs.
4. Pour the tea into the tub while the bathwater is running so that it will mix well. The tea turns the bathwater a light green, with the very pleasant scents of rosemary and peppermint. Run the herbal bath as hot as you usually run a bath for the child, but make sure the temperature of the bath is not too hot after adding the brewed tea.

APPLICATION: Have the child bathe for at least 20 minutes and deeply inhale the steam rising from the bathwater. Most children enjoy herbal baths, especially if there are fresh or dried herbs floating around in the water for them to play with. Repeat the bath once each day until the symptoms abate.

If the child seems listless after the bath or runs a high fever (103 degrees and above), he or she may have a more serious disorder than a cold, such as pneumonia or bronchitis. If you suspect this to be the case, consult a physician.

Pennyroyal Bath
To rehydrate during fever, clear the sinuses, and relieve muscle aches

Preparation Time: 20 minutes
Yield: 1 treatment
Children's Enjoyment: ☺

If your child has a fever as well as body aches, use a Pennyroyal Bath, which will also help clear mild head congestion. One of the folk names for pennyroyal is squaw mint, and many Native Americans use it in their sweat baths to treat themselves for colds, rheumatism, and kidney problems. Pennyroyal belongs to the mint family and has a peculiar, camphorous smell. You will probably recognize the smell immediately, since pennyroyal oil is a common ingredient in many commercial insect repellents. This herb is used in Europe and America to promote sweating at the onset of a cold. Pennyroyal also relaxes sore muscles and refreshes the skin when used in a bath.

        2 ounces dried pennyroyal
        2 quarts water

1. Combine the pennyroyal and water in a large, covered pot, bring to a boil, and simmer slowly for 20 minutes.
2. Strain out and discard the herbs.
3. Pour the tea into the bathtub while the water is running so that it

35

will mix well. Run the herbal bath as hot as you usually run a bath for the child or infant, but make sure the temperature of the bath is not too hot after adding the brewed tea. The bathwater is light green and smells strongly of peppermint and camphor.

APPLICATION: Put the child in the bath and gently play with him or her for at least 20 minutes. There is no need to wash the child during the bath. Explain to the child that this bath makes the skin feel slightly tingly. Let the child soak in the tub for 20 minutes. You can add some dried leaves of pennyroyal to the bath water for the child to play with, but make sure you cover the drain of the bathtub with a strainer when you empty the tub. This bath can be repeated once each day in the early evening until the cold disappears (usually 1 week).

If a high fever (above 103 degrees), lassitude, or nausea are present, or if the cold persists or gets worse after 1 week, consult a physician.

COUGHS AND LUNG CONGES-TION

During a cold, the lungs and bronchial tubes will sometimes become congested, causing the chest to feel tight and breathing to be difficult. Poultices and oil rubs are good for congestion because they stimulate the circulation in the lungs and chest muscles.

Comfrey and Eucalyptus Poultice
To bring up phlegm and relieve dry cough

Preparation Time: 20 minutes
Yield: 1 treatment
Children's Enjoyment: ☺

If your child has a harsh, dry cough — like a seal barking — the warming, expectorant properties of this Comfrey and Eucalyptus Poultice will aid the lungs in expelling excess mucus. Eucalyptus tea and oil are traditional remedies that reduce inflammation of the bronchial tubes and relieve spasmodic coughing.

  1 ounce eucalyptus leaves
  1 ounce comfrey root pieces
  1 quart water
  Clean piece of muslin

1. Bruise the eucalyptus leaves with your hands, or a mortar and pestle, before using.
2. Combine with the comfrey root in a covered pot, add water, bring to a boil, and simmer for 5 minutes.
3. Strain out the herbs and place them in a colander to let excess moisture drain. Discard the water.
4. Dampen the muslin, put the steaming herbs in the center, and fold the cloth over the herbs lengthwise, so that it is approximately 5 inches wide, with the herbs forming a mound in the center. Fold the ends of the towel over the center to form a secure herbal pouch.
5. Cool the poultice until it can be applied without burning the child's skin.

APPLICATION: The poultice is most effective on congested lungs when it is applied as warm as the child can stand, but be careful not to burn the child's skin. Explain to the child that the poultice will feel a little hot. Put the poultice on the child's chest until the blood rises to the surface of the skin, turning it a bright pink (about 5 minutes). Then have the child lie on his or her stomach and put the poultice directly between the shoulder blades, pressing down gently. Leave the poultice on until the herbs have cooled, then discard them. Repeat this procedure once each day until a loose, rattling cough sets in that brings up mucus (2 to 4 days). This indicates that the lung congestion is breaking up. You may also dose the child with Onion Syrup, page 40, or Licorice Tea, page 76, to speed recovery and soothe a mild sore throat resulting from coughing

If the child is unable to sleep at night, refer to SLEEPLESSNESS, page 41. If a dry cough persists after 3 days of treatment, or if a fever develops, consult a physician.

Eucalyptus Oil Rub
To soothe a child and stimulate the lungs

Preparation Time: 5 minutes
Yield: 3 treatments
Children's Enjoyment: ☺

Eucalyptus oil is excellent for children with coughs and lung conges-tion. Many commercial cough lozenges and syrups use eucalyptus oil as an ingredient because of its mucous-expelling qualities. The pun-gent aroma of eucalyptus, combined with a loving massage, relaxes a child and helps break up congestion in both the head and the lungs.

    5 teaspoons olive or other vegetable oil
    1 teaspoon eucalyptus oil

1. Combine the vegetable and eucalyptus oils in a small dish or jar lid.
2. Stir with your index finger to make sure the oils are thoroughly mixed and will not irritate the child's skin. The oil is ready to use when it makes your finger tingle slightly, but not burn.
3. Store the oil in a dated, labeled jar out of the reach of children. Discard any unused portion after 6 months.

APPLICATION: Apply this oil once each day, just before bedtime, until the cough abates (about 1 week). Place a palmful of the oil in your hand and rub your hands together to warm the oil before apply-ing it. Have the child lie on his or her back, then rhythmically rub the oil into the chest, following the contours of the rib cage. Hum or gently talk to the child while you massage, and encourage the child to inhale deeply through the nose. Turn the child over and repeat the pro-cess, rubbing between the shoulder blades and again following the contours of the rib cage. Most children drift off to sleep during this process. When you complete the treatment, dress the child in an old, cotton T-shirt and cover the child warmly.

If the child has a persistent dry cough that does not show any sign of improvement after 1 week of treatment, consult a physician.

A sore throat is often the first symptom of an oncoming cold and is usually caused by mucus draining from the head down the back of the throat, irritating the delicate tissue. As the cold progresses, a child can develop a persistent cough, which irritates the throat and causes it to feel dry and raspy. Swollen glands can also create pain in the throat when swallowing. The following remedies will help soothe sore throats from coughs or throat irritation. (See also CHAPTER TWO — EAR, NOSE, AND EYE DISORDERS and CHAPTER THREE — SORE THROATS.)

SORE THROATS

Plantain Syrup
To strengthen the immune system and soothe sore throat

Preparation Time: 15 minutes
Yield: 15 treatments
Children's Enjoyment: ☺

This syrup is perfect for a sore throat that accompanies a rattling, loose cough. Plaintain is well known as a demulcent — a substance that soothes and heals membranes. It is also considered an alterative — a term describing herbs which favorably alter or change unhealthy conditions of the body and restore them to normal. Administered as a syrup, plantain is a tasty vitamin supplement. Plantain is a very common herb, found in backyards, roadsides, and empty lots all over the United States and Europe. Do not gather plantain from roadsides or any public lands unless you know it has not been sprayed or poisoned. This is a good syrup to let a child help you make, especially if you use your own fresh plantain.

    1 ounce dried or 2 ounces fresh plantain
    2 cups water
    1 1/2 pounds (approximately 3 cups) brown sugar

39

1. If you use fresh plantain, bruise the leaves with your hands or the back of a wooden spoon.
2. Put the water in a pot and immerse the fresh or dried plantain in it. Simmer, covered, for 10 minutes.
3. Strain out the herbs and discard them.
4. Add the sugar to the dark green liquid. Bring the mixture to a gentle boil and cook it until the sugar is completely dissolved.
5. Cool the mixture to room temperature. The syrup has a mild, grassy smell and is dark brown in color. Pour it into a glass jar with a tight-fitting lid, and label and date the jar. Discard the syrup after 6 months.

APPLICATION: Give the child 1 tablespoon 3 times each day, between meals, until the sore throat disappears. This syrup tastes sweet and grassy and, while it is unusual, it is not unpleasant. Most children like its taste and are usually cooperative at medicine time.

If the sore throat grows worse, if there are white spots on the back of the throat, or if other symptoms such as high fever (above 103 degrees), paleness, and listlessness appear, consult a pediatrician.

Onion Syrup
To soothe a sore throat from a dry cough

Preparation Time: 2 hours
Yield: 15 treatments
Children's Enjoyment: ☺

This syrup sounds like a contradiction in terms, but it is very easy to make and actually doesn't taste bad. Since it is very effective for drying up congestion while soothing the throat, Onion Syrup is indicated when your child's cough is involuntary and tickly, and yet fails to bring up much phlegm. Onion juice combined with honey is also excellent for sore throats and coughs. Onions are an abundant source of vitamin C and are often eaten raw, like apples, in the cold lands of the north. Onion juice is an excellent external and internal germ killer, digestive aid, and substance that expels mucus.

> 1 medium yellow onion
> 3 cups honey

1. Peel and dice the onion, and place it in an ovenproof dish that has a tight-fitting lid.
2. Pour the honey over the onion, cover the dish, and place it in a 300° F. oven for 2 hours.
3. Remove the dish from the oven, and pour its contents into a wide bowl. Mash the onion to a pulp with a potato masher, then thoroughly strain out the onion pulp and discard.
4. Pour the syrup into a glass jar and cool to room temperature. This syrup has a light consistency and must be kept refrigerated. Warm the syrup for each use and discard it as soon as the child's sore throat has abated.

APPLICATION: Give the child 1 tablespoon 3 times each day, before each meal, until the sore throat and cold are relieved. Some kids like this syrup but others do not, so you may need to keep some golden raisins on hand to use as a chaser. I learned this trick from my Chinese herbalist friends, who have a genius for developing the most awful-tasting herb brews. A good way to prepare children for the syrup's taste is to let them help make the syrup. If a child complains of an onion aftertaste, reduce the dosage.

If the sore throat persists after 1 week or grows significantly worse, consult a pediatrician.

SLEEPLESSNESS

Conjure up the image of a St. Bernard rescuing the frozen, half-dead, snow-covered skier. What does our faithful and furry friend always have around his neck? A keg of brandy. Brandy has warming, restorative powers that are nothing short of miraculous. Depending on its quality, brandy can be very effective for warming the stomach and the intestines. It also has a positive effect on the lungs, helping them to expectorate mucus. The following recipe is excellent for a child who is having difficulty sleeping because of a cold and cough.

Hot Toddy
To relieve sleeplessness from a cold

Preparation Time: 10 minutes
Yield: 2 treatments
Children's Enjoyment: ☺

Brandy is a widely available, old-fashioned remedy for sleeplessness because of a cold. When brandy is mixed in a tincture with warming herbs such as ginger or licorice, it is doubly effective, not to mention delicious. Because of the alcohol content of brandy, a racking spasmodic cough — the kind that keeps you and your kid up at night — can be eased enough to allow sleep. Mixed with honey, brandy is easy to give to children. Use high-quality brandy for this purpose.

> 1 cinnamon stick or 1/8 teaspoon powdered cinnamon
> 1 1/2 cups water
> 2 thin slices fresh ginger or 1/4 teaspoon powdered ginger
> 2 tablespoons brandy
> 2 teaspoons lemon juice
> Honey to taste

1. Combine the cinnamon stick or powder and water in a small pot and simmer for 5 minutes.
2. Add the fresh ginger or ginger powder to the pot and simmer for 5 minutes more.
3. Remove the pot from the heat, allow to cool for 5 minutes, then add the brandy, lemon juice, and honey.
4. Stir with the cinnamon stick or a stainless-steel spoon to combine.
5. Allow the mixture to cool to a comfortable temperature for your child, then serve.

APPLICATION: Give 1 cup of the hot toddy once a day at bedtime to help your child (and you) sleep comfortably until the cold goes away.

If a high fever (above 103 degrees), lassitude, or nausea are present, or if the cold persists or gets worse after one week, consult with a physician.

Please do not worry that, by giving your child an occasional hot toddy for a cold, you may be sculpting a future alcoholic. A little brandy can be highly beneficial, even for infants. In fact, it was a common practice at the turn of the century to let a teething child suck on a clean rag that had been soaked in sugar syrup and brandy. It safely relieved the pain and ended the incessant crying that can sometimes be caused by teething.

WHEN TO SEE THE DOCTOR

✚ FLU: Influenza, or flu, is caused by a mutating virus that goes through many stages and phases throughout the world. There seems to be a new type of flu every year, but the general symptoms are the same: sudden, acute fever; gastrointestinal disorders such as vomiting or sudden and distressing diarrhea; runny nose and rattling cough; muscle aches and pains; and occasional depression or nervous disorders. Usually a child will be over the flu within a matter of days, the disease leaving as quickly as it arrived. The sudden, acute nature of flu is what distinguishes it from a common cold, but flu symptoms resemble symptoms of many other conditions. If your child's recovery is slow, or if the symptoms become severe, a physician's examination is necessary.

✚ SINUSITIS: Sinusitis is an infection of the mucous membranes that line the sinuses. The symptoms of a full-blown sinus infection differ from a common runny nose in several ways. The nasal passages are completely blocked, and X-rays reveal opaque areas where clear sinuses should be. The mucus is thick and yellow-green in color, and the sense of smell is gone. Facial swelling from infected sinus cavities is sometimes present around the brow and upper jaw, and your child may complain of soreness while chewing. The most constant symptom of sinusitis is a headache located around the forehead and eyes, caused by the swelling of the upper sinus cavities and the resulting pressure on the eyeballs. Other symptoms include low chronic fever, general listlessness, blurred vision, and a spaced out, confused feeling. If you think your child has sinusitis, you should see a health professional as soon as possible, since antibiotics may be necessary. There can be dangerous complications in sinus infections and it is a particularly miserable condition for your child to be in. Generally, sinusitis does not develop suddenly; it is usually the result of a persistent cold combined with low immune resistance. Sinus problems can sometimes be an inherited condition, so care should be taken with diet and prevention. (See also CHAPTER TWO — EAR, NOSE, AND EYE DISORDERS; DIETARY GUIDELINES, page 229.)

✦ BRONCHITIS: Bronchitis is the inflammation of the bronchial tubes, or bronchi. A child suffering acute bronchitis will have fever, tightness and stuffiness in the chest, and a severe, continual cough. Mucus gathers and causes a wheezy breathing and coughing. There can also be shortness of breath. Bronchitis can be the effect of a persistent cold or flu, or may be a complication of measles, whooping cough, or chicken pox. Untreated bronchitis can result in pneumonia. A child exhibiting any of these symptoms should be examined at once by a health professional.

✦ PNEUMONIA: Pneumonia is an infection of the lungs. Symptoms include fever, chest pains, and a spasmodic, bubbling cough. There is sometimes high color on the cheeks, with the rest of the face pale. The infection of the lungs may be around the bronchial tubes (bronchopneumonia) or it may affect the entire lung (lobar pneumonia). If your child's resistance is low, pneumonia may be caused by bacteria that is usually present in the mouth and throat. Pneumonia is frequently a complication of other illnesses, and it can also be caused by aspiration of foreign matter, such as food, into the lungs. The different diagnoses are made by medical professionals upon examining the color and quality of the mucus discharged by the lungs. Pneumonia can become serious quite suddenly, with very high fever and difficulty in breathing. If you suspect that your child has developed pneumonia, get him or her to an emergency medical center promptly.

CHAPTER TWO

EAR, NOSE, AND EYE DISORDERS

INFANTS

Ear Infections

Eye Problems

CHILDREN

Ear Infections

Styes

Conjunctivitis

Sinus Congestion

Nosebleeds

among the most common ear, nose, and eye disorders experienced by children are outer ear infections (swimmer's ear) and middle ear infections, occasional nosebleeds, and minor eye infections such as styes and conjunctivitis (pink eye). Although ear, eye, and nose problems are sometimes caused by injuries, they usually develop as complications of colds and infections. Ear infections are most often caused by food allergies, upper respiratory infections, or blockage of the eustachian tube owing to swelling of the adenoids or tonsils. Nosebleeds are frequently the result of injury, but some children suffer from epistaxis — chronic nosebleeds — because of nasal polyps or dilated, delicate blood vessels in the nose. Eye problems can be caused by rubbing the eye with dirty fingers or by contagious diseases such as conjunctivitis. Letting your child's hair hang down into the eyes will irritate them and give bacteria a chance to grow, often resulting in inflamed eyes.

All of these conditions can be frightening, especially to inexperienced parents, but they rarely develop into anything serious. It is very important to keep your child's ears, eyes, and nose clean so that bacteria do not have a chance to grow. Show your children how to clean their own ears and eyes in order to keep infections to a minimum. A child who develops a complication from one of these conditions or who seems to be in severe pain should be taken to a health-care center immediately. (See also WHEN TO SEE THE DOCTOR, page 67.)

INFANTS

Many infants have bloodshot or draining eyes for their first week as a result of the drops put into their eyes at birth. Swollen eyelids are also a common reaction to this treatment. Parents should not be overly concerned unless these symptoms seem prolonged or abnormally severe. With my three infants, all symptoms were gone within three days.

A newborn infant's eyes usually remain closed most of the time for the first three to five days. After this, most babies start to look around at the world and try to focus — especially on the eyes and face of whoever is feeding them. Parents should test the strength and focus of their infant's eyes by waving objects such as a finger about eighteen inches in front of the child. The infant's eyes should follow the movement. Mild strabismus — crossed eyes — is common in infants at this age, and parents should not be overly concerned. If you feel your infant is not focusing or showing any interest in moving objects within his or her field of vision, consult with your pediatrician.

Your infant probably had hearing tests in the hospital shortly after birth. If your infant is born at home, make sure that the presiding midwife or doctor conducts a hearing test. Any sharp noise in the room should disturb or surprise the infant, although a steady, droning noise like a vacuum cleaner is usually ignored. If you notice any strange discharge coming from your infant's ear, besides the normal ear wax, consult your pediatrician. Also, if your infant is overly restless, has a runny nose with a fever, or is eating poorly, an ear infection may be present and a visit to the pediatrician or health-care clinic is in order.

EAR INFECTIONS

Infants with ear infections may exhibit such symptoms as runny nose, irritability, poor appetite, and fever. Bottle-fed infants may have a greater risk of getting middle ear infections than breast-fed infants, perhaps because their bottle is often in their mouth when they are lying flat on their back. The horizontal position hinders drainage of the eustachian tubes, and milk and other secretions can be aspirated into the middle ear. Always hold an infant in your lap with its head raised slightly during bottle-feeding until it is old enough to do it for itself.

An infant should be examined by a health professional whenever an ear infection is suspected. Infants under the age of three months cannot localize infections, which presents the danger of meningitis (an infection of the lining of the brain) or mastoiditis (an infection of the mastoid area). Premature infants are especially at risk. Antibiotics are usually administered for ear infections, and parents should have their physician explain to them what kind of antibiotic is being prescribed and how infants generally respond to it. Keep a record of what kind of drugs your children receive and monitor the response. Knowledge of prior, possibly ineffective or overly harsh drugs is of vital importance as your child grows.

Once your infant is diagnosed with an ear infection and antibiotics are administered, it is important that you complete the entire course of antibiotics, even if your infant seems completely recovered after a few days of treatment. In the meantime, there are some herbal procedures and remedies that help speed healing and relieve discomfort.

Rosemary and Wintergreen Oil Rub
To reduce pain or swelling from ear infections

Preparation Time: 5 minutes
Yield: 3 treatments
Children's Enjoyment: ☺

Rosemary and wintergreen oils, combined, make a painkilling rub for ear infections and mumps. Rosemary oil is a nervine — a substance that numbs the nerves. Wintergreen is a popular ingredient in liniments because of its ability to reduce swelling. Rubbing this combination of oils around the ear and throat reduces pain and inflammation of swollen lymph glands and delicate inner ear tissue.

> 1/4 teaspoon rosemary oil
> 1/4 teaspoon wintergreen oil
> 2 1/2 teaspoons olive oil (for infants)

1. Combine all the ingredients in a small dish or jar lid.
2. Stir with your index finger for 2 minutes to make sure oils are completely mixed and will not irritate tender skin. When the oil makes your finger tingle slightly but not burn, it is ready to use.
3. Warm the oil to skin temperature before applying. Store the oil in a labeled jar with a tight-fitting lid, away from children. Discard any unused portion after 6 months.

APPLICATION: For an infant's ear infection, rub the oil into the skin and scalp. Start behind the ear, come around to the point of the jaw, and trace the line of the ear up to the hairline. Repeat the rubbing from the front to the back of the ear until the oil is absorbed. Most infants enjoy this process, especially if you hold them securely while rubbing gently. Humming and singing to infants helps relax them, making this therapy more beneficial. Repeat this treatment twice each day until the pain and swelling subside.

Ear infections in infants under the age of 3 months should always be diagnosed by a physician. Let the physician know you are using the herbal oils in conjunction with prescribed medication.

Wintergreen Tea
To relieve fever and discomfort from ear infections

Preparation Time: 20 minutes
Yield: 8 treatments
Children's Enjoyment: ☺

Wintergreen is an analgesic, or painkilling herb, which makes Wintergreen Tea excellent for relieving the pain of infant ear infections. Wintergreen has a pleasant taste, and the tea can be sweetened with corn syrup to make it more palatable. Dried wintergreen is brownish green and has very little smell. It is available in health food and herb stores.

> 1/2 ounce dried wintergreen leaves
> 2 cups water
> 1/2 teaspoon light corn syrup

1. Combine the wintergreen leaves and water in a covered pot, bring to a boil, and simmer for 5 minutes.
2. Remove the pot from the heat, and steep the herb mixture for 15 minutes.
3. Thoroughly strain the tea through a cheesecloth-lined sieve and discard the herb. The tea is gray-green in color, smells minty, and should have no floating particles in it.
4. Cool the tea until it is the right temperature to give to an infant. When you test a few drops of the tea on the inside of your wrist, it should feel comfortably warm.
5. Measure out 1/4 cup of tea and add the corn syrup before serving.

Refrigerate the tea and reheat with each use, adding the corn syrup as the tea warms. Discard any unused portion after 2 days.

APPLICATION: Give an infant 1/4 cup of tea 3 times each day, by bottle or teaspoon, for 1 to 3 days until the earache is gone. Most infants enjoy the sweet, minty taste of this tea, so it is very easy to administer.

An infant's ear infection should always be diagnosed by a physician. Be sure to let the physician know that you are using wintergreen tea as a painkiller in conjunction with any prescribed medication.

EYE PROBLEMS

Infants should be thoroughly examined by health professionals when they are born so that obvious eye problems can be discovered and treated immediately. As most parents know, infants have silver nitrate dropped in their eyes as a prophylactic measure against eye diseases contracted from the mother during birth. Many infants develop what is known as chemical conjunctivitis as a result of these eyedrops. The eyes appear bloodshot and swollen, and may be tearing a little. This condition should clear up within one to three days with no assistance from the parents or a health professional. If it does not, or if the condition gets worse, a visit to a pediatrician is necessary. Your infant may have developed neonatal conjunctivitis in spite of the drops received at birth, and prompt treatment with antibiotics is indicated to prevent blindness owing to corneal erosion.

Infants' eyes will run, along with their nose, during the course of a normal cold. It is important to keep the mucus from crusting around the eyes and to keep the eyes very clean. Infants also develop sore or red eyes if they have been crying for an extended period of time. If your infant experiences red or running eyes, there is a safe and comforting herbal procedure for you to try. (See also WHEN TO SEE THE DOCTOR: VISION PROBLEMS, page 67.)

Eyebright Eyewash
To dry up eye excretions and soothe inflammation

Preparation Time: 25 minutes
Yield: 1 treatment
Children's Enjoyment: ☺

Eyebright is a parasitic plant, like mistletoe, that is used traditionally in lotions and washes for eye disorders. Eyebright derives its name from the healing and soothing effect it has upon eyes. It is slightly astringent and can draw the inflamed tissues of the eye together, drying up discharges.

>   1/2 ounce eyebright
>   1 cup water
>   Paper coffee filter
>   Clean cotton washcloth

1. Combine the eyebright and water in a covered pot and simmer for 20 minutes.
2. Strain the liquid very thoroughly through the coffee filter and discard the herbs. There should be no floating particles in the solution.
3. When the tea has cooled to a tepid temperature, comfortably warm for the eyes, it is ready to use.
4. This herbal wash is to be used only once. Discard any leftovers and make a fresh batch each time.

APPLICATION: Make sure the infant is not hungry or tired before proceeding with the application. Hold the infant securely in your arms and place yourself in a comfortable position on the floor or on a bed. Put the washcloth into the pot of warm tea and place it close to you. Wring out the washcloth with one hand so that it is not dripping but is still quite moist. Gently lay the washcloth across the infant's eyes and hold it there with very minimal pressure. The infant will close his or her eyes. This is normal and the tea will still be of benefit. Leave the cloth in place over the eyes for 3 minutes, let the infant rest for 3 minutes, then rinse the cloth in the tea and repeat the process 2 more times. The infant will relax at first, then may try to remove the cloth. Keep replacing it gently until the skin around the eyes gets a little red. This is a good sign since it means that blood is circulating in the area. This process may be performed once or twice each day until the infant's eyes have returned to normal (up to about 1 week).

If the infant's eye disorder seems to cause severe discomfort, or if it persists or gets worse after 1 week of treatment, consult a physician.

CHILDREN

As children grow, they become more active and curious about the world around them. When they are toddling, they usually experience nothing more than a few bumps and bruises because their parent or caretaker is nearby. Children who are old enough to be running around on their own, however, are prone to more serious injuries that can involve the ears, nose, and eyes. A child who has sustained this type of injury should be taken to a doctor or clinic immediately. Often, just the speed with which an injury is treated can be a deciding factor in the healing process. Also, injuries to these parts of a child's body may not appear as serious as they really are, so a thorough examination by a health professional is essential.

Many children experience middle ear infections, styes, sinus congestion, conjunctivitis, and nosebleeds in the process of growing. These disorders rarely develop into anything serious, but they should be watched and treated carefully. There are many effective herbal remedies and procedures for you to rely on to help ease your child's discomfort. If any ear or eye condition appears to get worse or does not respond to treatments, consult your pediatrician or primary health care center for advice. (See also WHEN TO SEE THE DOCTOR, page 67.)

The two most common ear problems among children are external oti-tis — also known as swimmer's ear — and otitis media, which is an infection of the middle ear right behind the ear drum. External otitis is usually a result of inflammation of the ear canal, often resulting when water is trapped in there after swimming. This kind of earache usually produces discharge, itching deep inside the ear, and pain when the ear is pulled. An abnormal buildup of ear wax can also cause pain and in-flammation in the external ear canal. Middle ear infections can be caused by sinusitis, food allergies, injury to the inner ear, and foreign bodies in the ear. If your child has inserted something in the ear that will not dislodge easily, do not, under any circumstances, try to re-move it yourself. Irreparable ear damage can occur when parents try to remove things such as beads, peas, and erasers from their children's ears by using hairpins, tweezers, or their own fingers. The tympanic membrane — or ear drum — is very delicate, so the hands of a skilled professional should be employed to extract foreign objects from a child's ear. If your child is suffering from an outer or middle ear in-fection there are several herbal procedures to try.

EAR INFECTIONS

Garlic Oil Ear Drops
To draw out and relieve outer and middle ear infections

Preparation Time: 2 days
Yield: 6-month supply
Children's Enjoyment: ☺

Garlic oil is an effective remedy for relieving infections of the outer and middle ear. Garlic has been used for centuries to heal all kinds of disorders, including respiratory infections, gastrointestinal problems, and high blood pressure. Fresh, firm cloves of garlic and pure olive oil are required for this mixture, which is good to make up in advance of any illness.

4 cloves garlic, peeled
1/4 cup olive oil

55

1. Mash the garlic or press it through a garlic press.
2. Combine the garlic with the olive oil in a glass jar with a tight-fitting lid.
3. Let the mixture stand at room temperature or in the sun for at least 1 day, but not more than 3 days.
4. Thoroughly strain out and discard the garlic, making sure there are no floating particles left in the oil. The ear drops will have a slightly opaque look and the smell of garlic, but their scent is not overpowering.
5. Store the oil in a labeled, dated glass jar, with a tight-fitting lid, out of the reach of children. Discard any unused oil after 6 months.

APPLICATION: When a child complains of an earache, warm the oil so that a drop applied to the inside of the wrist feels comfortably warm. Have the child stand in the light and tilt the head to one side. Put 2 drops in each ear, even if only one ear hurts. This keeps the eyes from watering and helps maintain the sense of balance. Place cotton balls in the ears after applying the oil to make sure none of it drains out. Perform this procedure twice each day, in the morning and at bedtime, for no more than 4 days.

If the child's earache persists or gets worse after 4 days of treatment, or if a fever sets in at any time, consult a physician.

STYES Adults, as well as children, often get a sty in their eye. Styes are small red sores caused by staphylococcus bacteria. Some styes are located on the inside of the eyelid. These are usually quite painful, since the lid of the affected eye becomes red and swollen. External styes, located on the rim of the eyelid, are usually small and superficial, and will hardly be noticed by you or your child. Instruct your child to avoid rubbing the eyes with dirty hands, and to keep hair out of the eyes. Giving your child a lesson in how to get a particle out of the eye without rubbing is useful. If your child has a sty, there is an effective herbal remedy you can try.

Witch Hazel Fomentation
To dry up excretions from the eye and shrink styes

Preparation Time: 20 minutes
Yield: 1 treatment
Children's Enjoyment: ☺

Witch hazel wash is widely used for skin irritations, bruises, insect bites and stings, minor burns, and poison ivy. As a tea, it is effective against diarrhea and can be gargled for a sore throat. This versatile herb is very astringent, causing contraction of the tissue, and is soothing to all membranous surfaces — of which the eye is one. I use it successfully for both my children and myself whenever styes or inflamed eyes are a problem. Do not buy commercially prepared tincture of witch hazel for this procedure; tinctures are made with alcohol and should never come in contact with the eye.

> 1 ounce witch hazel bark pieces
> 2 cups water
> Paper coffee filter
> Clean cotton washcloth

1. Combine the witch hazel bark and water in a covered pot, bring to a boil, and simmer for 20 minutes.
2. Thoroughly strain the liquid through the sterile coffee filter and discard the herb. The solution should have no floating particles in it.
3. Cool the fomentation to a comfortably warm temperature for applying to a child's eyes. However, since heat is part of this healing treatment, make sure the fomentation is not cold.

APPLICATION: Dip the washcloth in the witch hazel solution until saturated. Gently wring out the washcloth so it is not dripping but is still quite moist. Explain to the child that the washcloth will feel a little warm on the eyes. Have the child lie down comfortably on a couch or bed. Put the washcloth on the child's eyes, or have the child put it on unassisted, if desired. Apply gentle pressure to the closed eyes until the washcloth cools, then immerse the cloth in the solution and reapply. Repeat the procedure once more. Discard the rest of the solution and make a fresh batch each time you need it. Perform the fomentation once each day until the eye disorder clears up, usually in 2 to 4 days.

If the child suffers severe discomfort, or if the disorder does not respond or gets worse after 4 days of treatment, consult a physician.

CONJUNC-
TIVITIS

Conjunctivitis is the most common eye disease in the United States. It is an inflammation of the mucous membrane of the eye, and can develop from infections, glaucoma, scratches on the cornea, or as a side effect of allergies. If this is the case, a visit to a physician is necessary. Infectious conjunctivitis can also be caused by bacterial infections and that is the type discussed here. If your child wakes up one morning with sore, inflamed, and runny eyes, but no fever or other problems, the conjunctivitis can be treated easily at home with herbal preparations.

Camomile Compress
To soothe swollen, inflamed eyes

Preparation Time: 15 minutes
Yield: 1 treatment
Children's Enjoyment: ☺

At the turn of the century, camomile was used commonly in this country to treat children's illnesses. It is still used in many herbal preparations for children in Europe, especially cough syrup and stomach preparations. It has recently appeared again in the United States as a skin freshener and firming agent, and as a hair rinse, but with its mild painkilling and muscle-relaxing properties, it makes an especially excellent children's herb. I recommend this compress made of camomile for a child's swollen, inflamed eyes because it is mild and will draw out the infection without further irritating sensitive eyes. Gently explain to your child that this compress will make his or her eyes feel better. I've found that when children hurt, especially around the eyes, they don't want to be touched by anything or anyone. The heat of this compress relaxes and relieves eye discomfort and speeds recovery.

> 2 cups water
> 2 ounces dried camomile flowers
> Paper coffee filter
> Clean muslin washcloth

1. Put the water in a covered pot and bring to a boil.
2. Remove the pot from the heat and immerse the camomile flowers in the hot water.
3. Cover the pot and steep for 10 minutes.
4. Strain the liquid through the coffee filter and set the herb aside. You may either discard the light yellowish-green camomile tea or serve it as a digestive aid or as a mild calmative before bedtime.

APPLICATION: Fold the steaming herb in a damp washcloth to form a 5 by 2-inch-wide strip with the herb in the center. Cool the compress until it is warm but not too hot to place on the child's eyes. When the compress has cooled sufficiently, explain to the child that it will feel a little hot. Have the child lie down and get comfortable. Place the compress over the closed eyes and press gently. The child will relax as soon as the compress is applied and will probably want to hold the compress in place unassisted. When the compress is cold, remove it and discard the herb. Repeat this treatment twice each day until the conjunctivitis has disappeared (up to about 1 week).

If the conjunctivitis is extremely uncomfortable or severe, consult a physician.

Plantain Wash

To speed recovery and remove dried excretions from the eye

Preparation Time: 20 minutes

Yield: 1 treatment

Children's Enjoyment: ☺

This wash can be alternated with the Camomile Compress (page 58) or used alone. Plantain is mild, yet effective, when used in a wash for children's delicate eye tissues. It reduces inflammation and irritation, which makes it ideal for treating conjunctivitis. Plantain is available in health food and herb stores, and grows commonly all over the United States in backyards, empty lots, and fields. If you harvest your own plantain, make sure it grows in an area that has not been sprayed with insecticides.

        1/2 ounce dried or fresh plantain
        1 cup water
        Paper coffee filter
        Cotton balls or a clean washcloth

1. Put the water in a covered pot and bring to a boil.
2. Add the plantain to the boiling water, cover the pot, and simmer for 5 minutes.
3. Remove the pot from the heat, and steep the herb for 10 minutes.
4. Thoroughly strain the liquid through the coffee filter and discard the herb. The wash should have no floating particles in it.
5. Cool the wash to a tepid temperature before using. This wash should be used only once. Discard any remaining tea.

APPLICATION: Soak 2 cotton balls or a clean washcloth in the wash. Have the child lie down in a comfortable position. Explain to the child that the wash will feel slightly warm but will not hurt the eyes in any way. Apply the cotton balls or washcloth to the eyes until cool, dip into the wash, and reapply. Repeat the process 3 times. Perform this treatment once or twice each day until the eye condition clears up, usually in about 1 week. Children who are old enough can apply the soaked cotton balls or washcloth themselves, or you may help them if they desire. I have found that if you let children become active participants in their own healing processes, they get quite involved and interested. Let them apply the wash to their eyes as often as they like until the symptoms abate. The important thing is to get children to relax for the treatment.

If the conjunctivitis is severe or does not improve after 1 week of treatment, consult a physician.

SINUS CONGESTION

Sinus congestion is often a side effect of allergies, a cold, or flu. If your child has chronic sinus congestion, however, it could be caused by improper diet. Too much overprocessed or highly refined food and food additives, sugar, concentrated starch, and fat — along with improper elimination — will cause all kinds of physical problems. A child's diet should be as unrefined as possible. If your child has gotten used to fast food and frequent treats, you might have to gradually switch him or her to a healthier selection of foods. Do not try to do this all at once; it will not work. Your child will probably pretend to be full after a few bites and then sneak off to a friend's house for a quick fix. I have found that with patience and firmness you can change children's attitudes toward food, and they will actually start to prefer healthy things, refusing cake and soda because it tastes too rich and sweet. Parents should, of course, try to set an example with their own eating habits.

If a change in diet does not seem to work, you might need to have your child tested for allergies. Many children are allergic to pollen, cat hair, or dust, which can all trigger chronic sinus congestion. After your child is examined by a health professional for allergies and is well on the way to a healthy change in eating habits, there are herbal remedies available to help bring symptomatic relief from the stuffiness and discomfort of sinus congestion. (See also CHAPTER SEVEN — ALLERGIC REACTIONS; DIETARY GUIDELINES, page 229; WHEN TO SEE THE DOCTOR: SINUSITIS, page 43.)

Head Congestion Facial
To relieve mucous congestion in the sinuses

Preparation Time: 20 minutes
Yield: 1 treatment
Children's Enjoyment: ☺

The inhalation of steam mixed with the head-clearing aromas of pennyroyal, wintergreen, and rosemary make this treatment excellent for head congestion. The essential oils of these herbs have powerful decongestant properties and help reduce inflammation of the mucous membrane lining the nose. Children enjoy this facial, but must be familiarized with the strong smell of the oils before the treatment.

        2 quarts water
        2 drops oil of wintergreen
        2 drops oil of pennyroyal
        2 drops oil of rosemary
        Large bath towel

1. Put the water in a pot and bring to a boil.
2. Take the pot off the heat, let the water cool for 10 minutes, and add the essential oils. The oils will naturally remain on the top of the water.
3. Stir with a stainless-steel ladle to combine them as fully as possible.
4. Place the pot on a table or workbench that is comfortable for a child to sit or stand at, and bend his or her head over the pot.

APPLICATION: Perform this treatment once each day, with adult supervision, until your child's head congestion is relieved (up to 1 week). Explain to the child that the steam will make the face feel a little hot and it's all right to come up for a cooling breath of air. Drape the towel over the head and shoulders to form a tent over the pot as the child bends over to inhale the steam. Have the child inhale the steam for 2 or 3 minutes, then take a break. During the break, cover the pot so that the water stays hot and no steam escapes. Jumping around temporarily unblocks the sinus cavities and passages and renders the facial far more effective. If the child feels up to it, have him or her do 20 jumping jacks during breaks. Repeat the process of facial and jumping jacks at least 3 times within 30 minutes, then discard the water and oil. This treatment clears a child's head for several hours.

If the child's head congestion shows no sign of improvement after 1 week, if the child is feverish or fatigued, or if a sinus infection is suspected, consult a physician.

Carrot Juice
To increase immune resistance and relieve mucous congestion
throughout the body

Preparation Time: 10 minutes
Yield: 4 treatments
Children's Enjoyment: ☺

Carrot juice is good for helping the body get rid of excess mucus, and it is recommended for children with sinus congestion from allergies, cold, or flu. It is also a great way to get your child to consume good-tasting, healthful juice without too much fuss. Carrots contain high amounts of beta-carotene, which increases the body's resistance to infections, particularly in the eyes, ears, tonsils, sinuses, and lungs. The juice helps normalize the digestive processes, and its nutrients are rapidly assimilated by the body. Make sure it is as fresh as possible. When you are buying carrots to juice, make sure they are organic and get them in bulk at a health food store. Three pounds will stay fresh for five days' worth of juice. Make only enough juice for one day's treatment. Refrigerate any portion that is not drunk immediately. If you buy fresh carrot juice, you need only to open the container and pour it for the child, but check the date on the container to be sure the juice was made within the past twenty-four hours.

APPLICATION: Give the child 1 cup of carrot juice 3 times each day, between meals, for 5 days. Bring the juice to room temperature before serving. If the taste is too strong for the child, dilute the juice with water. Never serve the juice before bedtime because it contains a lot of natural vegetable sugar and is slightly stimulating. Do not give more than three 1-cup servings a day, even if the child likes the taste and asks for it. Your child will urinate more frequently, and the urine might be a bright yellow color during this treatment. This is no cause for concern. Once the sinus congestion has cleared up, your child may drink carrot juice as part of the regular diet, but limit it to no more than 1 cup of juice daily.

If the sinus congestion is severe or prolonged, or if symptoms such as lassitude, fever, or cough are present, consult a physician.

NOSEBLEEDS

Nosebleed, or epistaxis, rarely occurs in infants but is quite frequent in young children, more so in boys than in girls. The main causes are trauma to the nose, picking the nose, nasal polyps, and dilated blood vessels in the nose. If your child's nose is bleeding because of a blow to the nose in the course of play, the following steps will stop it: Calm your child and place him or her in a sitting position. Tilt the head back slightly and hold the nose closed firmly but gently, using your thumb and forefinger. Apply gentle pressure continuously for ten minutes — this is how long it normally takes for blood to clot. Tell the child to breathe through the mouth during this procedure. If the bleeding does not stop, apply an ice pack over the bridge of the nose and insert a dry piece of cotton into the nose for ten minutes or so. If the bleeding still persists, take your child to a clinic or pediatrician. For occasional minor nosebleeds, there are some herbal preparations you can try. (See also WHEN TO SEE THE DOCTOR: SEVERE NOSEBLEED, page 68.)

Oak Bark Snuff
To speed the clotting of blood during a nosebleed

Preparation Time: 5 minutes
Yield: 20 treatments
Children's Enjoyment: ☺

Oak bark is highly astringent, which makes it an excellent remedy for nosebleeds. Oak bark is also used commonly in tea form to reduce fever and wash out sores in the mouth. As a snuff, oak bark quickly closes up a burst vessel in the nose and helps clot blood. It strengthens and disinfects the tissue in the nose, and taken in combination with Calcium Tea (page 66), it helps prevent future nosebleeds. Oak bark pieces are available in health food and herb stores.

1/2 ounce oak bark pieces

1. Place the oak bark in a clean coffee grinder or food mill and grind to a powder.
2. Sift the powder to remove any large or irregularly shaped pieces.
3. Pour the sifted snuff into a snuff box or any little container that is easy to get 2 fingers into. Store it away from small children. Discard any unused snuff after 6 months

APPLICATION: Whenever a nosebleed occurs, have the child dip into the snuff with forefinger and thumb, take out a pinch, and sharply inhale it. Two or 3 inhalations, with a 1-minute pause between snuffs, may be necessary to stop the bleeding. However, the child should not inhale so much snuff that it causes sneezing. If the nosebleeds are frequent, have the child keep the snuff tin in a pocket, but make sure the child knows how to use it correctly. If the nosebleeds are infrequent, keep the snuff dry and fresh in the tin or a small, labeled jar with a tight-fitting lid. Use this snuff only in the instance of nosebleed.

If the child suffers frequent or severe nosebleeds, consult with a physician.

Calcium Tea
To increase the strength of the blood vessels within the nose

Preparation Time: 20 minutes
Yield: 3 treatments
Children's Enjoyment: ☺

The inner nose is a very delicate area, with blood vessels that are close to the surface. If this area is weak, nosebleeds can occur when a child experiences quick changes in altitude, such as in an elevator, has a good sneeze, gets roughed up when playing, or even for no reason at all. Therefore, strengthening the lining of the nasal passage is of primary importance when nosebleeds are a chronic problem. Calcium Tea is useful in treating recurring nosebleeds and all wounds that are slow to heal. The primary ingredient is oat straw, which is very high in calcium and valuable for strengthening and regenerating the tissue lining the inner nostrils. The tea can also be used as an external wash for flaky skin and eye problems.

> 1/2 ounce dried oat straw
> 1/2 ounce dried horsetail
> 2 cups water
> Honey to taste (optional)

1. Place the herbs and water in a covered pot, bring to a boil, and steep for 20 minutes.
2. Strain out the herb and discard it. The tea is dark yellow in color and smells like wet grass or hay.
3. Cool the tea to room temperature before serving. Refrigerate the remaining tea and reheat it to a tepid temperature with each use. Discard any unused tea after 1 week.

APPLICATION: A child with recurring nosebleeds should drink 1/2 cup of the tea 3 times each day until the nosebleeds occur less frequently or stop altogether (up to about 2 weeks). Morning is the best time to take the tea, and it may be sweetened with honey to taste. The tea has a grassy, mildly bitter taste, even with honey added, so the child may need some kind of chaser such as orange juice.

If the nosebleeds do not show any sign of improvement after 2 weeks, or if they become worse, consult a physician.

WHEN TO SEE THE DOCTOR

✚ VISION PROBLEMS: Vision impairment in children can occur from injury to the eye and diseases such as cataracts or glaucoma. It can also be due to congenital visual disorders such as albinism, extreme myopia (nearsightedness), amblyopia (one eye is "lazy" and does not focus as it should), astigmatism (one eye is bigger than the other), and strabismus (crossed eyes). Color blindness is also quite common in boys. Many of these conditions are spotted at birth so, if the disease or condition is curable, parents and doctors can embark on eye-patterning exercises, surgery, or other forms of therapy to correct the disorder.

✚ EYE INJURIES: A child who has experienced any form of trauma to the eye, such as a cut or puncture wound, should be taken to the hospital immediately. Modern methods of dealing with eye injuries are nothing short of miraculous, especially if there has been little time lost.

✚ HEARING LOSS: About 10 to 20 percent of all hearing loss in infants is due to congenital abnormalities. A doctor will screen an infant who appears to be hearing-impaired for maternal rubella; prematurity; abnormalities of the skull, neck, musculoskeletal system, and face; a negative Rh; and abnormal renal (kidney) function. If your child seemed to have normal hearing at birth and a hearing loss appears later, the causes could include meningitis, recurrent middle ear infections, or mumps encephalitis. You should suspect hearing loss if your children seem to have speech difficulties that are not related to any physical impairment in the mouth or if your children do not hear speech directed at them unless there is visual contact as well. Many hearing problems acquired later in a child's life can be reversed by surgery, so a thorough examination by a qualified physician is very important.

✦ SEVERE NOSEBLEED: A severe nosebleed is usually caused by an injury to the nose or face. Parents should not try to stop a nosebleed that seems very serious because the child may lose too much blood during the process. If a child's nose is bleeding severely, call an ambulance and get professional care as quickly as possible. Epinephrine drops, a Vaseline gauze pack, or local cauterization of a blood vessel within the nose may be necessary to stop the bleeding, and will be administered by a doctor or health professional. Children with severe nosebleeds may swallow a lot of blood before the bleeding is checked, so parents should not be alarmed if their child later vomits bloody material or passes dark, tarry stools for a day or two after the nosebleed.

✦ OBJECTS IN THE EAR, NOSE, OR EYES: If a child has gotten something lodged in the ear, nose, or eye, you should not try to remove it by yourself. Further injury can be caused by inexperienced or clumsy parents trying to remove an object from a squirming, panic-stricken child. Extreme care must be taken when removing objects from eyes, and a thorough examination and treatment are needed to prevent infection. If your child has sustained a severe injury, such as a tear or puncture wound in the eye, call an ambulance. Removing objects lodged in the ears or nasal passages may require flushing or curettage (use of a long, slim instrument known as a curette to dislodge the object). Health professionals have the special tools and methods needed to do this.

CHAPTER THREE

SORE THROATS

CHILDREN

Hoarse Throat

Swollen Glands

Sore Throats from Colds and Flu

Sore throats are rare in children under one year of age and uncommon in children under two. After children are two years old, the incidence of sore throats gradually increases, with a peak between the ages of six and twelve.

A sore throat often accompanies a cold. It is also one of the first signs of tonsillitis, strep throat, and scarlet fever. If your child has a sinus infection or postnasal drip, a sore throat can be caused by mucus draining back into the throat. Also, a hacking cough — such as the kind that accompanies bronchitis or any type of lung congestion — can irritate the throat and make it sore.

CHILDREN

When your child complains of a sore throat, the first thing to do is place him or her under a light, tilt the head back, and examine the throat and tongue. The throat is probably red and the tongue slightly coated in back. Gently feel your child's neck at the base of the jaw. There may be some glandular swelling, which feels like soft marbles under the skin surface. Determine the severity of your child's discomfort. If there is a mild fever, do not be alarmed. On the other hand, if your child is listless, with a fever of 103 degrees or higher, very swollen tonsils, or white spots on the tonsils, take him or her to a physician or clinic for diagnosis and throat cultures. (See also WHEN TO SEE THE DOCTOR, page 79.)

HOARSE THROAT   A child's hoarse throat can have a number of causes. Children can scream themselves hoarse at a ball game or party. A hoarse throat can also be the sign of an oncoming cold. Sometimes, excessively dry air in the bedroom at night, especially during the winter when air is artificially heated, can cause hoarseness. If you think this might be the cause, place a vaporizer in the room at night to bring immediate relief. There are also a number of effective herbal remedies that you can use to relieve your child's hoarseness.

Licorice Lollipops
To soothe and relieve hoarse throat

Preparation Time: 10 minutes
Yield: 1 treatment
Children's Enjoyment: ☺

Licorice root is chewed by many professional singers to soothe their throats, and in China, licorice has been used to treat coughs and colds for thousands of years. Licorice is excellent for relieving sore throats and helping expectorate mucus from the head and lungs. Because it tastes good, licorice is easy to give to fussy children, especially with a light honey coating; and sucking on a lollipop always appeals to a child. Buy licorice root that is large enough for a child to suck on. If you can, get Chinese licorice which has been presoaked in honey, another substance that is good for the throat. These lollipops are delicious!

 1 five-inch-long piece licorice root
 2 tablespoons honey
 1 cup water

1. Place the licorice root, honey, and water in a covered pot, bring to a boil, and simmer for 5 minutes. (Omit the honey if you use Chinese licorice.)
2. Strain out the herb and set it aside to cool. You can keep the licorice tea to drink, or discard it if you wish.
3. When the softened licorice root is cool enough to hold comfortably in the hand, give it to the child to suck on. Keep the dried licorice root in a labeled jar with a tight-fitting lid, away from children. Discard any unused root after 6 months.

APPLICATION: Give a child with a hoarse throat softened licorice root once each day in the morning or afternoon to suck on for as long as he or she wishes. Remember that licorice root is slightly stimulating and a mild laxative, so it should be eaten only in the morning or early afternoon. The hoarse throat usually disappears after 2 days.

If the hoarseness does not abate or grows worse after 2 or 3 days, or if a fever over 103 degrees develops at any time, consult a physician.

Marshmallow Tea
Good for rebuilding and soothing the membranes of the throat

Preparation Time: 20 minutes
Yield: 4 treatments
Children's Enjoyment: ☺

This tea is good to use in combination with Licorice Lollipops (page 71). Marshmallow, also known as mallow, is very soothing to membranous surfaces, which makes it perfect for hoarse throats. Marshmallow is also high in calcium, which heals and regenerates damaged tissue anywhere in the body. The leaves and stems of marshmallow are used medicinally and smell and look like mown grass.

> 2 cups water
> 1 ounce dried marshmallow
> Honey or syrup (optional)

1. Put the water in a covered pot and bring to a boil.
2. Take the pot off the heat, add the marshmallow, and replace the pot lid. Steep the herbs for 20 minutes. The tea is light gray-green in color and smells like wet grass.
3. Cool the tea to a tepid temperature before serving. Refrigerate leftover tea and reheat it for each use. Discard any unused portion after 2 days.

APPLICATION: Give your child 1/2 cup of tea twice each day, in the afternoon and before bedtime, for 3 days. You can sweeten the tea with honey or syrup. This tea tastes unusual, but not unpleasant, and most children like it.

If the hoarse throat persists or gets worse after 3 days, or if a fever above 103 degrees develops at any time, consult a physician.

Your child may complain of a sore throat at times when there is no redness or swelling apparent. Ask your child if the throat hurts all the time or only when swallowing. If the reply is that it hurts only when swallowing, the lymph glands in the throat may be swollen and irritated. The lymphatic system is responsible for filtering bacteria and other toxins from the bloodstream. As the body cleanses itself of these wastes, the lymph glands, particularly in the throat, swell and become tender. Swollen glands are usually not serious unless the swelling is extreme or pain is present. If your child has similar pain and swelling in the armpit or the groin area, a checkup by a physician is needed to determine the cause. After you know that you can safely treat your child at home, there are some excellent herbal remedies you can make.

SWOLLEN GLANDS

Flannel Muffler Wrap
To relieve pain and swelling in the throat area

Preparation Time: 10 minutes
Yield: 1 treatment
Children's Enjoyment: ☺

Flannel mufflers are a traditional remedy for sore throats and swollen glands. Warming the throat area can reduce swelling and encourage healing, especially when some diluted eucalyptus oil is rubbed onto the throat beforehand. Any old flannel shirt will do for this process, but make sure it is clean.

> 1 five-inch-wide strip of flannel, long enough to comfortably tie around the child's throat
> 1 application of Eucalyptus Oil Rub (page 38)

APPLICATION: Perform this treatment just before bedtime. Apply a palmful of the Eucalyptus Oil Rub on the child's throat, starting at the point of the jaw slightly behind the ears and continuing down to the collar bone. Rub gently but vigorously. Encourage the child to tell you where it hurts as you rub, so that you can apply the oil where it will do the most good. When the oil is applied and absorbed, warm the flannel muffler briefly in the oven and wrap it around the child's throat. Tie the muffler loosely in the back and make sure the child can sleep comfortably with it on. Leave the wrap on all night. In the morning, wash all the unabsorbed oil off the child's throat and wash the flannel. Repeat the procedure once each night with the same clean piece of flannel until the sore throat or swollen glands have disappeared (up to 1 week). Even very young children get a kick out of this procedure, and their brothers and sisters often try to get in on the act by pretending to have sore throats, too. You may want to have some placebo flannel wraps around to prevent possible "sicker than thou" competitions.

If the swollen neck glands persist after 1 week of treatment or are very painful, or if glandular swelling occurs anywhere else in the body, such as the armpit or groin, consult a physician.

Apple Juice and Clove Tea
To reduce throat pain and flush the lymphatic glands

Preparation Time: 15 minutes
Yield: 8 Treatments
Children's Enjoyment: ☺

This beverage is good to use in combination with the Flannel Muffler Wrap. Apple juice is a lymphatic-system flush that helps the body rid itself of toxins. This makes apple juice especially useful to treat swollen glands and mumps. Fresh apple juice is alkaline and helps balance the body if too many acid-forming foods, such as red meat or sugar, are ingested. Cloves act as a topical painkiller, and when taken with apple juice, help to reduce pain and discomfort from swallowing. Try to get fresh, unfiltered juice. If you juice your own apples, use McIntosh or Granny Smith apples that have not been waxed or sprayed.

8 whole cloves
1 quart fresh apple juice

1. Add the cloves to the juice and simmer slowly in a covered pot for 15 minutes.
2. Strain out the cloves and discard. The tea will look and smell like spiced apple juice and may have some essential oil of cloves floating on top. Stir the tea to recombine the oil.
3. Cool the tea to room temperature before serving. Refrigerate any remaining tea and warm it to room temperature for each treatment. Discard any unused portion after 5 days.

APPLICATION: Have the child drink 1/2 cup of the tea twice each day, in the morning and afternoon (never at night, since it is slightly stimulating) until the swelling and sore throat subside. This combination is pleasant to drink, but tell the child that the tea will taste strongly of cloves and that there will be a slight numbness in the mouth and throat afterwards.

If swollen glands persist beyond 1 week of treatment, if there is glandular swelling in other parts of the body, or if there is severe pain, consult a pediatrician.

SORE THROATS FROM COLDS AND FLU

A sore throat can be the first symptom of a cold or flu. The throat is usually red and the tonsils may be slightly enlarged, but there should be no white patches in the throat, and your child should not feel any severe discomfort. Give your child soft food and soups to eat for a couple of days until the throat is no longer tender. Your child may not have any appetite for a day or two, anyway, and a liquid diet will be fine. It will keep a normal fluid balance in the body and speed the toxin-cleansing processes. Fruit juice popsicles are excellent for children with sore throats resulting from colds or flu. It is important that your child have bedrest and quiet during this time so that the body's resistance to infection can be restored to normal. If your child has a sore throat as a symptom of cold or flu, and you determine that it is nothing more serious than that, there are a number of comforting herbal therapies you can try.

Licorice Tea

To help perk up a child, and to relieve sore throat
and head and lung congestion

Preparation Time: 20 minutes
Yield: 4 treatments
Children's Enjoyment: ☺

Licorice Tea is a tasty antidote for sore throats, especially those that accompany colds and flu. Licorice is a mild stimulant and laxative. Besides soothing the throat and helping a child feel more comfortable, licorice helps reduce fever and expel mucus from the lungs.

> 1/2 ounce licorice root pieces
> 2 cups water

1. Combine the licorice root and water in a covered pot, bring to a boil, and simmer for 20 minutes.
2. Strain the liquid and set aside the herb. The tea is light brown in color and tastes and smells sweet and of licorice.
3. Cool the tea until comfortably warm before serving. Refrigerate the remaining tea and reheat it with each use.
4. Save the boiled root, since it is good for your child to suck on. Discard any unused portion after 2 days.

APPLICATION: Give the child 1/2 cup of the tea twice each day, in the morning and afternoon, for 3 days. Serve the tea as warm as is comfortable for the child since heat is soothing to the throat. No sweetener is necessary; licorice root is naturally quite sweet, even sweeter than sugar. Most children enjoy this tea very much.

If the sore throat persists or worsens after 3 days, if white spots appear on the tonsils or back of the throat, or if a fever above 103 degrees is present, consult a physician.

Sarsaparilla Syrup
To strengthen the immune system, relieve sore throat,
and bring down fever

Preparation Time: 1 hour, 30 minutes
Yield: 15 treatments
Children's Enjoyment: ☺

Sarsaparilla Syrup is a good-tasting and effective cough syrup that helps children overcome sore throats and colds. This syrup was a traditional spring tonic and, combined with wintergreen and sassafras, was used to make homemade root beer. Sarsaparilla was regularly used by Native Americans as a tonic for coughs and colds. The syrup base of this mixture soothes and coats a sore throat, while the sarsaparilla stimulates the circulation in the organs and systems of the body, induces sweat, and helps digestion. This syrup tastes wonderful and can also be mixed with sparkling water and ice to make a root beer-like beverage that cools a sore throat and helps bring down fever.

1 ounce dried sarsaparilla root
2 cups water
1 1/2 pounds (approximately 3 cups) brown sugar

1. Place the sarsaparilla root and water in a pot and soak the root for 1 hour before preparing the syrup.
2. Cover the pot and simmer the mixture for 20 minutes.
3. Strain out the herb and discard it. The mixture is dark brown in color and smells like root beer.
4. Add the sugar to the mixture and gently boil until it is completely dissolved.
5. Cool the syrup for 15 minutes, then pour it into a glass jar or bottle with a tight-fitting lid. Label and date the container, and store it in a closet, out of the reach of children. Discard any unused portion after 6 months.

APPLICATION: Give your child 1 tablespoon 3 times each day, between meals, for 1 week. The syrup soothes the sore throat, increases energy, and helps increase his or her resistance to infection. Children like the taste of this syrup very much.

If the child's sore throat or cough persists after 1 week of treatment or becomes severe at any time, or if the child exhibits fatigue or a high fever (103 degrees or above), consult a pediatrician.

Plantain Syrup
To relieve a lingering sore throat after a cold or flu

Preparation Time: 15 minutes
Yield: 15 treatments
Children's Enjoyment: ☺

Plantain is a very common herb, found in backyards, roadsides, and empty lots all over the United States and Europe. Administered as a syrup, plantain helps expel mucus from the lungs, coats the throat to relieve soreness, and is also a tasty vitamin supplement. Do not gather plantain from roadsides or any public lands unless you know it has not been sprayed or poisoned. This is a good syrup to let a child help you make, especially if you use fresh plantain.

> 1 ounce dried or 2 ounces fresh plantain
> 2 cups water
> 1 1/2 pounds (approximately 3 cups) brown sugar

1. If you use fresh plantain, bruise the leaves with your hands or the back of a wooden spoon.
2. Put the water in a pot and immerse the fresh or dried plantain in it. Simmer, covered, for 15 minutes.
3. Strain out the herb and discard it.
4. Add the sugar to the dark green liquid. Bring the mixture to a gentle boil and cook until the sugar is completely dissolved.
5. Cool the mixture to room temperature. The syrup has a mild,

grassy smell and is dark brown in color. Pour it into a glass jar with a tight-fitting lid, and label and date the jar. Discard the syrup after 6 months.

APPLICATION: Give the child 1 tablespoon 3 times each day, between meals, until the sore throat disappears. This syrup tastes sweet and grassy, and while it is unusual, it is not unpleasant. Most children like its taste and are usually cooperative at medicine time.

If the sore throat grows worse, if there are white spots on the back of the throat, or if other symptoms such as high fever (above 103 degrees), paleness, and listlessness appear, consult a pediatrician.

WHEN TO SEE THE DOCTOR

✦ TONSILLITIS: Tonsillitis can be frightening and uncomfortable for your child but is rarely life threatening. If your physician diagnoses your child's sore throat as tonsillitis, be aware that a tonsillectomy is not necessarily required. If your doctor insists on performing one, you should get a second opinion. While surgery of this type has become generally less common, tonsillectomies and adenoidectomies are still the leading causes of pediatric admissions in hospitals throughout the United States. Some good reasons for performing tonsillectomies and adenoidectomies include an obstructed airway, a tonsil enlarged enough to interfere with swallowing, a nasal obstruction that causes breathing difficulties or speech impediments, chronic ear infections from eustachian tubes blocked by adenoids, three or more bouts of strep throat in one year, or an abscessed tonsil. If your child has none of these conditions, work closely with your pediatrician to determine an alternative treatment.

✦ STREP THROAT: Streptococcal pharyngitis, or strep throat, comes on suddenly, with a high fever (103 degrees or above, rectally), a very sore throat, and white bumps on the back of the throat and tonsils. Headache and abdominal pain may also be present. A child with strep throat will appear quite ill. If your child has any of these symptoms, a visit to the doctor is in order. A throat culture will be taken and antibiotics will be administered for ten days to completely kill the bacterial infection. It is very important for your child to take the full ten days' supply of antibiotics, even if the infection seems to have cleared up. Otherwise the infection can reappear in a more resistant form. Parents and siblings of a child with a positive throat culture should also have cultures taken because they, too, may be harboring the bacteria. Strep throat should not be left untreated. It will not go away by itself, and complications of strep throat include scarlet fever and rheumatic fever.

✚ SCARLET FEVER: Before the discovery of antibiotics, scarlet fever was a very serious childhood disease that often resulted in death or permanent heart or kidney damage. Major symptoms of scarlet fever include a sudden fever of up to 104 degrees rectally, headache, sore throat, vomiting, and a characteristic bright red rash that sets in after one or two days. Your child's tongue will have a white coating, while its tip and edges are red. Since the discovery of antibiotics, the rates of mortality and serious complications from this disease have fallen to less than 1 percent. Along with antibiotics, the usual treatment includes bed rest, fluids, and fever-reducing drugs. Although scarlet fever is now a relatively rare disease in the United States, it is quite contagious and can require hospital supervision.

✚ RHEUMATIC FEVER: Acute rheumatic fever has symptoms such as swollen nodules beneath the skin, tender and swollen joints, uncontrollable shaking, fever, runny nose, and sore throat. Rheumatic fever can permanently weaken the heart, and before the discovery of antibiotics, it was often fatal. It is a streptococcal infection of the upper respiratory tract and is often the result of untreated strep throat. Treatment for rheumatic fever consists of antibiotics, bed rest, and gradual daily exercise.

CHAPTER FOUR

FEVERS

INFANTS

Fevers from Colds

Fevers from Infections

Fevers Caused by Teething

CHILDREN

Fevers from Colds

Fever as a Symptom of Other Childhood Diseases

fevers in children are generally mild, with temperatures below 100 degrees and a duration of no more than three days. Fever is not a signal for panic; instead, it can be used to monitor the health of your child's immune system, since fever is usually the first symptom of an illness. An infection anywhere in the body can generate a fever, and fever is one of the first symptoms in childhood diseases such as colds, measles, and chicken pox. To check your child for fever, don't rely on putting your hand to your child's forehead. Instead, keep both oral and rectal thermometers in the medicine cabinet and learn to use them.

Occasionally, I give my kids children's aspirin or liquid acetaminophen (Tylenol) for fever, especially when they wake up in pain during the night. I prefer, however, to handle fevers with safer and more effective baths and teas whenever possible. Children often think of children's aspirin as candy because of its color and sweetness, and will go to great lengths to find the bottle no matter where you store it. Be sure your child knows that children's aspirin is not candy, but medicine to be taken only when sick, with an adult handing it out. Also, keep in mind that childproof caps are not always childproof.

Most of the time a mild fever in a child can actually be beneficial. Fever, in effect, puts the whole body on what might be called "yellow alert." When the body's temperature rises, the metabolism speeds up and the body can move healing nutrients to a malfunctioning area more efficiently. Fever also helps the body burn off and flush out unwanted materials by triggering perspiration. Many of the toxins present in the body are expelled through the pores of the skin in this way. In fact, sweatbaths, saunas, and hot tubs can promote health by artificially inducing fevers and causing toxins to be sweated out. As a result, a mild fever can actually be a sign of good health in a child because it proves that the immune system is alert and responsive enough to battle infections. If, however, your child looks flushed or pale, develops a fever suddenly, or has a fever that steadily rises to over 103 degrees, consult a physician immediately. (See also WHEN TO SEE THE DOCTOR, page 100.)

INFANTS

When infants have a fever, they exhibit symptoms such as irritability, restlessness, paleness, redness around the eyes, and of course, an elevated body temperature. The most common causes of infant fevers are colds, measles, chicken pox, gastroenteritis, ear infections, and — although this is still not a scientifically documented fact — teething. Parents should know that any infant under three months of age does not have the ability to localize infections. Instead, infections in infants can spread to other parts of the body. For example, a middle ear infection in an infant can spread to the brain and cause meningitis. Infants with an unexplained fever that might be due to an infection should be taken to a doctor or pediatric clinic promptly. Frequently, however, infants will develop mild fevers when they are exposed to colds and when they are teething. Most of these mild infant fevers can be treated safely and effectively at home.

FEVERS FROM COLDS

Infants who have caught a cold sometimes develop a mild fever. Parents should try to manage the fever to make sure it does not go over 103 degrees. However, they should remember that mild fever in an infant with a cold is a sign that the immune system is on the alert trying to combat the cold virus. A mild fever should be allowed to run its course to help the body recover faster. Feverish infants should be kept lightly covered and their hands and feet should be kept warm. Heavy blankets or sleepers will only make them hot and uncomfortable. I have two favorite fever-soothing herbal remedies for infants with colds.

Catnip Tea
To reduce fever and help an infant relax

Preparation Time: 20 minutes
Yield: 5 treatments
Children's Enjoyment: ☺

Catnip Tea is indicated for infants with low fevers from colds, flu, or chicken pox. Catnip is a mild sweat inducer that helps cool the body and excrete wastes through the skin. Catnip is mildly tranquilizing and can also soothe colic and settle an upset stomach. Do not use catnip that is packaged for pets.

> 1/2 ounce dried catnip
> 2 cups water
> 1 tablespoon light corn syrup

1. Combine the catnip and water in a covered pot and simmer for 20 minutes.
2. Strain out the herb and discard. The tea is a light gray-green color and smells slightly grassy and bitter.
3. Sweeten with corn syrup. Cool the tea to room temperature before serving.

APPLICATION: For an infant with a low fever, administer 6 tablespoons of tea twice each day, just before nap and at bedtime, until the temperature returns to normal (2 to 4 days). If the infant will not take a bottle, use a teaspoon to spoon the tea into the mouth. Remember to hold the infant in a comfortable, secure position to receive the medicine. In this way, the infant will get used to the routine and there will be less resistance at tea time. Catnip Tea is very mild, so don't worry about giving your infant too much.

If the fever shows no improvement after 1 week of treatment, or if it rises above 103 degrees at any time, consult a physician.

Pennyroyal Bath
To soothe muscle aches and pains and reduce fever

Preparation Time: 20 minutes
Yield: 1 treatment
Children's Enjoyment: ☺

Baths are an excellent and easy way to cool and soothe mild fever in your infant. Pennyroyal belongs to the mint family and has a peculiar, camphorous smell. You will probably recognize the smell immediately, since pennyroyal oil is a common ingredient in many commercial insect repellents. It is mildly diaphoretic, which makes this bath an excellent cold remedy. This bath is very effective in combination with the Catnip Tea.

    2 ounces dried pennyroyal
    2 quarts water

1. Combine the pennyroyal and water in a large, covered pot. Bring to a boil and simmer slowly for 20 minutes.
2. Strain out and discard the herb.
3. Pour the tea into the bathtub while the water is running so that it will be well combined. Run the herbal bath as hot as you usually run a bath for the infant, but make sure the temperature of the bath is not too hot after adding the brewed tea. The bathwater is light green and smells strongly of peppermint and camphor.

APPLICATION: Put the infant in the bath and gently play with him or her for at least 20 minutes. There is no need to wash the infant during the bath. This bath can be repeated once each day in the early evening until the cold disappears (usually 1 week). Both you and your infant should enjoy this treatment very much.
    If a high fever (above 103 degrees), or lassitude are present, or if the cold persists or gets worse after 1 week, consult a physician.

85

FEVERS
FROM
INFECTIONS
If an infant under three months of age develops a fever, a prompt examination by a health professional is always necessary. A fever in a three- to six-month-old infant without any external symptoms, such as a runny nose or cough, may be due to an infection somewhere in the body. In such a case, a doctor's examination is necessary to determine if the fever is the first symptom of a cold or a disease such as measles, or chicken pox, or if it is caused by a specific infection. In either case, parents should not become alarmed or distressed, but should work with their doctor to determine the best way to bring the fever down and combat the infection. The most common problem areas for infant infections are the ears, bronchial tubes, and urinary tract.

When an infant is feverish, parents should not apply ice packs or use alcohol rubs. Ice packs can shock a body that is already weakened by a cold, and the inhalation of alcohol fumes has been linked to the development of hypoglycemia and coma in infants. In addition, the chilling effect of both of these methods may cause shivering that can actually increase the body's core temperature. Ice packs and alcohol rubs should be used on infants only in cases of very high fever and always under the supervision of a medical professional. The following bath is very effective for reducing fever and making your infant feel more comfortable.

Peppermint and Comfrey Bath
To soothe itching and fever from chicken pox or measles

Preparation Time: 30 minutes
Yield: 1 treatment
Children's Enjoyment: ☺

This is a particularly good bath for an infant with a fever resulting from measles, chicken pox, or any illness that produces a skin rash. Peppermint, like pennyroyal, produces the cooling sensation common to all the mint family. It is also a mild topical anesthetic, which can reduce itchiness and discomfort on your infant's skin. Comfrey root is very high in calcium and a substance called allantoin. When applied to your infant's skin in the bathwater, it can help heal eruptions, sores, and rashes, as well as regenerate tissue. Keep in mind that the skin, the body's largest organ, performs very important excretory and respiratory functions. By keeping your infant's skin vital and glowing you help the immune system operate at its most efficient level. Another of the healing attributes of comfrey root is its ability to lower an elevated body temperature. Mixed with peppermint in a bath-tea combination, comfrey lowers a temperature in infants at the same time as it relieves minor aches and pains, and soothes and softens the skin.

> 2 ounces dried comfrey root
> 2 ounces dried peppermint
> 2 quarts water

1. Combine the comfrey root and water in a large, covered pot and bring to a boil.
2. Simmer the comfrey for 10 minutes, remove the covered pot from the heat, and add the peppermint.
3. Steep the mixture for 20 minutes.
4. Strain out the herbs and discard them. The bath tea is dark brown and smells mostly of peppermint. Pour the bath tea into the tub while the water is running so that it will be well combined. Run the herbal bath as hot as you usually run a bath for your child, but make sure the temperature is not too hot for the infant's skin after adding the brewed tea.

APPLICATION: Let the infant soak for at least 20 minutes. Repeat the bath once each day just before bedtime until the fever is lowered to normal, usually 1 to 3 days.

If the fever persists for more than 3 days, or rises above 103 degrees at any time, consult a physician.

FEVERS CAUSED BY TEETHING

An infant's first teeth appear between the ages of three to six months. The front teeth usually come in first, with four on the top gum and four on the bottom. Most infants will not have any difficulty breaking these incisors through the gum, although some infants might exhibit a change in behavior or sleep habits. It is when the molars are breaking through — at twelve to sixteen months of age — that side effects such as fever occur, though some infants never have any problems. All of my children developed fevers while they were teething. The fevers lasted three to four days, never went over 101 degrees, and were always accompanied by fretful, whining behavior. With all three, the fever broke as soon as the molar — it was always a molar — broke through the gum. Other reactions to watch for during teething are excessive diaper rash, nasty temperament, sleeplessness at night, and loss of appetite.

If your infant exhibits fever or any of the symptoms mentioned above, and you suspect it is due to teething, there are several things you can do. Use your index finger — with a short fingernail and clean, of course — to rub your infant's top and bottom gums in the back of the mouth. If they are red or swollen, there is probably a molar on its way to the surface. By firmly rubbing your infant's gums, you hasten the molar's breakthrough. As you do this, your infant might involuntarily bite down on your finger because the pressure feels good. I gave my children hard biscuits to chew. Give infants as many biscuits as they want and repeat the gum-rubbing process at least three times each day. There are also very effective herbal remedies for the symptoms of teething.

Willow Bark Tea
To relieve the pain and mild fever of teething

Preparation Time: 20 minutes
Yield: 4 treatments
Children's Enjoyment: ☹

White willow bark has been used since prehistoric times to kill pain, bring down fever, reduce inflammation, and reduce water retention. Willow bark contains salicin, which is converted in the body to salicylic acid, a substance that closely resembles synthetic aspirin. This versatile herb can be used in tea or tincture form and is available in health food and herb stores. Try to get whole pieces of bark — as opposed to powdered willow bark — since this is easier to brew as tea. There are also several varieties of white willow bark tablets available, which can be used whole for children, or crushed up and mixed with juice for infants.

>   1/2 ounce white willow bark pieces
>   2 cups water

1. Combine the willow bark with the water in a covered pot, bring to a boil, and simmer for 20 minutes.
2. Strain out the herb and discard it. The tea is a dark burgundy color and has a slightly bitter, astringent taste.
3. Do not sweeten. Cool the tea to room temperature before serving. Store remaining tea in the refrigerator and reheat with each use. Discard any unused portion of the tea after 2 days.

APPLICATION: Administer 10 drops 3 times each day to your infant, by sterile dropper or by teaspoon, until pain or fever disappears (1 to 3 days). The effect of the tea will be felt immediately and a restful night's sleep should ensue. Because this tea is slightly astringent, too much may cause constipation. If your infant becomes constipated during treatment, reduce the dosage.

If pain becomes severe or fever rises above 103 degrees at any time, consult a physician. If your infant has been found to be aspirin sensitive or allergic, do not use this tea.

Clove Oil Gum Rub
To calm an infant or toddler and reduce the pain of teething

Preparation Time: 5 minutes
Yield: 8 treatments
Children's Enjoyment: ☹

This is my favorite remedy for a teething child because it is by far the easiest one to prepare and administer. Clove oil can be used to allay the pain of teething and to soothe colic and upset stomachs. Whole cloves can also be sucked on to refresh the breath. They contain hot carminative oils that aid digestion, which is why cloves are often combined with meats that are high in fat, such as ham. Clove oil is a powerful pain reliever when used in a dilute solution in the mouth or on the skin. Essential oil of cloves is a clear, amber color. It is available in many drugstores as well as health food and herb stores. The label on the bottle should state clearly that the oil is suitable for internal consumption, since some methods for extracting essential oils can involve harmful chemicals.

>   1/2 teaspoon essential oil of cloves
>   2 teaspoons fresh olive, corn, or other vegetable oil

1. Combine all the ingredients in a small dish or jar lid.
2. Stir with your index finger for 2 minutes to make sure the oils are thoroughly mixed and will not burn the skin. When the oil makes your fingertip tingle mildly, it is ready to use.

APPLICATION: For a teething infant, wash your hands, trim your nails, and coat your fingertip with the oil. Rub firmly wherever a tooth is trying to erupt through the gum, which is evident by swelling and redness of the gum and your ability to feel the tooth under the gum tissue. Most infants do not like the flavor of this rub, so you need to hold them firmly and croon to them. After about a minute, they will feel the anesthetic effect and will begin to calm down. My infants often slept after clove oil was applied. This treatment may be repeated as often as needed until the tooth erupts (2 to 5 days).

Teething infants are rarely in danger of complications, and the oil should help to relieve pain while the tooth erupts. If a child complains of a painful toothache, consult a dentist before applying the oil.

CHILDREN

A mild fever after playing outdoors all day is common in children. Strenuous physical activity can raise their body temperature, especially on a hot day. This mild fever is no cause for alarm as long as the temperature returns to normal after the child cools off indoors. Fever also usually accompanies colds and flu, and is often the first sign of a childhood illness such as mumps, measles, chicken pox, colds, ear infections, and upper respiratory infections. Fever in conjunction with these disorders should not alarm you unless the temperature is 103 degrees or above. High fevers in children can trigger convulsions. A child with a high fever should be examined by a healing professional to determine the cause of the fever and supervise the administration of fever reducing drugs. (See also WHEN TO SEE THE DOCTOR, page 100.)

FEVERS FROM COLDS

Fever usually sets in about twenty-four to thirty-six hours after exposure to the cold virus. Herbal teas can make children with colds and cold-related fevers more comfortable. If getting teas — even good-tasting ones — into your child is a problem, there are other remedies you can try. Sweet syrup is often the best way to get a finicky child to take medicine, and herbal syrups are easy to make. Herbal baths can also be specially formulated to allay discomfort from fever while providing an external — and very pleasant — form of relief for small children. Herbal baths for fevers should always be run warm, never too hot to avoid increasing the fever and never too cold to avoid chilling your child. I have several favorite fever remedies for children with fevers from colds.

Catnip Tea
To rehydrate during fever and induce sleep

Preparation Time: 20 minutes
Yield: 2 treatments
Children's Enjoyment: ☺

Catnip induces sleep in children and helps relieve the discomforts of a cold with its gentle expectorant, or mucus-expelling, qualities. This tea is widely used in Europe to treat the symptoms of children's colds and fevers, to soothe distressed or overexcited children, and to relieve stomachaches. If your child is restless at night because of a fever, one cup of this tea just before bedtime is indicated. In addition to reducing fevers, this tea also replenishes any fluids that may be lost. Children with fever often have no appetite. Don't try to force-feed them when they are sick. When their appetite returns, it is a good indication that they are getting well. Catnip Tea is indicated for infants and children with low fevers from colds, flu, or chicken pox. It is a mild sweat inducer that helps cool the body and excrete wastes through the skin. Catnip is mildly tranquilizing and can soothe colic and settle an upset stomach. Do not use catnip that is packaged for pets.

    1 ounce dried catnip
    2 cups water
    Honey to taste (optional)

1. Combine the catnip and water in a covered pot and simmer for 20 minutes.
2. Strain out the herbs and discard. The tea is a light gray-green color and smells slightly grassy and bitter.
3. Honey can be used to sweeten the tea for children over the age of 18 months. Cool the tea to room temperature before serving.

APPLICATION: Most children tolerate the taste of the sweetened tea. Give them 1 cup of tea twice each day, before nap and at bedtime, until the fever is gone (2 days to 1 week).

If the fever shows no improvement after 1 week of treatment, or if it rises above 103 degrees at any time, consult a physician.

Black Currant Syrup
To strengthen resistance to viral infection and reduce fever

Preparation Time: 2 minutes
Yield: 20 treatments
Children's Enjoyment: ☺

If your child simply will not take tea for whatever reason, this delicious syrup should be used. Black currant, also known as quinsy berry, is widely cultivated in Europe and is used in jams, jellies, spreads, and syrups. It is high in vitamin C and iron; and has diaphoretic, or sweat-inducing, and diuretic, or water-eliminating, qualities. This syrup is excellent for a child with a fever from a cold. The syrup reduces fever, causes wastes to be discharged through the pores of the skin, and helps the body resist the cold virus. A tablespoon of this syrup can also be given to a healthy child two or three times a week as a good-tasting, overall tonic. Black currant syrup is available in some gourmet food stores and most health food stores. There are many brands available, but I prefer those that are imported from Europe, especially from Switzerland and West Germany, where preservatives are not commonly used in syrups. The syrup does not need to be refrigerated, but write the date it was opened on the label and store it in a child-proof place. Discard the syrup 6 months after it was opened.

APPLICATION: Administer 1 tablespoon of the syrup 3 times each day, before meals, until the cold and fever symptoms disappear. As an alternative, 1 tablespoon of the syrup mixed in a glass of sparkling water helps combat the loss of fluids brought on by fever. This is an extremely good-tasting medicine, and children may try to convince you they are sick enough to need it.

If the child's fever persists after 1 week, or if paleness, listlessness, or very high fever are present, consult a pediatrician.

Pennyroyal Bath
To rehydrate and reduce fever, muscle aches, and pains

Preparation Time: 20 minutes
Yield: 1 treatment
Children's Enjoyment: ☺

Pennyroyal belongs to the mint family and has a peculiar, camphorous smell. You will probably recognize the smell immediately, since pennyroyal oil is a common ingredient in many commercial insect repellents. This herb is used in Europe and America to promote sweating at the onset of a cold. Pennyroyal also relaxes sore muscles and refreshes the skin when used in a bath. This remedy is good to use in combination with the black currant syrup.

2 ounces dried pennyroyal
2 quarts water

1. Combine the pennyroyal and water in a large, covered pot; bring to a boil and simmer slowly for 20 minutes.
2. Strain the tea for the bath, but do not discard the pennyroyal herbs. Instead, wrap the herbs in a washcloth and tie up the 4 corners with a rubber band, forming a scrub pad. Have your child use the herb-filled washcloth to scrub the skin all over the body. This will stimulate the skin and open the pores, making the bath doubly effective as a fever reducer.
3. Pour the tea into the bathtub while the water is running so that it will be well combined. Run the herbal bath as hot as you usually run a bath for the child, but make sure the temperature of the bath is not too hot after adding the brewed tea. The bathwater is light green and smells strongly of peppermint and camphor.

APPLICATION: Explain to young children that this bath makes the skin feel slightly tingly. Let the child soak in the tub for 20 minutes. You can add some dried leaves of pennyroyal to the bathwater for the child to play with, but make sure you cover the drain of the bathtub with a strainer when you empty the tub. This bath can be repeated once each day in the early evening until the cold disappears (usually 1 week).

If a high fever (above 103 degrees), lassitude, or nausea are present, or if the cold persists or gets worse after 1 week, consult a physician.

Fever is a common symptom in many childhood diseases. A child with a fever will be listless, have no appetite, and may have soreness and puffiness around the eyes. You need not be concerned about childhood fevers unless they go too high — above 103 degrees — or last more than three days. Fevers in children can come and go with amazing swiftness, sometimes running their course in a single, sleepless night. A child with a fever may feel anxious and afraid, but an informed parent's assurance and lovingly prepared herbal remedies can soothe the child and hasten the healing process. There is an herbal soda and several teas that can work wonders on children's fevers, while relieving other symptoms, as well.

FEVER AS A SYMPTOM OF OTHER CHILDHOOD DISEASES

Angostura Soda
To rehydrate the body, reduce fever, and relieve diarrhea

Preparation Time: 5 minutes
Yield: 1 treatment
Children's Enjoyment: ☺

If your child has both a fever and an upset stomach — as in the case of flu — this is an excellent remedy. It is easy to make, good tasting, and a good way to get extra fluids into your child's system. Angostura Soda is excellent for relieving both fever and diarrhea. Angostura Bitters is a popular flavoring and mixer in cocktails such as an old-fashioned and a Manhattan. The primary ingredient in Angostura Bitters is gentian root, which is known for its worm-killing, fever-reducing, stomach-strengthening, and liver-stimulating properties. It is also a topical and internal antiseptic, and is used in gentian violet, a topical medicine for canker sores, minor cuts, and scrapes. Angostura Bitters is available in any liquor store and in many grocery stores. I let my children prepare Angostura Soda to their own individual tastes.

> 1 cup any brand sparkling water
> 5 to 10 drops Angostura Bitters
> Mint sprig (optional)

1. Fill a glass with sparkling water.
2. Let the child shake the Angostura Bitters drops into the soda and stir it. The soda is light pink in color. You can garnish it with a sprig of mint if you like.

APPLICATION: This soda can be served plain or on the rocks. It has an aromatic, slightly sweet taste that children love. Give the child the soda once or twice each day between meals until the fever or diarrhea is gone. Store Angostura Bitters in the liquor cabinet or any place that is out of the reach of children.

In cases of very high fever (103 degrees and above), severe vomiting or gastrointestinal pain, or paleness and lassitude, consult with a physician.

Willow Bark Tea
To reduce fever and discomfort from flu and colds

Preparation Time: 20 minutes
Yield: 4 treatments
Children's Enjoyment: ☺

White willow bark has been used since prehistoric times to kill pain, bring down fever, reduce inflammation, and reduce water retention.

Willow bark contains salicin, which is converted in the body to salicylic acid, a substance that closely resembles synthetic aspirin. This versatile herb can be used in tea or tincture form. There are now several varieties of white willow bark tablets available, which can be used whole for children.

> 1 ounce white willow bark pieces
> 2 cups water

1. Combine the willow bark with the water in a covered pot, bring to a boil, and simmer for 20 minutes.
2. Strain out the herb and discard it. The tea is a dark burgundy color and has a slightly bitter, astringent taste.
3. Do not sweeten. Cool the tea to room temperature before serving. Store remaining tea in the refrigerator and reheat with each use. Discard any unused portion of the tea after 2 days.

APPLICATION: Give the child 1/2 cup 3 times each day, for 3 to 5 days, or until the pain or fever subsides. Because this tea tastes bitter and should not be sweetened, keep a good-tasting chaser such as golden raisins on hand.

If pain becomes severe or fever rises above 103 degrees at any time, consult a physician. Do not use this tea if your child is allergic or sensitive to aspirin.

Borage and Wintergreen Tea
To speed recovery in convalescence

Preparation Time: 20 minutes
Yield: 3 treatments
Children's Enjoyment: ☺

If your child is recovering slowly from an ailment that is causing fever, this tea is indicated. Borage and wintergreen are both good herbal aids for reducing fever and restoring vitality. Borage can induce a mild sweat, which helps rid the body of wastes. Wintergreen contains methyl salicylate, which closely resembles the painkilling ingredient in aspirin. This tea is also mildly tranquilizing and can promote appetite and digestion.

> 1 ounce dried borage
> 1 ounce dried wintergreen
> 1 quart water
> Honey to taste

1. Place the borage, wintergreen, and water in a covered pot and simmer for 20 minutes.
2. Strain and discard the herbs. There may be some essential oil of wintergreen floating on the tea that should be stirred in. The tea is light green in color and smells very minty.
3. Cool the tea to room temperature before serving. Refrigerate the remaining tea and warm it each time you use it. Discard any unused portion after 1 week.

APPLICATION: Give a child suffering from fever 1/2 cup of the tea 3 times each day, between meals, until the temperature is normal. This tea tastes slightly bitter and minty, so sweeten with honey to taste. Most children like this tea, and it is a good one to let them help to prepare.

   If, after a week of treatment, the child still has a low fever, or if the fever rises above 103 degrees at any time, consult a physician.

Peppermint and Comfrey Bath
To reduce fever and discomfort from measles,
chicken pox, and dermatitis

Preparation Time: 30 minutes
Yield: 1 treatment
Children's Enjoyment: ☺

This bath is indicated for a child with fever caused by measles and chicken pox, and can also be used to relieve the itching and discomfort of dermatitis and insect bites. Peppermint makes the skin feel cool. It is also a mild topical anesthetic. One of the healing attributes of comfrey root is its ability to lower an elevated body temperature. Mixed with peppermint in a bath tea, comfrey lowers a temperature at the same time as it relieves minor aches and pains, and soothes and softens the skin.

    2 ounces dried comfrey root
    2 ounces dried peppermint
    2 quarts water

1. Combine the comfrey root and water in a large, covered pot and bring to a boil.
2. Simmer the comfrey for 10 minutes, remove the covered pot from the heat, and add the peppermint.
3. Steep the mixture for 20 minutes.
4. Strain out the herbs and discard them. The bath tea is dark brown and smells mostly of peppermint.
5. Pour the bath tea into the tub while the water is running so that it will be well combined. Run the herbal bath as hot as you usually run a bath for your child, but make sure the temperature is not too hot for the child's skin after adding the brewed tea.

APPLICATION: Explain to the child that the bathwater will feel silky and tingly to the skin. Let the child soak for at least 20 minutes, while playing with fresh peppermint leaves in the water. Be sure to strain out the leaves before emptying the tub to prevent a clogged drain. Repeat the bath once each day just before bedtime until the fever is lowered to normal, usually 1 to 3 days.

If the fever persists for more than 3 days, or rises above 103 degrees at any time, consult a physician.

WHEN TO SEE THE DOCTOR

✚ SUDDEN FEVERS: Sudden fevers in children may be caused by infections, dehydration, overexertion, or drug reactions. Any child who suddenly develops a fever over 103 degrees should be taken promptly to an emergency health facility. Once the cause of the fever has been isolated for treatment, lowering the fever may also be necessary. The most commonly used fever-reducing drugs are acetaminophen (Tylenol, Tempra, etc.) and aspirin. Both of these drugs can have side effects, particularly in children, and dosages should be determined by an expert.

✚ PROLONGED OR HIGH FEVERS: A child or infant with a high fever — over 103 degrees, rectally — should be taken to a clinic or primary health-care center for observation. Most short-term fevers are caused by acute infections such as upper respiratory infections, meningitis, ear infections, viral or bacterial gastroenteritis, pneumonia, and urinary tract infections. A thorough physical examination should be performed with emphasis on the ears, neck, throat, and chest. This will usually reveal the site of infection, if there is one. The danger of dehydration in young children is present in cases of high or prolonged fever. This will often require the administration of replacement fluids. If an infant under twelve months of age has a fever with vomiting or diarrhea, urine and stool cultures should be taken. A child with a high fever should not leave the clinic until health professionals determine that the temperature is not rising. Usually, fever-reducing drugs and sponging decrease the child's temperature by at least one degree within thirty minutes.

CHAPTER FIVE

DIGESTIVE DISORDERS

INFANTS

Colic

Diarrhea

CHILDREN

Indigestion

Nausea

Constipation

Diarrhea

Intestinal Parasites

gastrointestinal upsets are common in infants and young children, but they rarely develop into anything serious. Sometimes children get well by themselves in a few hours; other times it takes a day or two. Occasionally, children use a "tummyache" to express their need for a little extra affection, but this can become a bad habit. While children benefit from herbal remedies, they also need to learn independence and a healthful, positive frame of mind. It's good for parents to know when the best medicine for their children is sitting down for a game of Monopoly or taking them out on a "date."

INFANTS

I can't think of any aspect of child care that causes more anxiety in parents than choosing what to feed their infant to prevent colic and other gastrointestinal problems. At this time, the two most common infant food choices in the United States are breast milk and formula, with goat's milk increasing in popularity. I tried a different feeding method with each of my three babies. With my first, I breast-fed very successfully. I supplemented the breast-feeding with goat's milk at times when I needed to go out or her father wanted to help feed her. She experienced no abnormal gastric upsets as an infant, and progressed to solid food very normally. With my second child, I was unable to produce enough breast milk and had to resort to goat's milk. He did very well with this diet, but gained weight a little too quickly as an infant, owing to the higher fat and protein content of goat's milk. He seemed to suffer more gastrointestinal upsets when he went through teething. Also, he now experiences some minor allergies which could stem from his infant diet. With my third child, I was again unable to produce enough breast milk, and I decided to use formula. She did very well on this, once I adjusted the ratio of powdered formula to water. An overconcentrated mixture can cause stomach upsets and even kidney problems, and can result in an overweight infant. I found that a little less than the "normal" ratio of formula to water was perfect for keeping her weight under control and her bowels regular.

No matter which feeding method you choose, your infant will probably experience some digestive upsets. The most common digestive problems among newborns are swallowed air, or wind that causes burping, milk allergies, hiccups, and colic.

Wind is to be dealt with at almost every feeding, whether it's of breast milk, goat's milk, or formula. Infants often swallow air when sucking, which forms a bubble in their stomach. An infant should be burped at least once during a feeding, between breasts or halfway down the scale on the bottle. My favorite method is to put the child, stomach down, on my knees and gently bounce, while rubbing the back. As soon as you hear the obligatory belch, you can proceed with the feeding. Of course, sometimes you will bring up more than a belch. If this is frequently the case, you may decide on a different arrangement. Forgetting to burp an infant results in his or her stomach filling with air. This causes infants to feel full before they consume a proper amount of breast milk or formula, and they will wake up more frequently than normal for feedings.

Hiccups are very common in newborns, and an infant is rarely upset by them. Sometimes, though, the hiccups can be annoyingly persistent — especially at christenings and portrait sittings. If you encourage your infant to burp or suck a little bit, the hiccups will usually stop.

Two of the less common infant digestive problems are gastroenteritis and vomiting because of infection or obstruction in the digestive tract. Infants with severe diarrhea or continual vomiting must be examined promptly by a health professional.

Premature infants have immature digestive systems and may not gain weight as quickly as full-term infants. They may also need vitamin supplements. Premature infants are usually kept under hospital care until they reach a weight of four to six pounds and are strong enough to be bottle or breast-fed at home on a regular schedule. (See also WHEN TO SEE THE DOCTOR: ACUTE DIARRHEA AND GASTROENTERITIS, page 127; and EXPLOSIVE OR CONTINUAL VOMITING, page 128.)

COLIC

Colic, the primary disorder in newborns, is a severe abdominal pain that affects most infants between the ages of two weeks and three months. Infants with colic scream and draw up their legs to their stomach while tightly clenching their fists. This bane of the newborn has one common characteristic: nobody is quite sure what causes it. I have consulted M.D.s, N.D.s, R.N.s, midwives, Chinese herbalists, grandmothers, and hundreds of mothers. All of them have an opinion, of course, but it seems to me that no two people can agree on either the cause or the cure. The most interesting and believable theory is that colic has nothing at all to do with the gastrointestinal system, rather, it is the result of mild hypoxia (not enough oxygen in the bloodstream) during or shortly after the infant's birth. Hypoxia can cause mild injury to the central nervous system, resulting in the spasms of colic. The colic abates as soon as the central nervous system has had a chance to regenerate.

To deal with colic, keep infants warm by swaddling them in warm receiving blankets and holding them close, humming, and crooning, and bouncing all the while. I have administered a few drops of red wine with an eye dropper to a colicky infant with a measure of success. Red wine relaxes the intestinal tract and aids the digestive process. Also, the alcohol in the wine helps soothe a child and trigger sleep.

The most difficult challenge in handling a colicky infant is keeping a firm hold on yourself. A feeling of guilt and helplessness may set in, which could have an adverse effect on your infant. I have actually ended up crying myself when one of my infants was having an attack of colic. When these feelings arise, remember that sooner or later your infant will fall asleep and harmony will be restored to your home. Try to think about the future — flying kites or raising bunny rabbits — that you will have with the screaming little scrap in your arms. If the infant's crying persists or increases in intensity, there are a number of herbal remedies you can try that are quite effective.

Colic Tea
To calm and soothe the spasms of colic

Preparation Time: 10 minutes
Yield: 5 treatments
Children's Enjoyment: ☺

This is an easy-to-prepare and effective remedy that relieves the bloat and gas of colic, and helps an infant sleep. The onion tea recipe was given to me by another mother, who had it passed down from her mother, and so forth. The muscle-relaxing, stomach-strengthening, and digestion-regulating properties of onions make them perfect for treating colic. Onions are available everywhere, but try to get fresh, firm, organic yellow onions for this tea. Do not use onion powder or flakes.

> 4 (1/4-inch) slices yellow onion
> 2 cups water

1. Combine the onion slices and water in a covered pot and simmer for 10 minutes.
2. Strain the tea through a cheesecloth-lined sieve. Discard the onion slices. The tea is a clear, light yellow and smells mildly of onions.
3. Cool the tea to tepid before administering. Refrigerate any unused portion of the tea and reheat to tepid before each use. Discard any remaining tea after 2 days.

APPLICATION: Administer 4 tablespoons of unsweetened tea to the infant twice each day, by bottle or teaspoon, during an attack of colic. You will have to hold the infant firmly and reassuringly, and keep a grip on yourself, too. Your infant may not like the taste of this tea. If this is the case, administer it by spoon or dropper. When I used this with my son, he slept for 4 hours after taking just a few tablespoons. Many infants like the tea's taste and suck it right away. The infant will relax 30 minutes to 1 hour after drinking the tea, and may sleep for several hours. Do not give an infant more than 3/4 cup of tea each day. If you are breast-feeding, it is a good idea to get your infant used to feeding from a bottle for this and many other purposes.

If the infant does not respond to 2 consecutive doses of the tea, if the colic seems unusually severe or painful, or if the infant fails to gain weight, consult a pediatrician.

Hot Castor Oil Rub
To calm infant and expel pockets of gas

Preparation Time: 10 minutes
Yield: 15 treatments
Children's Enjoyment: ☺

This remedy is good if your infant's belly is tight and bloated and/or gas is being passed. In India, a newborn is thoroughly rubbed down with warm castor oil at birth to help expel meconium (fetal feces) and help relax the infant after the trauma of birth. Castor oil is a well-known and powerful purgative for the bowels. Warmed and massaged into an infant's belly, however, castor oil is comforting and effective for relieving colic and expelling intestinal gas.

> 1 6-ounce bottle castor oil
> 1 pot half-filled with water

1. Loosen the cap and place the bottle of castor oil in the pot of water.
2. Warm the water until little bubbles form on the pot bottom.
3. Apply a test drop or 2 to the inside of your wrist to test the temperature. The oil should be as warm as possible, but not so warm that it burns an infant's tender skin.
4. Write the date you opened the bottle on the lable, and store the oil in the medicine chest, well out of the reach of children. Warm the oil when needed, and discard it after 6 months.

APPLICATION: Arrange yourself comfortably on the floor or a bed with the bottle of warmed oil nearby. Lay the diapered infant on his or her back in your lap. Make sure the room is warm because the infant's belly is exposed. Hum and croon to calm the infant, pour out a palmful of oil, and gently apply it to the belly. Start at the navel and rub in a clockwise direction until you cover the infant's entire abdominal area. Rub for 10 to 15 minutes, applying more oil as needed. The infant will calm down as soon as you start rubbing and may pass gas or have a bowel movement.

If the infant has unusually long or severe attacks of colic, or fails to gain weight, consult a physician.

Infant's Calming Herbal Bath
To calm a tense or wakeful infant

Preparation Time: 20 minutes
Yield: 1 treatment
Children's Enjoyment: ☺

Once the colic has abated somewhat, your infant may be restless and slightly ense. Lavender and camomile are a good combination to calm and soothe an infant with colic. Both herbs have mild sedative substances and lend a wonderful fresh scent to bathwater. Most infants enjoy this bath very much and come to associate its scent with pleasant relaxation.

> 1 quart water
> 1 ounce dried lavender buds
> 1 ounce dried camomile flowers

1. Bring the water to a boil in a covered pot.
2. Remove the pot from the heat and add the herbs, being sure to cover the pot again. Let the herbs steep in the hot water for 20 minutes.

3. Strain and discard them. The bath tea is dark yellow and smells pleasantly of lavender.
4. Pour the tea into an infant bathtub and add enough warm water to fill it. The herbal bath should be as hot as a normal bath for the infant.

APPLICATION: Make sure the room is warm before the bath. Place the infant in the bathwater and hold him or her reassuringly, humming and crooning all the while. Soak the infant in the bath for at least 10 minutes. Do not try to wash the infant during an herbal bath. Gently pour the water over the belly and legs, and just let the infant play and splash. Use this bath as often as necessary to reassure and calm an upset, colicky infant.

If the infant still has severe or frequent bouts of colic after trying this bath or Colic Tea, page 105, or is failing to gain weight, consult a physician.

DIARRHEA   Infants may have frequent bowel movements, whether they are bottle or breast fed. As they grow, their bowel movements may become less frequent, occurring once every other day or even every two or three days. Parents should not worry about this if their infant seems comfortable and happy. If you notice that your infant is having more bowel movements than usual, and that there is a distinct change in the color and consistency of the feces, you should try to determine the cause. If you are breast-feeding, your infant's diarrhea could be due to elements in your own diet, such as caffeine and alcohol. To help prevent this, drink coffee and alcohol in limited quantities, if at all. Vegetables such as cabbage and asparagus in your diet may also have an adverse effect on your infant's bowel movements. If you are bottle-feeding your infant, make sure the formula you use is the right one for your infant. Gradual diarrhea is often the result of careless formula mixing — too much sugar is usually the culprit. Pay close attention to the directions on formula containers. Finally, be certain that the bottles, bottle caps, and nipples are clean. Let them soak in a solution of baking soda and water, or boil them once a week to safeguard against bacteria that can cause diarrhea. If your infant's diarrhea is severe, it is probably due to an infection. This is a serious condition in an infant and prompt medical attention is necessary to prevent nutrient loss and dehydration. For mild, intermittent infant diarrhea, I have discovered two excellent herbal remedies.

Rosemary Tea
To correct infant diarrhea

Preparation Time: 20 minutes
Yield: 16 treatments
Children's Enjoyment: ☹

This is the quickest remedy for diarrhea I know of, as well as the easiest to prepare. Rosemary is antispasmodic and astringent, so a mild tea made from this herb is excellent for infant diarrhea. The antispasmodic property relaxes painful abdominal cramping, and the astringent quality helps tighten the lower intestine and solidify the stool. The medicinal part of the rosemary plant is its flowering top, where most of the oil is. Do not buy rosemary in a grocery store for this treatment, since the culinary and medicinal methods of curing the herb are quite different.

        1/4 ounce rosemary
        1 cup water

1. Combine rosemary with the water in a covered pot, bring to a boil, and simmer for 5 minutes.
2. Take the pot off the heat and steep the herb for 15 minutes.
3. Thoroughly strain out the herb through cheesecloth and discard it. There should be no floating particles in the light green tea.
4. You may see some essential oil floating on top. Stir this back in and cool the tea to tepid before serving. Do not sweeten. Refrigerate the unused tea and reheat with each use. Discard any remaining tea after 3 days.

APPLICATION: Bottle-feed an infant suffering from diarrhea 1/4 cup of tea 3 times each day, for 3 days, or until the diarrhea is checked. Most infants do not like the taste of the tea, so you may have to use a teaspoon or sterile dropper to administer it.

Diarrhea in an infant can become a serious condition owing to dehydration. If the diarrhea is severe, dehydration can occur in less than 24 hours. If mild diarrhea does not improve after 3 days of treatment, or if the diarrhea is severe, with frequent uncontrolled bowel movements and painful cramping, consult a physician.

Slippery Elm and White Rice Pablum
To correct diarrhea in older infants and toddlers

Preparation Time: 45 minutes
Yield: 4 treatments
Children's Enjoyment: ☺

If your infant is old enough to eat from a spoon, you can prepare this dish to correct mild diarrhea. This mixture is very soothing to the lining of the intestinal tract and also bulks out in the colon to solidify the stool. Powdered slippery elm bark is nourishing and soothing for an infant or toddler with diarrhea. Combined with watery white rice, which is used throughout the world to combat diarrhea, slippery elm gently and effectively soothes lower bowel irritation and solidifies the stool. The naturally sweet taste of slippery elm bark combines with the white rice to make this pablum easy to administer to an older infant. Do not use pre-cooked or instant rice.

1/4 cup white rice
2 cups water
4 teaspoons powdered slippery elm bark
4 teaspoons light corn syrup

1. Combine the rice with the water and bring to a boil in a covered pot.
2. Simmer the rice until it is completely cooked, about 30 minutes. The consistency resembles oatmeal.
3. Cool the cooked rice enough to be eaten and spoon out a serving.
4. Add 1 teaspoon slippery elm bark and 1 teaspoon corn syrup to each serving. Store the remaining cooked rice in the refrigerator and add the corn syrup and powdered slippery elm bark each time you reheat a portion for the infant. Discard any unused pablum after 4 days.

APPLICATION: Give an older infant or toddler with diarrhea 1/2 cup of the pablum each day for breakfast until the diarrhea disappears (1 to 4 days). Most infants like this mixture since it is naturally sweet and mild tasting.

Diarrhea in an infant can become a serious condition owing to dehydration. If the diarrhea is severe, dehydration can occur in less than 24 hours. If mild diarrhea does not improve after 3 days of treatment, or if the diarrhea is severe, with frequent uncontrolled bowel movements and painful cramping, consult a physician.

CHILDREN

If your child has frequent digestive problems — stomachaches, diarrhea, constipation, gas, or nausea — the most obvious place to begin your search for their cause is in the diet. Many foods, especially dairy foods containing lactose, simply cannot be tolerated by young digestive systems. High-fat, low-fiber diets also create an acid condition in the blood. This acid-forming diet includes too much fried food, meat, sugar, salt, and overprocessed, low-nutrient foods such as white bread and junk cereals. Common symptoms of acid conditions in the blood include loss of appetite or poor appetite, poor elimination, acid stomach and sour breath, and headaches.

The environment in which your child eats can also be an important factor in digestive problems. (Are mealtimes often hectic and off schedule? Does everyone sit down together for a meal, or is it every man, woman, and child for himself? Does your child constantly crave snacks at all hours of the day and night, even after just eating a meal?) To many children, food is love and security. An eating-in-the-fast-lane lifestyle can easily contribute to your child's digestive upsets, either real or imagined.

As frequently as you can, try to have a home-cooked, sit-down dinner with the TV off and the answering machine on. Encourage your child to eat slowly, chew thoroughly, and not overeat. Food should be eaten with as little added liquid as possible. Drinking cold beverages with meals greatly reduces the stomach's digestive capacity. The best time for children to have something to drink is between meals. These drinks will keep children going until mealtime and not interfere with the digestive process. If your child simply must have juice or milk with meals, try to keep amounts to a minimum and never give either to them refrigerator-cold. Exercise control over your child's snacking. Keep healthy snacks such as celery, carrots, fresh fruits, and whole-grain crackers available at all times.

INDIGESTION   Stomachaches are probably the most common childhood complaint — after boo-boos, of course. More than half the time, children complaining of a stomachache are just tired or need some love and attention. However, consider their complaint carefully; they might actually be suffering from indigestion or gas pains.

Fennel and Orange Peel Tea
To relieve the discomfort of indigestion

Preparation Time: 20 minutes
Yield: 3 treatments
Children's Enjoyment: ☺

This tea is a great one to let your kids help you make, since they often forget about their tummyache in the process of concocting its cure. Fennel and orange peel both contain hot oils known as carminatives. These carminative oils stimulate intestinal peristalsis, the wavelike contractions that move food through the intestine, and promote the expulsion of gas from the gastrointestinal tract. Buy the orange peel at a health food or herb store. Do not use the peel of a storebought orange to make this tea, since pesticides may be present.

> 1 tablespoon fennel seed
> 1 tablespoon dried sweet orange peel
> 2 cups water
> Honey to taste

1. Combine the fennel seed, orange peel, and water in a covered pot.
2. Bring the mixture to a boil and simmer for 20 minutes.
3. Strain out the herbs and discard them. The tea is light green in color and smells mostly of fennel.
4. You may see some essential oils floating on the top of the tea. Stir the tea to recombine the oils before serving. Keep any unused portion of tea in the refrigerator and reheat for each use. Discard any remaining tea after 2 days.

APPLICATION: Serve this tea as warm as is comfortable for the child, since heat aids the intestines to expel gas. Sweeten it with honey to taste. Most children enjoy the taste of this tea. Give the child 1/2 cup of tea every 2 hours whenever he or she experiences stomach pain from gas.

If the child continues to complain of stomach pain after drinking 1 or 2 cups of the tea, check for other possible conditions, such as diarrhea, constipation, or gastroenteritis.

NAUSEA

Nausea is a common complaint in children of all ages. Many times, it is caused by overindulgence in sweets, bad combinations of foods, and ingestion of strange or highly spiced foods. Nausea is also a side effect of gastroenteritis, severe colds, scarlet fever, whooping cough, flu, and bacterial meningitis. It is important to have cultures and/or blood tests done if your child seems very ill and you suspect he or she might have one of these diseases. Any time your child feels severely nauseated, it is important that you investigate the cause. Of course, the most dangerous cause is that he or she was exposed to or swallowed something poisonous. Children who have a fever accompanying their nausea, and who exhibit other symptoms such as facial pallor, sore throat, mouth burns, lassitude, headache, or spots anywhere on their body, should be taken to a medical center promptly. When children complain of feeling nauseated, and you determine that the nausea is not severe, there are a number of herbal remedies that you can use. (See also WHEN TO SEE THE DOCTOR: ACUTE DIARRHEA AND GAS-TROENTERITIS, page 127; and POISONING, page 128.)

Sweet Basil Tea
To relieve nausea in children

Preparation Time: 20 minutes
Yield: 4 treatments
Children's Enjoyment: ☺

Just the smell of this tea will probably help fight nausea. Basil has several healing attributes that make it perfect for nausea in children. It is astringent, mildly antiseptic, and helps kill unwanted bacteria in the gastrointestinal system. Basil is carminative, meaning it helps relieve gas pains and cramping and helps settle and cleanse the stomach. Basil is also an herb that acts as a mild sedative. Cut dried basil is a familiar culinary herb, but for medicinal uses buy the herb in a health food or herb store.

> 2 ounces dried basil leaves
> 1 quart water

1. Combine the basil and water in a covered pot, bring to a boil, and simmer for 5 minutes.
2. Remove the pot from the heat, and steep the herb for 15 minutes. Strain out the herb and discard it. The resulting tea is light green in color and smells pleasantly of basil.

3. Cool the tea to a comfortable temperature for drinking before serving. Store the remaining tea in the refrigerator and reheat with each use. Discard any unused tea after 4 days.

APPLICATION: Serve the tea as warm as the child can stand, since heat can also help relieve nausea. Let the child drink the tea freely until the nausea disappears, usually after 1 or 2 cups. The tea has a pleasant taste and does not need to be sweetened.

If the nausea persists or grows worse, it may be a side effect of some other disorder. Consult with a physician for correct diagnosis and treatment.

Peppermint and Red Raspberry Syrup
To correct nausea due to flu, cold, or bad food combination

Preparation Time: 20 minutes
Yield: 20 treatments
Children's Enjoyment: ☺

This is a good syrup for a variety of ills. I would not, however, give this to a child who is experiencing nausea because of overindulgence in sweets; the Sweet Basil Tea (page 114) is a better remedy for that. This syrup is for a child who is nauseated because of flu, a cold, or indigestion resulting a bad combination of foods. Peppermint and Red Raspberry Syrup is a tasty and effective remedy to have on hand for upset stomachs. Peppermint and red raspberry leaves are stomach-settling herbs that are mild and easy to administer to children.

1/2 ounce fresh or dried peppermint leaves
1/2 ounce fresh or dried red raspberry leaves
1 1/2 pounds brown sugar
2 cups water

1. Combine the peppermint and raspberry leaves and the water in a covered pot. Simmer covered for 20 minutes, then strain and discard the herbs.
2. Add the brown sugar to the clear tea and reheat until the sugar is melted, approximately 5 minutes.
3. Cool the syrup to room temperature, then store in a tightly lidded, dark glass jar for future use. This syrup does not have to be refrigerated, but you should lable and date the jar, and keep it in a dark place such as a medicine cabinet. The syrup is dark brown in color and tastes delightful. Discard any unused portion of the syrup after 6 months.

APPLICATION: Give 1 tablespoon of the syrup to children complaining of nausea. They will enjoy the taste and usually feel better within 30 minutes. If the child still complains of nausea after 1 hour, give another tablespoon of the syrup. If there is no relief after the second dose, discontinue and try to determine the cause of the nausea. It could be a disorder such as gastroenteritis, food poisoning, flu, diarrhea, or constipation. If a child has already vomited, a tablespoon of this syrup both settles the stomach and relaxes the child. Two or 3 tablespoons can be administered each week to a healthy child as a good-tasting vitamin supplement.

If the nausea persists for several hours, or if repeated vomiting occurs, or if a fever accompanies the nausea, consult a physician.

Nutmeg Milk
To warm and coat the stomach during cold or flu

Preparation Time: 15 minutes
Yield: 1 treatment
Children's Enjoyment: ☺

This is my children's favorite remedy for nausea — and mine, too. Nutmeg is a good stomach settler, so this beverage is indicated for nausea in children. It is especially good for children suffering nausea from eating too much rich food. The warm milk coats the stomach lining, which may be irritated. This is also an excellent remedy for a child who is experiencing nausea as a side effect of a cold or flu. One cup will usually relieve the upset stomach. This beverage is great for just sharing a warm, loving moment with your child. Nutmeg is slightly stimulating, so do not administer this beverage just before bedtime. It's good to have whole nutmeg that can be grated by hand for this tea, but preground nutmeg is also fine. Buy the whole or ground nutmeg in a health food store so that you can be sure it has not been sprayed with insecticides.

> 1/2 cup water
> 1/8 teaspoon ground or grated nutmeg
> 1/2 cup milk
> 1 teaspoon honey

1. Combine the water and nutmeg in a covered pot, bring to a boil, and simmer for 5 minutes.
2. Add the milk and simmer for an additional 5 minutes. The beverage looks like watery milk with the ground herb floating on top and smells very pleasantly of nutmeg.
3. Cool the nutmeg milk to tepid. Add the honey, stir, and serve.

APPLICATION: Give 1 cup of warm Nutmeg Milk to a child complaining of nausea. If the nausea persists for an hour after the first cup, you can give the child another cup, but make sure it is not too close to bedtime. Do not give more than 2 cups of the tea in 1 day. If the nausea still persists, try to determine its causes.

If the nausea persists for several hours, if repeated vomiting occurs, or if a fever accompanies the nausea, consult a physician.

CONSTIPATION

Parents must be responsible for monitoring their child's regularity. Healthy children should have one bowel movement at least every other day. The stools should not be consistently dark colored or difficult to pass. When children are constipated, they usually show symptoms of irritability, hyperactivity, inability to sleep, poor appetite, or constant

117

mild pain in the lower tract. If your child is frequently constipated, you should include more fiber in the diet. Foods rich in fiber include whole grains, fresh fruits (eaten skin and all), and fresh, leafy green vegetables such as cabbage and spinach. Foods rich in unrefined starch, such as white potatoes, sweet potatoes, squash, and carrots, are also high in fiber. To help prevent constipation in children, give them unfiltered fruit juices, such as apple and prune juice, plenty of water, and always serve whole-grain breads, never white bread. There are two excellent herbal remedies for constipation that I use for for my children.

Black Cherry Agar Gelatin
To relieve chronic constipation in children

Preparation Time: 30 minutes
Yield: 4 treatments
Children's Enjoyment: ☺

This is a delicious and effective dietary aid for permanently correcting constipation. Agar gelatin is a soluble fiber that bulks out the colon. Agar, also known as kanten, is an extract of seaweed and is a popular jelling agent in Asian cuisine. It is a nutritious extract from seaweed that can absorb up to two hundred times its own weight in water. Black cherry juice is a mild laxative and lends a pleasant flavor to the gelatin. This is my favorite constipation remedy because it trains the colon to have a regular cycle of elimination and can permanently correct constipation.

> 2 sticks agar
> 1 quart water
> 1 quart black cherry juice (approximately; refer to directions
>   on agar package)

1. Break the agar sticks in halves or quarters and soak them in the water for 1 hour before preparing the gelatin.

2. Place the black cherry juice in a pot and bring to a boil.
3. Add the drained, soaked agar and stir continuously until it is completely dissolved.
4. Pour the liquefied gelatin into a bowl. For convenience, you might want to divide the gelatin into individual 1-cup servings.
5. Refrigerate for at least 1 hour until the gelatin has set. Once it sets, the gelatin is ready to eat. Store the gelatin in the refrigerator. Discard any unused portion after 1 week.

APPLICATION: Give a child suffering from constipation 1 cup of the gelatin, no more, each day for 1 week. At this point, bowel movements are usually regular and easy for the child to pass. Children like this remedy very much. Discontinue its use when regularity is achieved, but let the child have an occassional serving as a healthy treat.

If constipation continues after 1 week of treatment, or if severe pain and discomfort are present, consult a physician.

Coffee Sips
For immediate relief of constipation

Preparation Time: 20 minutes
Yield: 1 treatment
Children's Enjoyment: ☺

Coffee is well known for its laxative properties, which makes this an excellent temporary treatment for constipation. If your child needs immediate relief from the discomfort of constipation, Coffee Sips are very helpful. Use it only if your child's constipation is causing stomach cramps and irritability. Coffee is also a "bitter" herb, which means it can stimulate the liver to produce bile in quantities that speedily digest food. Coffee can be obtained in any grocery store but try to use whole-bean coffee instead of ground, freeze-dried, or instant coffee. Avoid extremely strong coffees such as French Roast or Viennese coffee; Mexican or Colombian coffees are best suited for this treatment.

1/2 cup freshly brewed coffee
1/2 cup milk
1 teaspoon honey

1. Combine the coffee, milk, and honey in a pot. Heat the mixture until it is warm, but not too hot for your child to drink. Heat is a necessary ingredient to stimulate the bowels to move, so the drink should be as warm as the child can tolerate. The beverage is a light tawny color and smells like sweetened, milky coffee.
2. Serve immediately.

APPLICATION: Have the child sip 1 cup of the mixture until it is consumed. Encourage the child to get up and take a brisk walk or to go outside and play after finishing the *café au lait*. The child should have a bowel movement within an hour. Children enjoy this beverage and usually want more. Please remember that, like any laxative, caffeine can be addictive, and this treatment is only for cases of abdominal discomfort caused by constipation. Morning is the best time to give this remedy. Never administer this stimulating beverage before bedtime.

If the child has recurring constipation, the Black Cherry Agar Gelatin (page 118) is needed. If the constipation persists after a week of treatment with the gelatin, or if severe abdominal pain is present at any time, consult a physician.

DIARRHEA   Occasional diarrhea in older children is usually not very serious. While there are several serious diseases that have diarrhea as a symptom, simple diarrhea can be brought on by a number of things including eating improperly combined foods, overeating, and taking antibiotics. Beverages and foods that are good for your child during a bout with diarrhea include ginger ale, crackers, carrot and celery sticks, and applesauce. Ginger ale is reputed to be effective in maintaining the body's electrolyte balance, which diarrhea frequently upsets. These foods should be given to your child in small amounts fairly frequently throughout the day. By the third day, your child should be tolerating a normal diet. There are a number of safe and effective herbal remedies for diarrhea. (See also WHEN TO SEE THE DOCTOR: ACUTE DIARRHEA AND GASTROENTERITIS, page 127.)

Red Raspberry Leaf Tea
To cleanse the gastrointestinal tract and relieve diarrhea

Preparation Time: 20 minutes
Yield: 4 treatments
Children's Enjoyment: ☹

If your child has eaten something that cannot be easily digested, or has eaten an improper amount or combination of foods, this tea is helpful. I have found a strong brew of this tea to be very comforting and quick to relieve diarrhea. Red raspberry leaf settles upset stomach and is mildly astringent, which makes this tea a good treatment for diarrhea. It is interesting to note that, while a tea made from its leaves will cure diarrhea, the red raspberry fruit has a laxative effect.

    1 ounce dried red raspberry leaves
    2 cups water
    Honey to taste (optional)

1. Combine the red raspberry leaves with the water in a covered pot and gently boil for 5 minutes.
2. Take the pot off the heat and steep the herbs for 15 minutes.
3. Strain out the herbs and discard them. The tea is gray-green in color, with a musty, green smell.
4. Cool the tea to a comfortable temperature for drinking and serve. Refrigerate the tea between servings and warm it for each use. Discard any unused portion of the tea after 2 days.

APPLICATION: Give the child 1/2 cup of the tea 3 times each day, an hour before meals, for 3 days. Red Raspberry Tea is not very tasty. You can try sweetening it with honey, but it's a good idea to have a ginger ale chaser on hand at medicine time.

If the diarrhea does not respond to treatment after 3 days, is severe, or if pain and bloating, fever, or vomiting occur, consult a physician.

Angostura Soda
To settle the stomach, reduce fever, and relieve diarrhea

Preparation Time: 5 minutes
Yield: 1 treatment
Children's Enjoyment: ☺

Angostura Soda is excellent for relieving both fever and diarrhea. Angostura Bitters is a popular flavoring and mixer in cocktails such as the old-fashioned and the Manhattan. The primary ingredient in Angostura Bitters is gentian root, which is known for its worm-killing, fever-reducing, stomach-strengthening, and liver-stimulating properties. It is also a topical and internal antiseptic, and is used in gentian violet, a topical medicine for canker sores, minor cuts, and scrapes. The soda is easy to make, has a pleasant taste, and is a good way to get extra fluids into a child. I let my children prepare it to their own individual tastes.

> 1 cup any brand sparkling water
> 5 to 10 drops Angostura Bitters
> Mint sprig (optional)

1. Fill a glass with sparkling water.
2. Let the child shake the Angostura Bitters drops into the soda and stir it. The soda is light pink in color. You can garnish it with a sprig of mint if you like.

APPLICATION: You can serve the soda plain or on the rocks. The soda has an aromatic, slightly sweet taste that children love. It is easy to make and keep on hand. Give your child two servings each day until the diarrhea has been relieved. Store Angostura Bitters in the liquor cabinet or any place that is out of the reach of children.

In cases of very high fever (103 degrees and above), severe vomiting or gastrointestinal pain, or paleness and lassitude, consult with a physician.

Goldenseal and White Rice Porridge
To relieve diarrhea caused by taking antibiotics

Preparation Time: 35 minutes
Yield: 4 treatments
Children's Enjoyment: ☺

This remedy is very palatable and nutritious, and can be prepared quickly and easily. It is especially helpful when your child is required to take antibiotics. Most antibiotics are indiscriminate in their elimination of microorganisms, killing off beneficial intestinal bacteria as well as harmful bacteria in the body, with diarrhea often the result. A pinch of goldenseal mixed with a watery white-rice porridge is very effective against diarrhea, since rice cooked with too much water is used worldwide to fight this disease. Red raspberry jam is a tasty addition and also provides astringent action that helps fight diarrhea. Yogurt rebalances the beneficial bacteria in the colon that aid digestion. Goldenseal is an excellent astringent and is a favorite herb among Native Americans for skin and mouthwashes and as a bitter tonic for the stomach and liver. Goldenseal also helps kill germs that can cause diarrhea.

> 1/2 cup white rice
> 3 cups water
> 1/2 teaspoon goldenseal powder
> 4 teaspoons red raspberry jam
> 4 tablespoons plain yogurt

1. Combine the rice with the water and bring to a boil in a covered pot.
2. Simmer the rice until it is completely cooked, about 30 minutes. The mixture is watery and resembles oatmeal in its consistency.

3. Cool the cooked rice and spoon out a 1-cup serving.
4. Add 1/8 teaspoon goldenseal, 1 teaspoon jam, and 1 tablespoon yogurt. Mix thoroughly and serve.
5. Store the cooked rice in the refrigerator and add the remaining ingredients each time you reheat a portion. Discard any unused porridge after 4 days.

APPLICATION: Give the child 1 cup of porridge each day for breakfast until the diarrhea disappears (1 to 4 days). The mixture tastes slightly bitter because of the goldenseal, but this is offset by the jam. Children generally like the taste of the porridge.

Always be sure a child with diarrhea takes in plenty of fluids. If the diarrhea persists or gets worse after 4 days of treatment, or if the child exhibits lassitude or low fever, consult a physician immediately.

INTESTINAL PARASITES

Threadworms, or pinworms are quite common in young children. These parasites are about 1/4 inch long and live in the intestines of humans. They resemble white threads, and can usually be seen in the feces. Symptoms of pinworm infestation include mild stomach pains, mild nausea, occasional mild diarrhea, and an urge to scratch around the anus. Pinworms are spread by hands, after scratching an infested area, and through contact with infected clothes and bedsheets. It is not unusual for epidemics of pinworms to occur in both public and private schools. If your child contracts pinworms, you may have to present a doctor's note to the school nurse proving that your child has received medication before he or she will be allowed to attend classes again. If a note from a doctor is not necessary, and if you feel strongly that your child should not ingest synthetic drugs, there is a very effective herbal remedy for pinworms. (See also WHEN TO SEE THE DOCTOR: ROUNDWORM, HOOKWORM, AND TAPEWORM, page 127.)

Wormwood Tea
To relieve intestinal pinworm infestation

Preparation Time: 20 minutes
Yield: 4 treatments
Children's Enjoyment: ☺

This tea has a nasty taste and is not effective in powdered form, so it doesn't help to give it to children in capsules. You may have to bribe children with some golden raisins to get them to swallow the tea, but it is hoped they will prefer the taste of the tea to the itching and discomfort of pinworms. Wormwood is an intestinal parasite killer that is used for pinworms in children. The oil of this herb was used in Europe and America in the nineteenth century to make an addictive narcotic drink called absinthe, and a powerful decoction of wormwood was administered in medieval times to calm hysteria and produce visionary dreams. Wormwood Tea is also good for the stomach and liver and relieves gas, indigestion, heartburn, and lack of appetite. Wormwood is not highly available because of its past use as a narcotic, but it can be found in large herb and health food stores.

    1 tablespoon wormwood
    2 cups water

1. Combine the wormwood and water in a covered pot, bring to a boil, and simmer for 20 minutes.
2. Strain out the herb and discard it. The tea is dark green in color and has an unpleasant, pungent smell.
3. Cool the tea to tepid before administering.

APPLICATION: Give a child 1/2 cup of tea 3 times each day, between meals, for 3 days. This tea is very unpleasant to drink, so a good tasting chaser is essential. Do not powder the herb and put it into capsules because it will not expel worms in this form. When using this treatment, give the child plenty of fluids and fruit to loosen the stool; this helps expel the worms and their eggs faster. Wormwood is a very bitter herb, so decrease the dose or discontinue the tea's use if the child complains of stomach cramps or irritation.

Always alert school officials if a child has pinworms. These parasites are highly contagious, and you may get rid of the pinworms one week only to have the child reinfected the next. If the pinworms persist, consult a physician. There are drugs available to combat pinworms. These drugs may be more effective against pinworms and easier for a child to ingest.

WHEN TO SEE THE DOCTOR

✚ MILK ALLERGY: If your infant suffers from frequent indigestion and vomiting, and shows no weight gain or very slow weight gain, it could be due to a milk allergy. Milk allergy is identified through a selective elimination diet and a series of lab tests. A nonmilk formula will be prescribed if this allergy is present. These formulas usually contain ingredients such as soybeans, corn and coconut oils, sucrose, and corn sugar. Most infants switched to a formula because of a milk allergy have fewer digestive problems and return to a normal rate of growth.

✚ FOOD ALLERGIES: Some digestive disorders in young children can be the result of food allergies. If you think your child has a food allergy, write down all the symptoms exhibited. In infants these can include vomiting, colic, and diarrhea. In older children, rashes, wheezing, runny nose, headache, and vomiting may occur. Note the foods you suspect, and consult a healing professional. There are many thorough allergy-testing methods available, should you decide that tests are necessary. Actually, relatively few foods account for the vast majority of food allergies in children. These include peanuts, cow's milk, eggs, fish, and soybeans. Foods such as strawberries and chocolate, which have a reputation for causing allergies, have not been confirmed as allergens.

✚ ROUNDWORM, HOOKWORM, AND TAPEWORM: Round-worms, hookworms, and tapeworms are considered generally uncommon in the United States. Children with chronic or acute diarrhea who have recently traveled to a place where parasites are common, or who have been in close contact with someone who has, should be checked for the presence of these parasites. Diagnosis is usually made by a laboratory examination of the fresh stool for eggs and adult parasites.

Roundworms invade the intestines, liver, and lungs. There may be no symptoms to indicate their presence unless there are many worms, in which case they may obstruct the bile duct. These worms are spread through eating contaminated food. Treatment for them is usually by drugs.

Hookworms are common primarily in tropical countries, although they do occur in parts of the southern United States. Reaching a length of 1/2 inch, hookworms attach themselves to the wall of the intestine and suck blood. Symptoms are an unusually large appetite, constipation alternating with diarrhea, anemia, and malnutrition. Treatment is with drugs to kill the worms and a high-protein diet with iron supplements to restore the health of the child.

Tapeworms are usually contracted from eating inadequately cooked contaminated beef, fish, or pork. Once the worms enter the digestive system, they attach themselves to the intestinal wall, producing severe complications. Treatment to eliminate tapeworms usually requires drugs.

✚ ACUTE DIARRHEA AND GASTROENTERITIS: Gastroenteritis refers to infections of the gastrointestinal tract, with symptoms of continual vomiting, diarrhea, abdominal discomfort, irritability, and occasionally fever. This condition can be caused by bacterial or viral infections and by the ingestion of contaminated foods. In infants, gastroenteritis is extremely serious because it presents the danger of dehydration from uncontrolled diarrhea. A child with gastroenteritis should be seen by a physician and quarantined. Treatment usually consists of antibiotics to fight the infection and supervised use of fluids to prevent dehydration and electrolyte imbalances.

Acute diarrhea or persistent diarrhea can also be a symptom of other serious illnesses including appendicitis, bacterial gastroenteritis, severe milk allergy, urinary tract infection, and severe emotional stress. The danger of dehydration is great, especially in infants. If your child is suffering from uncontrolled diarrhea lasting longer than ten to fifteen hours, prompt medical attention is essential.

✦ EXPLOSIVE OR CONTINUAL VOMITING: Explosive or severe vomiting is always a dangerous symptom. In cases of concussion, the vomit may actually shoot out a foot or more in front of the child. In cases of appendicitis, nausea and fever are common and vomiting may occur. The child may have tenderness in McBurney's Point, the soft part of the abdomen just above the right thigh. This is a distinctive feature of appendicitis. Severe vomiting can also be a symptom of infection in the kidneys and urinary tract. Get your child to an emergency medical facility if persistent vomiting occurs.

✦ SWALLOWED OBJECTS: If your young child or infant has swallowed an object, nine times out of ten it will pass right out through the other end within two to twelve days. Usually, if the object is small enough to swallow, it is small enough to move through the digestive tract and the anus without incurring any damage. Cases have been documented of children swallowing things like open diaper pins, nails, balls of string that unravel, and an amazing array of other objects. The danger here is that a swallowed item can lodge somewhere in the esophagus, stomach, or intestines, and cause swelling, pain, infection, and possible rupture of the stomach or intestinal lining. If you think your child has swallowed something — symptoms can be lassitude, fever, severe localized abdominal pain, gagging, vomiting, and/or blood in the stool — prompt medical attention is required. A simple X-ray will usually reveal whether or not a child has swallowed something and where it has lodged. Your doctor can then determine the most effective way of getting the object out.

✦ POISONING: Young children are particularly vulnerable to accidental poisoning because they are likely to put anything in their

WHEN TO SEE THE DOCTOR

mouths that is not nailed down — and even then they sometimes manage to take a bite. Usually, four types of substances are involved in poisoning: medicines and drugs, household products, garden and agricultural products, and certain plants and berries. The most common times for young children to poison themselves are when the home is disrupted, such as when guests are in the house or a parent is ill. You should have your local poison-control number posted by your phone long before your child is mobile.

Signs of poisoning include unusual sleepiness, a very red face, mouth burns, vomiting, convulsions, rapid deep breathing, stomach pains, diarrhea, and unconsciousness. After contacting a poison-control center or summoning emergency help, there are several things you can do.

If your child is unconscious, put him or her in a recovery position — on the stomach, head to one side, with the leg on that side pulled up till the thigh is at right angles to the body. This prevents suffocation from saliva or vomit. If you do not already know, look around to see what the possible poison might be. Keep a sample of any vomit and keep your child warm. If your child is fully conscious, you are certain what poison has been ingested, and you have already spoken with the poison-control center, you may be instructed to induce your child to vomit. If so, administer two tablespoons of salt or powdered mustard with a glass of warm water and then tickle the back of your child's throat; this will usually do the trick. Syrup of Ipecac is also a well-known emetic — a substance that induces vomiting — that you should keep on hand in a childproof place.

CHAPTER SIX

SKIN DISORDERS

INFANTS

Rashes

Bumps and Bruises

Flaking Skin and Cradle Cap

CHILDREN

Mild Burns

Bruises

Scrapes, Cuts, Blisters, and Minor Infections

Bug Bites

Rashes

Skin Parasites

Warts

Skin disorders are the most common and obvious health problems that children experience. Newborn infants can exhibit skin conditions that border on the bizarre, and they often upset new parents. These skin problems are usually not serious and can be effectively treated at home. From the time they are born, children have skin that changes, grows, stretches, and flexes. As they become more mobile in the world, they acquire bumps, bruises, scrapes, cuts, and burns, many of which require no medical care but will benefit from a concentrated dose of sympathetic attention.

Parents can experience feelings of accomplishment and pride in their ability to comfort and cure their little ones with home remedies and herbal procedures. A child with a skin injury that has been tended by the parent with a certain amount of pomp and ceremony — and herbs — will consider the healing process something special. However, if a child is seriously hurt or develops a skin condition that is severe or prolonged, it is essential to seek a physician's advice and skill. (See also WHEN TO SEE THE DOCTOR, page 156.)

INFANTS

Infants exhibit many harmless skin conditions shortly after birth. Many infants have little white spots on the head and face. These are called milia and are no cause for concern, even if there are many of them. With time, these spots are reabsorbed into the skin and disappear. Vernix, a whitish coating of the skin usually found on infants, is also a harmless, natural by-product of birth. No special attempt should be made to wash it off; it will disappear eventually with ordinary bathing. If your infant is born with a "strawberry" — a red-colored area usually owing to a pigmentation abnormality — or develops a severe rash, you need to work closely with your pediatrician to find the cause and remedy it.

RASHES Many infants will break out into a rash every now and then. This is actually a good sign because it shows the child's ability to discharge toxins through the skin. If a rash persists, it could be caused by prolonged irritation to the skin surface, as in the case of diaper rash. An infant with persistent diaper rash may have skin that is too sensitive for disposable diapers or commercial baby wipes dosed with chemical fragrances. Sometimes diaper rash can be an allergic reaction, from not bathing an infant enough, or possibly too much, or from cloth diapers that are not thoroughly disinfected before use. After you have investigated the possible causes, there are some effective herbal remedies that can help relieve the symptoms.

Diaper Rash Skin Ointment
To prevent diaper rash in infants

Preparation Time: 45 minutes
Yield: 20 treatments
Children's Enjoyment: ☺

This ointment is made from ingredients that will help keep the surface of an infant's skin dry, nourish the skin, and fight bacteria. Comfrey root, chickweed, and marshmallow root all have one thing in common: they contain large amounts of calcium, which can help stimulate tissue growth. Comfrey root, in particular, is noted for its healing powers, sporting common folk names like knitbone and bruisewort. These three herbs combined with goldenseal powder, which serves as a topical antiseptic, are an excellent combination for combating diaper rash. Beeswax and sweet almond oil both have skin nourishing and soothing qualities. This ointment is also good for mild abrasions, sunburns, and hives.

1 tablespoon chickweed
1 tablespoon marshmallow root
1 tablespoon comfrey root
1/8 teaspoon goldenseal powder
1 cup sweet almond oil
1/4 cup beeswax

1. Combine the chickweed, marshmallow root, comfrey root, and goldenseal powder in a cast-iron frying pan with the sweet almond oil.
2. Gently fry the mixture for 5 to 10 minutes. Be careful not to let the herbs burn.
3. When the mixture is hot, add the beeswax and melt it down.
4. When the beeswax is completely melted, strain the mixture through a cheesecloth into a small, labeled jar with a tight-fitting lid.
5. Refrigerate the ointment until it solidifies. The final ointment is an opaque tan color and smells of beeswax and comfrey root. Keep the ointment in a convenient place near the infant's changing table, away from heat. Discard any unused portion after 2 months.

APPLICATION: Apply the ointment by gently rubbing it on the diaper area each time the diaper is changed. This ointment is very soothing to a rashy infant. Three or 4 applications are usually enough to get rid of diaper rash.

If the infant's diaper rash does not respond to this treatment, or if it keeps reappearing, investigate factors such as the proper disinfection of diapers, changes in diet, or other skin disorders.

Cornstarch and Vitamin E Oil Rub
To soothe an infant's skin and keep moisture away

Preparation Time: 5 minutes
Yield: 10 treatments
Children's Enjoyment: ☺

This ointment is a little less labor intensive to prepare than the Diaper Rash Skin Ointment (page 133) and can be equally effective. You may want to alternate the two. This easy-to-make rub relieves and prevents diaper rash. Cornstarch has excellent moisture-absorbing and soothing qualities. Vitamin E oil is an emollient, or skin-nourishing oil. Deodorized cod liver oil can be used in place of the vitamin E oil.

1/4 cup vitamin E oil

1/2 cup (approximately) cornstarch

1. Put the vitamin E oil into a mixing bowl. Using your finger to stir, slowly pour the cornstarch into the bowl and stir until the mixture is a spreadable paste.
2. Store the rub in a glass jar with a tight-fitting lid, away from heat. Discard any unused portion after 1 week.

APPLICATION: Keep the rub near the changing table and apply generously to the diaper area each time you change the infant. Make a fresh batch each week. The rash usually starts to subside after 3 or 4 applications and be completely gone by 10 or 15.

If diaper rash shows no sign of improvement after 10 applications of the rub, investigate factors such as proper disinfection of diapers, changes in diet, or the presence of other skin disorders.

BUMPS AND BRUISES

Depending on how difficult the birth was, an infant may have some bruises, especially around the face. If a forceps delivery was required, there will almost certainly be bruises on the sides of the head. Generally, these bruises clear up very quickly and the best way to deal with them is to leave them alone. If they persist or are so ugly they are spoiling all the baby pictures, there is an herbal procedure you can try.

Comfrey Root Fomentation
To fade bruises and relieve tenderness

Preparation Time: 20 minutes
Yield: 1 treatment
Children's Enjoyment: ☺

A Comfrey Root Fomentation is just the thing for bruises because the healing elements of the herb are applied directly to the injury and absorbed into the skin. Comfrey root contains high amounts of silica and allantoin, both of which help promote tissue healing while inhibiting inflammation. The heat from the procedure also has a soothing effect on the skin.

> 2 quarts cold water
> 1/2 cup dried comfrey root pieces
> Muslin or plain linen towel

1. Place the cold water and comfrey root in a covered pot.
2. Bring to a boil and simmer for 15 minutes.
3. Strain out the comfrey root and discard it.
4. Cool the liquid until it is hot to the touch but not so hot that it burns or hurts the skin. Keep the solution warm throughout the process.

APPLICATION: Immerse a muslin towel in the comfrey solution and gently wring out the excess. Apply the towel to the bruise with gentle pressure. When the towel has cooled, dip it in the liquid and repeat the process. When the skin around the bruise turns bright red, discontinue. (The skin turns red because the heat of the fomentation draws blood to the area. This, combined with the medicinal qualities of comfrey, helps heal the bruise. The increased circulation in the bruised area disperses the clotted blood and promotes the repair of bruised tissue.) Infants usually enjoy this process as long as they are not hungry or tired and they are handled with assurance. Repeat the fomentation once each day until the bruise fades.

If an infant's bruise does not fade after 2 or 3 fomentations, or if any swelling or abnormal tenderness is apparent, consult a pediatrician.

FLAKING SKIN AND CRADLE CAP

All infants will have a bit of flaking skin after birth. Newborn skin has been wet up to the time of birth, and exposure to dry air will cause the outer layers to flake off. A virgin olive oil or any high-quality baby oil rubbed into the dry spot will solve the problem. You must repeat this treatment twice each day for two to four days. The Diaper Rash Skin Ointment (page 133) is good for more than diaper rash. Rub this ointment into your infant's skin two or three times each day until the flaking disappears.

Your infant may develop seborrheic dermatitis — or cradle cap — on the scalp. This is a dry skin rash usually accompanied by peeling, itching skin — sort of an infant dandruff. Olive oil rubbed directly into the scalp helps relieve cradle cap. If the cradle cap is persistent, try switching the baby shampoo you're using; it may be too harsh. I used a natural soap, not shampoo, on my infants. Later, I switched to a mild herbal shampoo and rinse. There is also a good herbal remedy you can try.

Comfrey Rinse
To relieve the itching and dryness of cradle cap

Preparation Time: 20 minutes
Yield: 4 treatments
Children's Enjoyment: ☺

When comfrey root is boiled, it yields mucilage, which gives this hair rinse a lotionlike consistency. Comfrey Rinse is excellent for returning moisture to the skin, promoting tissue regeneration, and soothing the itch and discomfort of cradle cap. Comfrey grows very well in a pot or garden plot, and is available in health food and herb stores.

> 1 quart water
> 2 ounces cut, dried comfrey root
> Washcloth

1. Put the water and comfrey root in a covered pot and bring to a boil.
2. Simmer the root for 20 minutes.
3. Strain out the root pieces and discard them. The remaining brew is dark brown, with a gummy, syruplike consistency.
4. Cool the rinse to tepid before using. Refrigerate the rinse between procedures and warm it to skin temperature before each use. Discard any unused portion after 4 days.

APPLICATION: Dip the washcloth in the warm rinse and gently pat it onto the infant's scalp or dry skin area, or bath the scalp with the rinse after shampooing. Most infants enjoy this procedure as long as the rinse is warm and you proceed with gentleness and assurance. Let the rinse air-dry on the scalp. Perform this treatment once each night until the symptoms disappear, usually about 1 week to 10 days.

If the cradle cap is severe or does not improve after 10 days of treatment, consult a physician.

Slippery Elm Ointment
To coat the skin and prevent itching and dryness

Preparation Time: 45 minutes
Yield: 2 weeks of treatments
Children's Enjoyment: ☺

Slippery elm is an herb that soothes and heals the skin surface while drawing out impurities. This herb was an important botanical for Native Americans and pioneers. As a powder, slippery elm is useful for skin disorders of all kinds; when used in ointment form, it is especially good for an infant's dry, flaky skin or cradle cap. Olive oil and cocoa butter are also good skin-treating substances and give this ointment its consistency. This ointment is good in combination with the Comfrey Rinse (page 137). Powdered slippery elm bark and cocoa butter are available in health food and herb stores, and olive oil is found at most grocery stores.

>1/2 cup olive oil
>3 tablespoons powdered slippery elm bark
>2 tablespoons cocoa butter

1. Combine the olive oil and powdered slippery elm bark in a cast-iron frying pan and gently fry for 5 minutes. Be careful not to let the oil or the herb burn.
2. Add the cocoa butter.

3. After the cocoa butter is completely melted, fry the mixture for an additional 10 minutes.
4. Strain the mixture through a sieve lined with cheesecloth and discard the herbs.
5. Pour the liquid ointment into a labeled, dated jar with a tight-fitting lid. Use a jar that is wide enough to insert 2 fingers into, such as a baby food jar or small olive jar.
6. Refrigerate the oil until it is solid. The final ointment has a tan, opaque look and smells like cocoa butter. Once the ointment is solid, keep it near the infant's changing table, away from heat. Discard any unused portion after 2 months.

APPLICATION: Gently rub the ointment into the flaky skin or scalp each time the infant is bathed or a diaper is changed, about 6 to 8 times each day. Most infants enjoy the applications and their skin usually starts to improve after 2 days.

If the rash or cradle cap does not respond after 3 or 4 days of treatment, or the condition spreads or gets worse, consult a physician.

CHILDREN

Children who can run about on their own will inevitably come home with bruises, cuts, and scrapes. This is all part of everyday life, and it is nice for a parent to know how to comfort a child with a small wound. Children love to make much of every little boo-boo; and if they can assist in making up a tea, salve, wash, or poultice for it, they will gain confidence in caring for themselves. I have had a lot of fun preparing these concoctions for my youngsters, and it has given me the opportunity to teach them about herbs. Severe wounds to the skin should be treated by professionals, and a child who has had a serious accident should be taken to a hospital or clinic promptly. (See also WHEN TO SEE THE DOCTOR, page 156.)

MILD BURNS

If a child is burned, it is up to the parents to determine the burn's severity. Most sunburns are what are called first-degree burns, where only the first layer of skin has been damaged. Second-degree burns are more severe and are marked by redness, swelling, and blistering. Burns that are more serious than this, usually caused by electricity or direct contact with fire or scalding water, require prompt medical attention. Once you have determined that your child does not need a professional's attention, there are two herbal remedies to try.

Plantain Poultice
To draw the heat from a burn and repair the skin

Preparation Time: 5 minutes
Yield: 1 treatment
Children's Enjoyment: ☺

This is a good poultice to apply if your child's fingers have been burned while helping you prepare dinner. It is also good for open and oozing blisters caused by burns. Plantain is a very common roadside weed, and you may be able to find some to store for these occasions. Have your child hold the burned area under cold running water. This will help ease the pain, prevent a blister from forming, and stop the burn from going into the deeper layers of the skin. A cold plantain poultice draws the heat from a burn and keeps the area disinfected while it assists skin regeneration. The cold poultice will also extract venom from bee and wasp stings and can be used to heal bedsores or any other sores that are slow to heal. Applied hot, the poultice quickly brings a boil to a head. It is best to use fresh plantain, but dried plantain works just as well.

4 ounces fresh or 2 ounces dried plantain

1. If you use dried plantain, place it in a bowl, wet it with a few drops of very cold water, and gently mash it with the back of a wooden spoon for 5 minutes.
2. If you use fresh plantain, rinse it in cold water and either bruise it with your hands or press it with the back of a wooden spoon on a chopping board until the leaves exude a little moisture.

APPLICATION: Take enough of the herb to completely cover the burn area and apply it directly to the burn. Cover the poultice with clean bandages or muslin strips. After 15 minutes, remove the poultice and replace it with a fresh, cold one. Leave this second poultice on for the rest of the day. You can leave the poultice on overnight, but remove it in the morning. Repeat the process each evening until the burn no longer hurts. Before you apply the poultice, explain to your child that it makes the burn feel better by keeping it cool and moist, so they shouldn't try to peek under the bandage every few minutes.

This poultice is only for treating mild burns that are red and painful but not open or oozing. Parents should get a physician's advice on how to treat second-degree burns, which are usually blistered and quite painful.

Slippery Elm Paste
To relieve burn pain and help protect and regenerate skin

Preparation Time: 5 minutes
Yield: 1 treatment
Children's Enjoyment: ☺

This paste is good for mild burns that are sore, but not open or oozing, because slippery elm is so beneficial to the skin surface. Slippery elm soothes and heals injured tissues. Vitamin E oil is a good medium for applying powdered slippery elm to mild burns, poison oak and ivy, and shallow cuts and abrasions. The paste clings to the burn or abrasion, relieves pain, and protects and helps regenerate the skin. Vitamin E oil is sold in many vitamin, health food, and herb stores and can be bought in liquid or capsule form. Note: The amount of vitamin E oil in this paste may vary, depending the consistency of the vitamin E oil; some vitamin E oils are heavier than others.

> 1/2 teaspoon vitamin E oil
> 1 teaspoon powdered slippery elm bark

1. Combine the ingredients in a saucer or jar lid until they form a spreadable paste.
2. Use your finger to stir the mixture. Test it by seeing if the paste clings to the tip of your finger when you lift it out; the paste should cling without dripping or sliding. It is dark brown in color, with a bland smell. Make a fresh batch of the paste each time it is needed.

APPLICATION: Spread a thin covering of paste on burns, minor abrasions and cuts, and poison oak and ivy. It does not have to be absorbed. Put a muslin bandage or regular Band-Aid over the paste and keep it from getting wet for at least 3 days. Some of the paste will dry out and crumble off. This is fine as long as a thin, scablike covering remains on the wound. The scab usually falls off within 1 week to 10 days, leaving no scar underneath — just pink, healthy skin.

This paste is for minor wounds only. If a serious cut or burn has been sustained, or if there is a danger of infection, consult with a physician.

BRUISES Bruises are unsightly and painful. Most of the time a bruise can be ignored, although your child will want to point it out to anyone within earshot. If the bruise is particularly large or sore, or if you just want to do something nice for your child, there is a comforting herbal procedure I have used with success.

> ## *Comfrey and Wintergreen Poultice*
> To fade a bruise and relieve pain and inflammation
>
> Preparation Time: 15 minutes
> Yield: 1 treatment
> Children's Enjoyment: ☺

Comfrey has long been used to heal torn ligaments, broken bones, burns, bruises, and even remove wrinkles from the face. It contains large amounts of calcium and allantoin, making it an excellent remedy for healing muscle, skin, and bone disorders. Wintergreen is used in poultice form to reduce pain and inflammation, and as an astringent wash for slow-healing ulcers and wounds.

> 1 ounce comfrey root pieces
> 1 ounce wintergreen leaves
> 1 quart water
> Clean muslin towel, approximately 12 inches square

1. Combine the herbs with the water in a covered pot, bring to a boil, and simmer for 5 minutes.
2. Strain out the herbs and place them in a colander to drain excess moisture. Discard the water.
3. Wet the muslin towel in warm water, lay it out, and put the steaming herbs in the center.
4. Fold the cloth over the herbs lengthwise, so that the towel is approximately 5 inches wide and the herbs form a mound in the center.
5. Fold the ends of the towel over the center, so that a secure herbal pouch is formed. Cool the poultice until it can be applied without burning the child's skin.

APPLICATION: The poultice is most effective on bruises when applied as warm as the child can stand, but be careful not to burn the child's skin. Explain to the child that the poultice will feel a little hot. Put the pouch of herbs directly on the bruise and press down gently. Leave the poultice on until the herbs have cooled, then discard them. Repeat this procedure once each day until the bruise stops being painful and starts to fade, usually 3 to 5 days.

If a bruise is very severe, or does not improve after 5 days of treatment, consult a physician.

SCRAPES,
CUTS,
BLISTERS,
AND MINOR
INFECTIONS

Children frequently experience scrapes, cuts, and minor infections as a result of falls, rough play, tree climbing, and the general business of being a kid. Blisters can appear on the lips as a result of sunburn or because of a cold, and on the hands and feet because of surface abrasion or minor burns. I have come to see an array of minor bruises and scrapes as the signs of a healthy child, since they indicate a high degree of physical activity and stamina. For any sore spot that really bothers your child, there are two herbal remedies I have used many times with success. (See also WHEN TO SEE THE DOCTOR: STUBBORN INFECTIONS, page 156; and DEEP CUTS AND PUNCTURE WOUNDS, page 156.)

Antiseptic Skin Wash
To relieve inflammation and prevent infection

Preparation Time: 20 minutes
Yield: 3 to 5 treatments
Children's Enjoyment: ☺

This wash is excellent for use on blisters, scrapes, shallow cuts, and minor skin infections. An antiseptic skin wash can lower the risk of infection and reduce the healing time. Clove and mint are topical pain relievers, and lavender and witch hazel have germ-killing and astringent qualities. The wash is refreshing and pleasant smelling. It is also good as a rinse for oily skin and acne, and as an herbal aftershave. If you plan to use this wash on the face, eliminate the cloves.

    5 whole cloves
    1 ounce peppermint
    1 ounce lavender
    1 ounce witch hazel bark
    1 quart cold water
    Cheesecloth

1. Combine the cloves, peppermint, lavender, and witch hazel bark.
2. Immerse the mixture in the cold water and simmer gently for 20 minutes in a tightly covered pot.
3. Place a strainer that is lined with a length of cheesecloth into a large bowl, and pour the hot tea into it.
4. After the liquid drains into the bowl, gather the corners of the cheesecloth and squeeze any remaining tea out of the herbs. Discard the cheesecloth and herbs. The wash is a clear brown and smells sharply of cloves and witch hazel.
5. Cool it to room temperature before use. Refrigerate any unused portion of the wash. Discard it after 1 week.

APPLICATION: Apply the tepid wash directly to the skin with a clean washcloth or muslin towel. Allow the wash to dry on the skin surface. The wash may sting a little, especially on a fresh cut or scrape, so explain this to the child before applying. Older children can sit by the pot of tea and apply the wash themselves for 5 minutes or so. Let the wash dry on the skin. You can repeat this procedure once each day until the scrape, cut, blister, or minor infected area is healed. This wash is also excellent for cleaning a fresh wound before bandaging.

Use this wash for fresh, minor wounds and mild skin irritations. Any wound that is extremely tender and painful, red, swollen, or running should be examined by a physician.

Slippery Elm and Comfrey Sprinkle
To form a protective scab over a wound

Preparation Time: 5 minutes
Yield: 5 treatments
Children's Enjoyment: ☺

Comfrey root and slippery elm bark are skin-nourishing herbs that, when combined with water, form a hard, healing scab. They are good for treating chicken pox, poison ivy, poison oak, minor burns, or a fresh wound or blister that has not yet formed a protective scab. It is a good idea to keep these two herbs on hand for such occasions. This herbal sprinkle relieves itching at the same time as it forms a scab and stops open sores from running. Powdered comfrey root was once used to coat wet bandages used in splints for broken limbs. When the bandages dried, the comfrey powder formed a hard cast that supported the bone at the same time as it helped knit the break.

> 1 ounce comfrey root
> 1 ounce powdered slippery elm bark

1. If you use these herbs in bulk form, use a coffee grinder or food processor to grind the herbs into a smooth, powdery consistency. There may some large pieces left in the powder, but these fall off when applied to the wound, leaving only the powder to form the scab.
2. Store the powder in a labeled, dated jar with a tight-fitting lid. Discard any powder after 6 months

APPLICATION: Gently wash the child's wound or skin eruption to remove any debris and get clean blood to the wound surface. Sprinkle the powdered herb combination generously over the wound or pox. The powder adheres immediately to the surface and stops any bleeding or running from the sore. It is not necessary to cover or bandage the wound. A child feels no pain when the herbs come in contact with the skin, and a hard, protective scab forms that is nearly impossible to scratch or pick off. The skin will be pink and healthy looking when the scab finally falls off, which, depending on the size and depth of the abrasion, is usually 1 week.

This sprinkle should be used only on fresh sores or wounds. If a child's wound is deep or bleeding profusely, or if it is not healing well or is infected, consult a physician.

BUG BITES

Almost all children will suffer mosquito or spider bites and bee or wasp stings at some time. In some rare instances, a child is so allergic to the venom of a bee or wasp that he or she must be immediately hospitalized. Symptoms you should watch for are severe flushing of the skin, severe coughing, severe anxiety, wheezing, blurred vision, loss of consciousness, vomiting, and shock. Most children, however, will experience nothing more than the immediate pain of the bite or sting, with mild swelling and aching afterward. If your child has been stung by a bee, you must try to remove the stinger if it is still lodged in the skin. Use clean tweezers for this purpose. Wasps can sting repeatedly but do not embed their stinger in the skin. There are several herbal remedies that have immediate effects on bug bites and stings.

Tobacco Poultice
To draw the venom from a bee or wasp sting

Preparation Time: 5 minutes
Yield: 1 treatment
Children's Enjoyment: ☺

This is a quick, easy, and effective remedy that draws out the venom from bee and wasp stings. It is a good field remedy, since children often get stung while on picnics or outings. If there are more than three adults in one place at a time, one of them will probably have a cigarette available.

An all-but-forgotten use for common tobacco is in drawing bee and wasp venom from a sting. Tobacco was also used in the Old West to extract snake venom from bites. Its drawing power is phenomenal; and when applied to a bite or sting, tobacco reduces swelling and pain immediately. It can be prepared as a poultice in the kitchen, as well. To obtain tobacco in an herb or health food store is very difficult. If you can't find any, you can use pouch cigarette tobacco for this purpose, since it is not as chemically processed as prerolled cigarettes. In an emergency, however, any brand of nonmentholated cigarette will do.

1/2 ounce pouch cigarette tobacco or 1 unrolled cigarette

APPLICATION:

Field dressing

1. Take a pinch of cigarette tobacco, put it in your mouth, and chew it for 1 minute. Tobacco tastes awful, but it is necessary to moisten and bruise it to obtain its beneficial effects.
2. If you are treating a bee sting, first remove the stinger from the skin.
3. Spit the moistened tobacco into the palm of your hand and apply it to the sting or bite with firm, but gentle pressure for 5 minutes.
4. Remove the poultice and examine the sting. There should be a noticeable reduction in swelling and pain, but you may reapply the poultice for 5 more minutes if necessary.
5. Discard the poultice and either resume your outing or go home, depending on how the child feels. Usually the poultice will soothe the sting enough so that you and your child can continue with your outdoor adventure.

Kitchen dressing

1. Take 1/2 ounce of pouch cigarette tobacco and place it on a chopping board.
2. Sprinkle enough water on the pile to moisten it and, with a cleaver, chop and mix it until it forms a moist wad.
3. If the child was stung by a bee, remove the stinger from the skin.
4. Apply the poultice directly to the sting or bite and put a Band-Aid or muslin bandage over it to keep it in place. Leave it there for 5 to 10 minutes, or until the sting stops hurting.
5. Discard the poultice and leave the sting or bite uncovered.

Usually wasp and bee stings are painful but not dangerous. If the child exhibits allergic symptoms such as dizziness, difficulty in breathing, blurred vision, flushing of the skin, or loss of consciousness, get him or her to an emergency health facility immediately.

Peppermint and Cleavers Bath
To cool and anesthetize itchy bug bites

Preparation Time: 20 minutes
Yield: 1 treatment
Children's Enjoyment: ☺

Cleavers and peppermint produce a cooling and anesthetic effect on the skin, which makes this a good combination for bug bites. A wash of cleavers has been used historically for many skin conditions, including acne, slow-healing wounds, and, of all things, freckles! The peppermint in the mixture also reduces the inflammation from mosquito bites and bee and wasp stings. Peppermint has a familiar minty smell, and cleavers has a bland, earthy aroma. Cleavers is an herb that is very high in calcium, one of the body's building blocks.

2 ounces dried peppermint
2 ounces dried cleavers
2 quarts water

1. Combine the herbs with the water in a large, covered pot and bring to a boil.
2. Slowly simmer the herbs for 5 minutes, then take the pot off the heat and steep the herbs for 15 minutes.
3. Strain out the herbs and discard them. The bath tea is greenish brown and smells like peppermint.
4. Pour the tea into the bathtub while running the water so that it will be well combined. Run the bath as hot as you normally would for a child, but make sure the temperature of the bath is not too hot after adding the brewed tea.

APPLICATION: Explain to the child that the bath will make the skin tingle slightly. Bathe the child once each day, in the morning or evening, until the itching and inflammation disappear (3 days to 1 week). Make sure the bathwater covers the child wherever there are bug bites on the skin. Have the child soak for 20 minutes. You can put some fresh mint leaves in the water for the child to play with, but don't let the leaves clog the drain when you empty the bathtub.

If the child has been severely bitten or exhibits an allergic reaction to an insect sting or bite, consult a physician immediately. Emergency treatment may be required.

RASHES A child's skin rash can be caused by measles, poison oak, poison ivy, drug reactions, allergies, eczema, herpes, impetigo, and chicken pox, among other things. Skin rashes are usually not very severe by themselves, but can be a side effect of other, more serious diseases such as scarlet fever. A skin rash accompanied by fever, sore throat, and listlessness may indicate an allergic reaction. If you suspect your child's skin rash is symptomatic of some other disorder, or if your child has a severe skin rash which is not responding to either of the following treatments, consult a pediatrician or dermatologist.

Sage Bath
To relieve itching and reduce bumps, excretions, and swelling

Preparation Time: 20 minutes
Yield: 1 treatment
Children's Enjoyment: ☺

Sage washes are a traditional external remedy for disorders of the skin and scalp, slow-healing wounds and ulcers, and chronic skin rashes such as eczema and psoriasis. As an internal medication, sage tea is used to dry up breast milk, rid the body of intestinal parasites, and calm the nerves. It is also good as a mouthwash.

  4 ounces dried sage leaves
  2 quarts water

1. Combine the sage and water in a covered pot, bring to a boil, and simmer for 5 minutes.

2. Remove the pot from the heat, and steep the herb for 15 minutes.
3. Strain out the herbs and discard them.
4. Pour the tea into the tub while the bathwater is running so that it will be well combined. Run the herbal bath as hot as you usually run a bath for the child or infant, but make sure the water is not too hot after adding the brewed tea. The tea turns the bathwater a light gray-green color, with the pleasant scent of sage.

APPLICATION: Soak the child or infant for 20 minutes, and allow him or her to play in the water. Let the skin air-dry after the bath, but be sure the room is warm enough to prevent a chill. Repeat the bath once each day until the skin condition clears up, usually 3 days to 1 week.

If the skin condition does not respond or worsens after 1 week of treatment, consult a physician.

Skin Food Bath
Excellent for moisturizing and healing dry, rashy skin

Preparation Time: 20 minutes
Yield: 1 treatment
Children's Enjoyment: ☺

Oats and barley are widely cultivated as edible grains, but cooked oats and barley can produce a soothing washing water that is healing to skin surfaces. This water is used to treat dermatitis, chicken pox, poison oak, poison ivy, eczema, dry skin, and sunburns. A bath tea made from oats and barley makes the skin feel soft and tender, dries up excretions, and speeds skin regeneration. Organic, pearled barley and rolled oats are available in health food stores.

> 1/2 cup rolled oats
> 1/2 cup pearled barley
> 2 quarts water

1. Combine the oats, barley, and water in a large covered pot, bring to a boil, and simmer for 20 minutes.
2. Strain out the oats and barley. Either discard them or save them in the refrigerator for breakfast or to use as a thickener for soups and stews.
3. Pour the tea into the tub while the water is running so it will be well combined. Make sure the temperature of the bathwater is not too hot after adding the brewed tea. The bathwater is milky and opaque, with a bland, grainlike smell, and feels soft and silky, as though bath oil were added.

APPLICATION: Bathe the child for 20 minutes once each day until the skin clears, which, depending on the condition, is usually 3 to 5 days. The skin will be soft and tender after bathing. Gently pat the skin with a washcloth; it is not necessary to wash with soap. Let the child air-dry after the bath, but be sure the room is warm enough to prevent a chill.

If the skin condition shows no improvement or gets worse after 5 days of treatment, consult a physician.

SKIN PARASITES

Ticks and head lice are the most common skin parasites that affect children. Ticks are more common in rural environments and can be easily removed. If your child has a tick anywhere on the body, take a wooden match and strike it. Let it flame for a second and then blow it out. While the match is still smoking and hot, gently apply it to the exposed body of the tick. The heat will cause the tick to immediately withdraw its head from the child's skin and drop off. It is necessary to make the tick drop off by itself, rather than to pick it off, because the tick's head can remain embedded in a child's skin and cause irritation and possible infection.

Head lice cannot be removed by washing with regular shampoo. They can be a big problem in schools, and parental participation is required to stem head-lice epidemics. Parents should examine their child's scalp if the child complains of itching. Head lice are easily visible to the naked eye. If you find them on your child, get rid of them immediately. Encourage your child to wash his or her hands as often as possible during the day, and let the school nurse know so that steps can be taken to prevent the head lice from spreading to other children. If your child has head lice, there is a safe herbal procedure that I have found to be effective in eliminating them.

Head Lice Hair Oil
A potent oil for removing head lice

Preparation Time: 10 minutes
Yield: 1 treatment
Children's Enjoyment: ☹

I used this mixture successfully on my daughter when she contracted head lice in school. Herbalists use this combination of herbal oils successfully to combat skin parasite infestations in both humans and animals. In addition to their many other medicinal qualities, pennyroyal, eucalyptus, and rosemary are all herbal insect repellents. The essential oils of these herbs are very hot, and should be diluted and applied cautiously to a child's tender scalp. The oils may smell unpleasantly strong even when diluted, so familiarize the child with the mixture before application to avoid difficulties during the treatment.

> 1/2 teaspoon oil of pennyroyal
> 1/2 teaspoon oil of eucalyptus
> 1/2 teaspoon oil of rosemary
> 8 teaspoons virgin olive oil
> Flea comb
> Cotton bandanna

1. Combine the oil of pennyroyal, eucalyptus, and rosemary, then mix them with the olive oil.
2. If the proportions are correct, when you test a drop of the mixture on your wrist it will tingle but not burn. If it burns, mix in more olive oil until you can apply it to your skin without burning.

3. Keep the mixture in a dated, labeled glass jar with a tight-fitting lid. Store it for no more than 6 months, well out of the reach of young children.

APPLICATION: Wash the child's hair with water as warm as he or she can stand and towel dry. Comb the oil through the hair and scalp with a regular comb, then use the flea comb to comb out any nits, or lice eggs that are firmly attached to the roots of the hair. They should be easy to remove because of the hot water wash and the oil in the hair. Tie the hair up in a cotton bandanna, and leave the oil on all night. The child may experience a tingling sensation on the scalp. If it burns, however, wash the oil out immediately. Reapply it in a more dilute solution. Wash the oil out of the hair the next morning with shampoo. Rub the shampoo into the child's dry hair, then wet the head. This technique helps cut the oil and makes the hair easier to shampoo. One application of the hair oil is usually enough to rid the child of head lice. If lice are still present, repeat the treatment the next night. I only had to do this once and there was no sign of head lice after that. Not only is this formula safe and nonpoisonous but it leaves the hair beautifully lustrous.

Remember to wash all of the used sheets, towels, and washcloths in the house to get rid of the nits. Lice are extremely contagious and can spread easily to siblings and parents.

WARTS Warts are very common in childhood and adolescence. There are several kinds of warts. The kinds your child is most likely to experience are common warts, usually found on the hands, and the sometimes painful plantar warts found on the soles of the feet. Usually, these warts disappear by the time a child is grown, but that doesn't comfort an embarrassed nine-year-old one bit. If your child has a large number of warts, or an extremely painful one, you may want to visit your pediatrician or dermatologist. There is, however, a poultice you can try to get rid of a wart.

Potato Poultice
For softening and removing warts

Preparation Time: 5 minutes
Yield: 5 to 6 treatments
Children's Enjoyment: ☺

Raw potato juice is a beneficial remedy for many skin blemishes, including warts. Potatoes contain high amounts of potassium, sulfur, phosphorus, and chlorine, all of which can wear down unhealthy wart tissue and normalize and heal the skin. Use fresh, firm white potatoes for this treatment.

>   1 small white potato
>   Muslin bandage or Band-Aid

1. Scrub the potato thoroughly, but do not peel it.
2. Grate enough potato to completely cover the wart or warts.
3. Gently pat the grated potato dry with a paper towel or a clean dishrag. One small potato usually yields 5 or 6 treatments. It can be wrapped in plastic wrap and saved in the refrigerator between treatments.

APPLICATION: Apply the grated potato directly to the wart and the skin around it. Cover the poultice with clean bandages or muslin strips and leave it on for 2 to 3 hours. The skin around the wart may take on a curious, bleached look. This is temporary and does not cause any damage. Let the skin rest for an hour, then apply more fresh, grated potato. Apply the poultice 3 to 4 times each day, but do not leave it on overnight. The wart tissue starts to soften after 2 or 3 days, and the wart usually disappears within a week.

If a wart is large, painful, or has noticeably changed color or shape, consult a physician.

WHEN TO SEE THE DOCTOR

✚ STUBBORN INFECTIONS: If your child has sustained a mild cut, there is usually nothing more required than cleansing the wound thoroughly with warm water. If you notice that the wound is healing poorly, or if it continues hurting after it should have started healing, it may be infected. Signs of wound infection include redness, swelling, warmth in the wounded area, and drainage. Staph bacteria are often involved in wound infections, and your child should be examined by a health professional so that the proper antibiotics can be administered.

✚ ANIMAL BITES: If your child has received a wound that is trivial, and has been inflicted by a family pet that is known to be healthy and immunized, it need not be reported, but should be cleaned thoroughly. Serious bites, bites from wild animals such as bats, foxes, and skunks, and bites from unknown dogs or cats must be reported to a doctor. Your child's tetanus immunization status must be checked and updated, and antibiotics may be prescribed, since they are effective against many mouth organisms. Pertinent information about the circumstances of the bite, such as whether the attack was provoked, what kind of animal it was, and the severity of the bite will determine whether a rabies vaccination is necessary. Children must be taught not to touch wild animals if they come upon them, nor should they approach strange dogs or cats.

✚ DEEP CUTS AND PUNCTURE WOUNDS: Parents must get their child to a hospital as quickly as possible if a deep cut or puncture wound has been sustained. The wound will require local cleansing. Also, a tetanus shot is needed if your child has not yet had the required primary immunizations, or if ten years have passed since the last immunization. If the wound is large or deep, stitches may be needed to close it. Parents should try to make sure that a young child does not have access to sharp or pointed objects. They must also teach their child that real utensils, such as forks and pocket knives, are never to be used as toys.

✚ **SEVERE BURNS:** Burns caused by chemicals, electricity, fire, and scalding water usually require hospitalization. Expert diagnosis is needed to determine the severity of the burn. Second-degree burns are shiny, red, blistered, and painful. Third-degree burns are dry, blanched or dark, leathery, and painless. Serious burns require liquids to replace fluid loss, increased nutrient levels to heal and grow tissue, pain control, and prevention of infection that can make the damage worse. Children under four years of age and toddlers are particularly at risk for burns. Parents should have smoke detectors in their houses and use flame-retardant clothing and bedding for their children.

CHAPTER SEVEN

ALLERGIC REACTIONS

INFANTS

Milk Allergy

Skin Rashes from Allergic Reactions

CHILDREN

Asthma

Hives

Head Congestion from Allergic Reactions

Contact Dermatitis

allergic reactions occur in many children and can be severe or mild, depending on the degree of hypersensitivity in a child. Allergic reactions may be accompanied by symptoms such as sinus congestion, skin rash, difficulty in breathing, headache, diarrhea, or vomiting. Both parents and children can be distressed by these reactions because they come and go without any warning or reason until the specific allergen — the substance known to cause the allergic reaction — is identified. Identification of an allergen can be easy, as in the case of hay fever. However, trying to identify specific food allergens or substances that cause contact dermatitis, a localized skin irritation, can be quite complicated.

Parents will need to work with a physician to find out if their child is experiencing a true allergic reaction. If an allergic reaction is confirmed, skin tests and environmental controls can help isolate the cause of the allergy and minimize a child's exposure to it. My son suffers allergic rhinitis (runny nose) and dermatitis on his scalp because he is allergic to animal hairs. I control his contact with cats and dogs and also give him plenty of fiber and fresh fruit to eat, which help cleanse his system. These simple environmental controls help to keep his allergic reactions minimal.

Some children can experience very severe allergic reactions such as difficulty in breathing, unconsciousness, and severe vomiting and diarrhea. Emergency medical attention is necessary in these cases. Parents with children who experience allergic reactions of this intensity should work closely with a physician to determine the cause of the reaction and to try to eliminate contact with the allergen. (See also WHEN TO SEE THE DOCTOR, page 176.)

INFANTS

Allergic reactions in infants are relatively rare, probably because the environment and diet of an infant are so closely controlled. Protective immunoglobulins are ingested by breast-fed infants, and these help decrease the possibility of hypersensitive reactions. Some infants are allergic to specific types of drugs, and these reactions must be monitored and controlled by a pediatrician. Parents should try to learn all they can about the drugs being given to their infants so they know what kind of reactions to expect and what alternatives exist.

Infants sometimes develop asthmatic-type reactions as a result of bronchiolitis — an inflammation of the bronchioles. Expert diagnosis is required because it is difficult to differentiate between asthma and bronchiolitis in children under one year of age. If your infant has a persistent cough, work closely with your pediatrician to determine its cause. (See also WHEN TO SEE THE DOCTOR: DETERMINING FOOD OR ENVIRONMENTAL ALLERGENS, page 176.)

MILK ALLERGY

Symptoms of milk allergy in infants include vomiting, colic, diarrhea, and a failure to thrive (showing no weight gain or very slow weight gain). All of the symptoms of milk allergy can signify some other disorder, so parents should be sure they are not overreacting to any of these symptoms. Some infants vomit regularly, despite an emotionally balanced environment and frequent variations in the amount and quality of food ingested. These infants will usually continue to grow at a normal rate. Chronic vomiting, however, can also signify an anatomical defect of the gastrointestinal system.

The most reliable symptom of infant milk allergy is a failure to gain weight. A physician's evaluation is necessary to determine this, since many parents think their infants are not healthy unless they are fat. Milk allergy must be identified by a series of lab tests, after which a non-milk formula will be prescribed. These formulas usually contain ingredients such as soybeans, corn and coconut oils, sucrose, and corn sugar. If your infant has been switched to a nonmilk formula because of a milk allergy, his or her rate of growth should return to normal, and the diarrhea, vomiting, and colic should subside.

SKIN RASHES FROM ALLERGIC REACTIONS

Infants sometimes develop skin rashes and irritations as a result of exposure to a contact allergen. This tends to occur less commonly in very young children and infants because they usually have infrequent contact with offending agents. Potential contact allergens are numerous, but a few to keep in mind for infants and toddlers are household cleaners, soaps and shampoos, and metals such as nickel often found in jewelry, leather, and plants.

Physicians use patch tests to identify the offending substance. This involves applying a small amount of the suspected material to the skin and keeping it there with impermeable plastic tape for twenty-four hours. If the skin beneath the patch becomes red and sore, identification is positive. Sometimes the offending agent will be obvious, such as a new brand of shampoo or soap. Infant contact dermatitis is usually not severe and causes the infant little discomfort. If an infant's skin becomes rough and scaly, or if the dermatitis seems to be spreading rapidly, a visit to the pediatrician is necessary. If your infant's skin reaction is a mild one, there are two herbal baths that can relieve the condition. (See also WHEN TO SEE THE DOCTOR: SEVERE ALLERGIC REACTIONS, page 176.)

> *Skin Food Bath*
> To soothe and moisturize an infant's irritated skin
>
> Preparation Time: 20 minutes
> Yield: 1 treatment
> Children's Enjoyment: ☺

This bath is very good for an infant with dry, flaky, or mildly irritated skin stemming from an allergic reaction. Oats and barley are widely cultivated as edible grains, but cooked oats and barley can produce a soothing washing water that is healing to skin surfaces. This water is used to treat dermatitis, chicken pox, poison oak, poison ivy, eczema, dry skin, and sunburns. A bath tea made from oats and barley makes the skin feel soft and tender, dries up excretions, and speeds skin regeneration.

> 1/2 cup rolled oats
> 1/2 cup pearled barley
> 2 quarts water

1. Combine the oats, barley, and water in a large covered pot, bring to a boil, and simmer for 20 minutes.

2. Strain out the oats and barley. Either discard them or save in the refrigerator for breakfast or to use as a thickener for soups and stews.
3. Pour the tea into the tub while the water is running so it will be well combined. Make sure the temperature of the bathwater is not too hot after adding the brewed tea. The bathwater is milky and opaque, with a bland, grain-like smell, and feels soft and silky, as though bath oil were added.

APPLICATION: Bathe the infant for 20 minutes once each day until the skin clears, which, depending on the condition, is usually 3 to 5 days. The skin will be soft and tender after bathing. Gently pat the skin with a washcloth; it is not necessary to wash with soap. Let the infant air-dry after the bath, but be sure the room is warm enough to prevent a chill.

If the skin condition shows no improvement or gets worse after 5 days of treatment, consult a physician.

Sage and Burdock Bath
An astringent wash to dry up excretions on the skin

Preparation Time: 20 minutes
Yield: 1 treatment
Children's Enjoyment: ☺

This is a good bath for an infant who seems to be uncomfortable because of itching and irritation. Sage baths are commonly used for the relief of itchy skin and eczema as well as to lend an herby scent to cosmetics and perfumes. Sage tea is an effective gargle for sore throats. Sage is highly astringent; it causes tissue to contract and reduces discharges and secretions. In a bath mixture, sage is excellent for healing rashes from chicken pox, poison oak, poison ivy, and allergic dermatitis. A wash of burdock leaves is also an effective remedy for sores, acne, and other disorders of the skin. The combination of these two herbs fortifies the skin surface and soothes itching and irritation.

2 ounces dried sage leaves
2 ounces dried burdock leaves
2 quarts water

1. Combine the herbs with the water in a large, covered pot and bring to a boil.
2. Simmer the mixture for 5 minutes, then remove the pot from the heat.
3. Steep the herbs for 15 minutes, then strain out and discard them.
4. Pour the tea into the bathtub while the water is running so that it will be well combined. The tea turns the bathwater greenish brown, with a strong smell of sage.
5. Run the herbal bath as hot as you usually run a bath for the infant, but make sure the temperature of the bath is not too hot after adding the brewed tea.

APPLICATION: Have the infant relax and play in the water for 20 minutes. There is no need to wash the infant, just use a clean wash-cloth to pat the bathwater gently on the skin. Let the skin air-dry after the bath, but make sure the room is warm enough to prevent a chill. Repeat this procedure once each day just before bedtime until the skin condition clears up (usually 1 week).

If an infant has a severe allergic reaction, or if the skin does not respond after 1 week of treatment, consult a physician.

CHILDREN

The most common allergic reactions experienced by children are asthma, skin disorders such as hives and contact dermatitis, and head congestion. The main environmental allergens that bring on these reactions are animal hair, dust, molds, pollen, pollutants such as car exhaust and smoke, and chemical odors such as paint fumes. Common food allergens include peanuts, cow's milk, eggs, soybeans, and fish. Many children will be sensitive to one or more of these things early in life, and then develop immunity as they get older.

Head congestion and skin rash are symptomatic of a variety of other disorders, so parents who suspect their child is suffering from an allergy must get a physician's evaluation to be certain. Skin tests, patch tests, and environmental and dietary controls will be performed to identify the allergen and minimize your child's exposure to it. Parents must be conscientious about reducing their child's exposure to confirmed allergens in the home, at school, and when playing outdoors.

Asthma is the most frequent chronic respiratory illness of childhood. Its main symptom is labored breathing caused by the production of excess mucus and spasms of the smooth muscle tissue in the lungs and bronchial tubes. Common asthma-causing allergens include foods, house dust, pollen, and molds. Attacks can be provoked by prolonged respiratory infections, vigorous physical activity, certain drugs such as aspirin, and emotional stress. Symptoms of asthma in the absence of labored breathing include chronic nighttime coughs and colds that persist for long periods. If your child exhibits any of these symptoms, a visit to your doctor is necessary to confirm the condition. You can then work with your doctor to determine the kind of therapy that is best for your child. If your child's asthma is not serious enough to require special treatment or hospitalization, there are two herbal teas that can make your child more comfortable during a mild attack.

ASTHMA

Chickweed and Elecampane Tea
To ease lung congestion and strengthen the respiratory tract

Preparation Time: 30 minutes
Yield: 4 treatments
Children's Enjoyment: ☺

Chickweed and Elecampane Tea is a good combination for a child with asthma. Chickweed derives its name from the fact that barnyard chickens make a special effort to eat it when they find it. It contains high amounts of calcium, which the chickens need to produce eggs. In humans, calcium is required to build and strengthen tissue. Chickweed is a common roadside herb that helps expel mucus from the lungs and bronchial tubes, and is a mild digestive aid. Elecampane root has long been used to quiet coughing and to ease respiratory tract inflammation.

> 1/2 ounce dried elecampane root pieces
> 2 cups water
> 1/2 ounce dried chickweed

1. Place the elecampane root and water in a covered pot and simmer for 10 minutes.
2. Add the chickweed, cover the pot, and remove from the heat.
3. Steep the mixture for 15 minutes.
4. Strain out the herbs and discard them. The tea is a dark yellow color and smells earthy.
5. Cool it to room temperature before serving. Refrigerate any unused portion and warm it to room temperature for each use.

APPLICATION: Administer 1/2 cup of the tea 3 times each day, between meals, for 2 weeks. This tea is not very pleasant tasting, so a child will probably enjoy a chaser of orange juice or natural soda. Sweetening the tea does not improve its taste, so it's best to give the tea straight. I've found that promising my children a favorite activity, such as cooking or taking a walk right after, is a good way to get them to take this medicine.

If the child shows no improvement after 2 weeks, is having difficulty breathing during an asthma attack, or if the asthma attack is prolonged, consult a physician.

Ephedra Tea

For relief during and after an asthma attack

Preparation Time: 20 minutes
Yield: 8 treatments
Children's Enjoyment: 😞

Ephedra Tea is helpful for children suffering from asthma. This herb was used by Native Americans and early pioneers to combat head and lung congestion, stimulate circulation in the kidneys, purify the blood, and soothe headaches and fever. The root has also been used for centuries in China to treat similar disorders.

2 ounces dried ephedra root
1 quart water

1. Combine the ephedra root and water in a covered pot and simmer for 20 minutes.
2. Strain out the herb and discard it. The tea is dark brown in color, with an earthy smell.
3. Cool the tea to room temperature and do not sweeten before serving. Refrigerate the unused tea and warm it to room temperature each time it is used. Discard any remaining tea after 1 week.

APPLICATION: Give a child with asthma 1/2 cup twice each day, between meals, for 2 weeks. The tea can also be given during an attack to help comfort the child and reduce breathing difficulties. You may have to bribe your child to drink the tea because it is not very tasty and should not be sweetened. A handful of golden raisins is healthy and useful for this, or some juice or soda as a chaser.

This tea should not be used for children suffering from high blood pressure, heart or kidney disease, diabetes, or thyroid trouble because ephedra is a strong stimulant. If the asthma attacks continue or worsen after 2 weeks of treatment, or if they are severe, consult a physician.

HIVES   Hives, or urticaria, is a condition marked by lesions that may be in one place on a child's body or all over the body. Normally, hives affects only the skin, but mucous membranes, such as those lining the eyes or nose, can also be affected. Hives can swell and be painful and will itch mildly when they start to clear up. Allergens in certain foods, drugs like penicillin and aspirin, pollen, fungi, insect stings, and animal hairs can all activate histamine production in a child's body, which can result in hives. For this reason, antihistamines are prescribed for mild cases of hives, and steroids are used for extreme cases. Physical factors such as extremes of temperatures, especially cold, may also trigger hives. A child who breaks out in hives should be examined by a doctor to determine whether an allergic reaction triggered them. If so, the allergen can then be identified and a child's exposure to it minimized. If your child breaks out in a mild case of hives, there is an ointment you can make to allay the discomfort and help return the skin surface to normal. (See also WHEN TO SEE THE DOCTOR: SEVERE ALLERGIC REACTIONS, page 176.)

Chickweed Ointment
To relieve the itching and irritation of hives

Preparation Time: 35 minutes
Yield: 15 to 20 treatments
Children's Enjoyment: ☺

Chickweed in ointment form is an excellent treatment for hives, chicken pox, and bruises. For centuries, fresh chickweed has been applied to skin wounds and open sores with good results, because of its healing effect on inflamed tissues. The base of this ointment is petroleum jelly (Vaseline), which can hold the active ingredients of the chickweed close to the skin for hours.

   1 1/2 ounces dried chickweed
   3/4 cup petroleum jelly (Vaseline)

1. Place the petroleum jelly in a cast-iron frying pan and melt it slowly over a very low heat.
2. When it is completely liquid, add the chickweed and gently fry the mixture. It is very important not to let it burn, so watch it carefully. The herbs should sizzle gently for 10 minutes.
3. Strain the mixture into a bowl or measuring cup through a cheesecloth-lined sieve and discard the herb.
4. Pour the strained ointment into a dated, labeled glass jar with a tight-fitting lid. The ointment can be left at room temperature to set or, if you are in a hurry, placed in the refrigerator for 30 minutes. Store the ointment away from heat and discard any unused portion after 6 months.

APPLICATION: This ointment may be generously dabbed onto hives, minor cuts, scrapes, chicken pox, and bruises. It is not necessary for it to be absorbed into the skin, so just dab it on and smooth it out. You can put a loose muslin bandage over the application to prevent messy clothes. The ointment wears off by itself and more can be applied until the skin irritation disappears (about 1 week or less, depending on the condition). The ointment looks like dark petroleum jelly and does not hurt when applied. Repeat the procedure until the hives subside. When applying the ointment, parents should remember that hives can be painful. Always apply the ointment gently and lovingly.

If the child's skin irritation is causing severe discomfort or the cause is not known, consult a physician.

HEAD CONGESTION FROM ALLERGIC REACTIONS

Head congestion resulting from allergies is classified as allergic rhinitis in the medical community. It is a common disorder among children and adults, and is manifested by watery eyes, nasal discharge, and headache. A child suffering with allergic rhinitis may have dark circles around the eyes and recurrent nosebleeds. This type of allergic reaction is usually caused by house dust, wool, feathers, animal hair, and indoor heating systems during the winter months. Children with allergic rhinitis are often mistakenly thought to have frequent colds instead of allergies.

If your child exhibits any of these symptoms of allergic rhinitis, a physician's evaluation is necessary to confirm an allergic reaction, and an effort must be made to identify the specific allergen. This may take a while, because so many different allergens can cause this condition. In the meantime, a high-fiber diet, which keeps the bowels moving freely, and plenty of fresh fruit and vegetable juice are helpful. This diet helps reduce mucus in your child's body as well as lower the hypersensitivity to whatever allergens are causing the reaction. There are two herbal procedures that can alleviate your child's discomfort from this type of head congestion. (See also WHEN TO SEE THE DOCTOR: DETERMINING FOOD OR ENVIRONMENTAL ALLERGENS, page 176.)

> ## Head Congestion Facial
> To clear the head and soothe the eyes
> during hay fever or other allergy attacks
>
> Preparation Time: 20 minutes
> Yield: 1 treatment
> Children's Enjoyment: ☺

This procedure is both comforting and fun for a child who has been suffering for days during hay fever season. A cup of peppermint tea for your child to drink during the facial will heighten the decongestant qualities of the herbs used in this procedure. The inhalation of steam mixed with the head-clearing aromas of pennyroyal, wintergreen, and rosemary make this treatment excellent for head congestion. The essential oils of these herbs have powerful decongestant properties and reduce inflammation of the mucous membrane lining the nose. Children enjoy this facial, but they must be familiarized with the strong smell of the oils before the treatment.

2 quarts water
2 drops oil of wintergreen
2 drops oil of pennyroyal
2 drops oil of rosemary
Large bath towel

1. Put the water in a pot and bring it to a boil.
2. Take the pot off the heat, let the water cool for 10 minutes, and add the essential oils.
3. The oils will naturally remain on the top of the water. Stir with a stainless-steel ladle to combine them as fully as possible.
4. Place the pot on a table or workbench that is comfortable for a child to sit or stand at and bend his or her head over the pot.

APPLICATION: Perform this treatment once each day, with adult supervision, until head congestion leaves (1 week). Have the child stand or sit in a position that allows him or her to comfortably bend the head directly over the pot. Explain to the child that the steam will make the face feel a little hot, and it's all right to come up for a cooling breath of air. Drape the towel over the head and shoulders to form a tent over the pot as the child bends over to inhale the steam. Have the child inhale the steam for 2 or 3 minutes, then take a break. During the break, cover the pot so that the water stays hot and no steam escapes. Jumping around temporarily unblocks the sinus cavities and passages and renders the facial far more effective. If the child feels up to it, have him or her do 20 jumping jacks during breaks. Repeat the process of facial and jumping jacks at least 3 times within 30 minutes, then discard the water and oil. This treatment usually clears a child's head for several hours.

If the child's head congestion shows no sign of improvement after 1 week, if the child is feverish or fatigued, or if a sinus infection is suspected, consult a physician.

Garlic Syrup

To purify the bloodstream and reduce the severity of allergic attacks

Preparation Time: 10 minutes
Yield: 30 treatments
Children's Enjoyment: ☹

This may not be your child's favorite remedy, but it is very effective for breaking up congestion anywhere in the body. Garlic can also purify the bloodstream and strengthen the immune system. This keeps allergic reactions from being so severe and may even stop some of them completely. Garlic Syrup is excellent for breaking up mucous congestion in the sinuses. Garlic also helps cleanse wastes that have built up on the intestinal walls and stimulates the circulation in the digestive organs, which allows greater absorption of nutrients.

1 small head garlic, peeled (about 10 cloves)
1 cup water
1 1/2 cups cider vinegar
1 1/2 pounds (approximately 3 cups) brown sugar

1. Dice the garlic cloves by hand or in a food mill or blender and combine with the water and vinegar in a tightly lidded jar.
2. Shake vigorously and let the mixture stand for 4 hours.
3. When the mixture is ready, strain out the garlic and discard it.
4. Put the strained solution in a pot with the brown sugar and heat until all the sugar is dissolved (about 10 minutes). The syrup is dark brown in color and smells lightly of garlic.
5. Pour into a glass jar, label and date the jar, and store in the medicine closet. Discard any unused portion after 6 months.

APPLICATION: Administer 1 tablespoon 3 times each day, 1 hour after each meal, until the nasal congestion is relieved. Relief from sinus congestion usually happens within 1 week. The syrup has a strong garlic taste for a child, so some golden raisins may be needed for a chaser. If your child complains severely about the taste, reduce the dosage. Because garlic cleanses the system of wastes, it may cause mild skin rashes, sweating, strong-smelling urine, and mild muscle aches and pains if used for more than 1 week. This kind of internal cleansing, however, may help the body to overcome many allergic reactions. Reassure the child that this treatment is temporary, and use other herbal remedies to help make the child more comfortable during this phase of healing. Do not administer the syrup for more than 3 weeks.

If the allergic reaction has not improved, or if it gets worse after 3 weeks of treatment, consult a physician.

CONTACT DERMATITIS

Some children experience contact dermatitis when their skin comes in contact with specific allergens. This type of allergic reaction may be nothing more than a mild redness of the skin, or it can manifest as painful, oozing blisters. Parents can usually determine what the specific allergen is on their own, but a patch test should be performed to be certain. This test is performed when a doctor applies a small amount of the suspect material to the skin and keeps it there with an impermeable piece of plastic tape for twenty-four hours. If the skin beneath the patch is red and sore, identification is positive. Parents should make sure that the allergen their child reacts to is removed from his or her environment so that the condition does not become severe. Skin that is dry, thick, and scaly is symptomatic of severe contact dermatitis and can be an embarrassment to a child. If your child's dermatitis is mild, there are two procedures that can help relieve the condition and strengthen the skin surface. (See also WHEN TO SEE THE DOCTOR: SEVERE ALLERGIC REACTIONS, page 176.)

Almond Oil Rub

To relieve the irritation, discharge, and flaking skin of dermatitis

Preparation Time: 5 minutes
Yield: 30 treatments
Children's Enjoyment: ☺

This rub smells wonderful and is soothing to a child's skin. Almond oil has been used since biblical times to soften the skin, and it is available in many health food stores and bath shops. This is a good remedy to let your child help you make. The oil of almonds is excellent for skin problems of all kinds because of its emollient — skin soothing and softening — properties. Rose petals and buds, which are used topically for their astringent qualities, can be taken internally in tea or jelly to stimulate the appetite. The combination of these two herbs is comforting and healing to irritated skin, as well as very sweet smelling. Look for sweet almond oil that is prepared for cosmetic use; it is also available in some bath shops. Fresh rose petals can be used in place of dry ones, but make certain they have not been sprayed with insecticides before harvesting. Most children will enjoy gathering the rose petals and preparing the oil.

> 1 ounce dried or 2 ounces fresh rose petals
> 2 cups sweet almond oil

1. Combine the fresh or dried rose petals with the almond oil in a clear glass jar with a lid.
2. Place the jar in direct sunlight for a day. Or, if it is overcast outside, either put the jar in a crockpot set to low, overnight or place the oil and petals in a covered ovenproof dish and bake in the oven on very low heat (200° F.) for 3 to 4 hours
3. After the mixture has "cured," strain out the rose petals and discard. The pale yellow, rose-scented oil is ready for use. Almond Oil Rub can be stored at room temperature in a labeled, lidded jar for up to 6 months.

APPLICATION: Apply the oil generously to a child's skin wherever there is roughness, redness, or mild itching. Use the oil right after a bath, and gently rub it into the skin until absorbed. This oil will soothe the redness and irritation of contact dermatitis or any other skin rash from allergies. Relief usually comes within 2 days, and skin irritation usually disappears completely after 2 weeks of applications. Most children enjoy this treatment very much.

If the child's skin irritation continues or grows worse after 1 week of applications, or if it is very painful, consult with a pediatrician or dermatologist.

Skin Food Bath
To regenerate skin after an outbreak of dermatitis

Preparation Time: 20 minutes
Yield: 1 treatment
Children's Enjoyment: ☺

This bath is very soothing to itchy, inflamed eruptions on the skin surface. Oats and barley are skin-nourishing herbs that relieve itch and irritation. Make sure you use rolled oats and pearled barley (hull removed). Oats and barley are widely cultivated as edible grains, but cooked oats and barley can produce a soothing washing water that is healing to skin surfaces. This water is used to treat dermatitis, chicken pox, poison oak, poison ivy, eczema, and dry skin. A bath tea made from oats and barley makes the skin feel soft and tender, dries up excretions, and speeds skin regeneration.

> 1/2 cup rolled oats
> 1/2 cup pearled barley
> 2 quarts water

1. Combine the oats, barley, and water in a large covered pot, bring to a boil, and simmer for 20 minutes.

175

2. Strain out the oats and barley. Either discard them or save in the refrigerator for breakfast or to use as a thickener for soups and stews.

3. Pour the tea into the tub while the water is running so it will be well combined. Make sure the temperature of the bathwater is not too hot after adding the brewed tea. The bathwater is milky and opaque, with a bland, grainlike smell, and feels soft and silky, as though bath oil were added.

APPLICATION: Bathe the child for 20 minutes once each day until the skin clears, which, depending on the condition, is usually 3 to 5 days. The skin will be soft and tender after bathing. Gently pat the skin with a washcloth; it is not necessary to wash with soap. Let the child air-dry after the bath, but be sure the room is warm enough to prevent a chill.

If the skin condition shows no improvement or gets worse after 5 days of treatment, consult a physician.

WHEN TO SEE THE DOCTOR

✚ DETERMINING FOOD OR ENVIRONMENTAL ALLERGENS: Parents should always take a child to the doctor when they suspect an allergic reaction. Patch tests, skin tests, and controlled food and environmental factors are all involved in positively determining specific allergens. Determining these at an early stage can prevent the condition from becoming worse. It also makes parents aware of what allergens must be eliminated from their child's environment to prevent further allergic reactions. Educated, alert parents can recognize a severe allergic reaction, should it occur, and can avoid panic and emotional distress for themselves and their child. Children with allergies should not be made to feel handicapped or traumatized, and an informed parent is mentally and emotionally equipped to keep this from happening.

✚ SEVERE ALLERGIC REACTIONS: A severe allergic reaction is characterized by deep flushing of the skin, severe coughing, wheezing, blurred vision, loss of consciousness, vomiting, and shock. If your child exhibits any of these severe symptoms after being exposed to a known or unknown allergen, call an ambulance and get your child to a hospital emergency room as quickly as possible. Don't delay, because the swelling in your child's throat from an allergic reaction can lead to suffocation. Immediate therapy in this situation calls for the administration of epinephrine, which will reduce the congestion in the throat area and ease breathing difficulties.

CHAPTER EIGHT

CHICKEN POX, MEASLES, AND MUMPS

INFANTS

Chicken Pox

Measles

CHILDREN

Chicken Pox

Measles — Rubella and Rubeola

Mumps

Chicken pox, measles, and mumps are acute, infectious diseases of childhood that rarely develop into anything serious. Mumps is no longer considered as common as chicken pox and measles because a mumps vaccine was licensed for use in 1967. However, if a child should happen to contract mumps — possibly by traveling to another country — it is good for parents to be familiar with the symptoms. Infants up to eight months of age are generally protected from mumps because of lingering maternal antibodies in their systems.

Chicken pox — known as varicella — is a benign, highly contagious illness that generally occurs in childhood but can happen at any age. One attack of the disease is enough to provide lifelong immunity. The younger a child is when exposed to chicken pox, the more severe the reaction. It is important to keep older siblings with chicken pox away from infants and toddlers, and not to allow your infant or toddler to play in the home of an infected child. Unfortunately, the disease is at its most contagious before the telltale skin eruptions are visible.

Measles comes in two varieties: German, or three-day measles, known as rubella; and ten-day measles, known as rubeola. Both of these disorders are mild in infants and young children. Rubella, however, is extremely dangerous to a fetus, especially during the first trimester. Rubella is now uncommon during childhood because of a vaccine that has been in use since 1969. Unfortunately, there are still many women of child-bearing age in this country who are not immunized and who did not contract the disease during childhood. Also, there are many children who have had an incomplete series of vaccinations or none at all. Parents must make sure their children are fully immunized to avoid the risk of spreading rubella to a pregnant woman who has not been vaccinated or previously exposed to the disease.

INFANTS

Infants should be vaccinated against rubella and rubeola by the time they are fifteen months old. If your infant has older siblings in the four- to eight-year range, however, there is a good chance of exposure to chicken pox or measles before reaching the age of twelve months, the usual age for infant immunizations. There is no vaccine for chicken pox commercially available at this time, although one is currently being tested. Chicken pox is considered a mild, although uncomfortable, disease in infants, with rare side effects.

Rubella — or German measles — is also mild, except to fetuses. If you think your infant has rubella, visit your pediatrician to confirm the diagnosis. You must then ascertain whether your infant has been handled or babysat by a woman who is pregnant. If there is any risk of infection, inform the woman immediately.

Rubeola is not considered particularly severe, although it can cause an infant a lot of discomfort. Care should be taken to isolate the child after diagnosis is confirmed, because the disease is highly contagious and can be transmitted to other infants and adults who are not immune. Chicken pox, rubella, and rubeola can, although they rarely do, have serious side effects. If your infant is not recovering quickly from any of these disorders, a thorough examination by a pediatrician is necessary. (See also WHEN TO SEE THE DOCTOR: COMPLICATIONS OF CHICKEN POX, page 204; and COMPLICATIONS OF MEASLES, page 204.)

Early symptoms of chicken pox in infants include loss of appetite, slight fever, irritability, and sleeplessness. A rash will break out approximately twenty-four hours after the onset of the early symptoms. It is important to keep your infant from scratching the eruptions, especially on the face, since scar tissue will form if the sores are opened repeatedly. Keep your infant's hands in mittens or covered by long sleeves at night to prevent this. The younger your infant is, the more severe the rash will be, but if the sores are not scratched, and you do all you can to keep your infant comfortable, there should be no need for stronger therapies such as cortisone cream. Change your infant's diaper as soon as it is wet or soiled, and keep your infant very clean with gentle bathing once or twice each day. This will relieve the itch and may keep the severity of the rash to a minimum. There are several herbal remedies that I have used successfully to relieve chicken pox symptoms in infants.

CHICKEN POX

Catnip Tea

To soothe a restless, feverish infant and speed the process of recovery

Preparation Time: 20 minutes
Yield: 5 treatments
Children's Enjoyment: ☺

Because it is a mild tranquilizer, this is a good tea for a restless, un-comfortable infant. Catnip is a blood purifier and fever reducer that hastens the process of toxin excretion through the skin. Catnip tea is indicated for infants with low fevers from colds, flu, or chicken pox. Catnip is a mild sweat inducer that helps cool the body and excrete wastes through the skin. Catnip is mildly tranquilizing and can soothe colic and settle an upset stomach. Do not use catnip that is packaged for pets.

1/2 ounce dried catnip
2 cups water
Light corn syrup to taste

1. Combine the catnip and water in a covered pot and simmer for 20 minutes.
2. Strain out the herbs and discard. The tea is a light gray-green color and smells slightly grassy and bitter.
3. Sweeten with corn syrup if the tea is for an infant. Honey can be used to sweeten the tea for children over the age of 18 months.
4. Cool the tea to room temperature before serving.

APPLICATION: For an infant with a low fever, administer 6 table-spoons of tea twice each day, just before nap and at bedtime, until the temperature returns to normal (2 days to 1 week). If the infant will not take a bottle, use a teaspoon to spoon the tea into the mouth. Remember to hold the infant in a comfortable, secure position to receive the medicine. In this way, he or she will get used to the routine and there will be less resistance.

If the fever shows no improvement after 1 week of treatment, or if it rises above 103 degrees at any time, consult a physician.

Peppermint and Burdock Bath
To anesthetize the skin and reduce scratching

Preparation Time: 20 minutes
Yield: 1 treatment
Children's Enjoyment: ☺

Peppermint is an effective anodyne, meaning it deadens sensation. It is used externally in a bath to relieve the itch of chicken pox, poison oak, or poison ivy. Burdock leaf tea makes a good wash for sores and also relieves itching conditions of the skin when used in a bath. This is a mild combination and good for infants, especially in combination with the Catnip Tea (page 182).

    2 ounces dried peppermint
    2 ounces dried burdock leaves
    2 quarts water

1. Combine the herbs with the water in a large, covered pot.
2. Bring the mixture to a boil, and simmer it slowly for 20 minutes.
3. Strain out and discard the herbs.
4. Pour the strained tea into an infant bathtub while running the bath so that it will be well combined. Run the herbal bath as hot as you usually run a bath for the infant, but make sure the bath is not too hot after adding the brewed tea. The tea turns the bathwater a light, tawny brown.

APPLICATION: Soak the infant in the bath for at least 20 minutes. Don't try to wash the infant; just let him or her play and relax in the bath. If the infant is old enough to sit up, you may add some fresh peppermint leaves to play with, but make sure the herbs do not clog the drain when you empty the tub. Bathe the infant once each day, just

183

before bedtime, until the itching subsides, which, depending on the condition, is usually in 1 week.

If the skin condition shows no improvement or is worse after 1 week of treatment, consult a physician.

Skin Food Bath

To dry and soothe the eruptions of chicken pox and measles

Preparation Time: 20 minutes
Yield: 1 treatment
Children's Enjoyment: ☺

This bath is very good for drying up the eruptions of chicken pox on the skin and reducing the itch. Oats and barley are widely cultivated as edible grains, but cooked oats and barley can produce a soothing washing water that is healing to skin surfaces. This water is used to treat dermatitis, chicken pox, poison oak, poison ivy, eczema, and dry skin. A bath tea made from the oats and barley makes the skin feel soft and tender, dries up excretions, and speeds skin regeneration.

    1/2 cup rolled oats
    1/2 cup pearled barley
    2 quarts water

1. Combine the oats, barley, and water in a large covered pot, bring to a boil, and simmer for 20 minutes.
2. Strain out the oats and barley. Either discard them or save in the refrigerator for breakfast or to use as a thickener for soups and stews.
3. Pour the tea into the tub while the water is running so it will be well combined. Make sure the temperature of the bathwater is not too hot after adding the brewed tea. The bathwater is milky and opaque, with a bland, grainlike smell, and feels soft and silky, as though bath oil were added.

APPLICATION: Bathe the infant for 20 minutes once each day until the skin clears, which, depending on the condition, is usually 3 to 5 days. The skin will be soft and tender after bathing. Gently pat the skin with a washcloth; it is not necessary to wash with soap. Let the infant air-dry after the bath, but be sure the room is warm enough to prevent a chill.

If the skin condition shows no improvement or gets worse after 5 days of treatment, consult a physician.

Chickweed Ointment
To reduce inflammation in the diaper area
of an infant with chicken pox

Preparation Time: 35 minutes
Yield: 15 to 20 treatments
Children's Enjoyment: ☺

This is an excellent ointment for the diaper area of an infant with chicken pox. Chickweed in ointment form is an excellent treatment for hives, chicken pox, and bruises. For centuries, fresh chickweed has been applied to skin wounds and open sores with good results, because of its healing effects on inflamed tissues. The base of this ointment is petroleum jelly (Vaseline), which holds the active ingredients of the chickweed close to the skin surface for hours.

> 1 1/2 ounces dried chickweed
> 3/4 cup petroleum jelly (Vaseline)

1. Place the petroleum jelly in a cast-iron frying pan and melt it slowly over a very low heat.
2. When it is completely liquid, add the chickweed and gently fry the mixture. It is very important not to let it burn, so watch it carefully. The herb should sizzle gently for 10 minutes.
3. Strain the mixture into a bowl or measuring cup through a cheesecloth-lined sieve and discard the herb.

4. Pour the strained ointment into a dated, labeled glass jar with a tight-fitting lid. The ointment may be left at room temperature to set, or, if you are in a hurry, placed in the refrigerator for 30 minutes.
5. Store the ointment away from heat and discard any unused portion after 6 months.

APPLICATION: This ointment may be generously dabbed onto hives, minor cuts, scrapes, chicken pox, and bruises. It is not necessary for it to be absorbed into the skin, so just dab it on and smooth it out. You can put a loose muslin bandage over the application to prevent messy clothes. The ointment wears off by itself and more can be applied until the skin irritation disappears (about 1 week or less, depending on the condition). The ointment looks like dark petroleum jelly and does not hurt when applied. The diaper area is especially susceptible to infection and irritation from chicken pox, so special care should be taken with each diaper change. Use your regular diaper ointment again when the chicken pox subsides.

If the child's skin irritation is causing severe discomfort or the cause is not known, consult a physician.

Rosemary and Marigold Wash
To dry up the eruptions of chicken pox and measles
and prevent infection

Preparation Time: 20 minutes
Yield: 4 treatments
Children's Enjoyment: ☺

This wash is excellent for combating any infection caused by repeated scratching of the chicken pox. The combination of rosemary and marigold has been used for centuries to keep the skin refreshed and free of topical bacteria. Both rosemary and marigold are mildly antiseptic and astringent, which makes this a particularly good wash for an infant's tender skin.

Rosemary is highly astringent and draws tissues together and dries out discharges from sores. These actions make rosemary excellent for treating chicken pox, poison oak, poison ivy, or any other oozing skin condition. Marigold flowers, also known in herb stores as calendula, acts as an antiseptic and decreases the chances of a sore becoming infected from scratching. Combined, these herbs are soothing and fast acting on tender infant skin. This wash may be used in combination with the Chickweed Ointment (page 185). While dried rosemary leaves are the familiar, spiky, dark green leaves used in soups and stews, medicinal rosemary should be purchased in a health food or herb store.

> 1 ounce dried rosemary
> 1 ounce dried marigold
> 1 quart water
> Clean washcloth

1. Combine the rosemary and marigold with the water in a covered pot, bring to a boil, and simmer gently for 5 minutes.
2. Take the pot off the heat and steep the herbs for 15 minutes.
3. Strain out the herbs through fine cheesecloth and discard them.
4. Cool the wash to a comfortably warm temperature for applying to an infant's skin. Refrigerate any unused portion of the wash and reheat with each use. Discard any remaining wash after 3 days.

APPLICATION: This wash is most effective when applied right after a bath. Apply the wash as warm as possible, but not so warm that it is uncomfortable to an infant's already irritated skin. Test a little on the inside of your wrist before applying it. Dip the washrag in the wash, and wring it out so that it is not dripping but is quite damp. Press it gently on the infant's skin where needed. Do not rub! This will only cause more oozing and irritation. Let the wash air-dry on the skin. Perform this treatment once each night until the skin is clear, which, depending on the condition, is usually 2 days to 1 week.

If the condition does not respond to treatment after 1 week, or if the infant experiences severe discomfort, consult a physician.

MEASLES
Symptoms of infant rubella — or German measles — include a distinctive spotty rash, mild fever, and occasional swollen lymph glands. These symptoms last for a week at most and complications are rare in healthy infants. Parents should be aware that the typical rubella rash does not always appear in infants and toddlers, and the disease can sometimes come and go unnoticed, being mistaken for a simple runny nose or fever. Treatment for rubella involves isolation and bed rest for an infant.

Rubeola — or ten-day measles — will cause much more discomfort to an infant than rubella. For the first four or five days, typical symptoms include low fever, conjunctivitis (pink eyes), cough and runny nose, and the appearance of little red spots on the skin, especially on the face, neck, and upper back and chest. Your infant may scratch at the mouth and suck the fingers because of little irritating bumps in the mouth known as Koplik's spots. These bumps are a sure sign of rubeola and usually break out within three days of the disease's onset. On the second or third day after the rash breaks out, your infant may have a fever, which is sometimes accompanied by a severe cough, puffy red eyes, and a runny nose. The symptoms begin to disappear after the sixth day, and by the tenth day, they should be gone completely. The infant should be examined by a health professional if any of these symptoms become severe or prolonged, especially the fever.

If your infant's discomfort from rubella or rubeola is severe, a physician's help is needed. If the symptoms are not severe or you wish to herbally complement the medications prescribed by the doctor, there are several procedures that will soothe and calm an infant with measles.

Eyebright Eyewash
To reduce inflammation of the eyes during measles

Preparation Time: 25 minutes
Yield: 3 treatments
Children's Enjoyment: ☺

Eyebright derives its name from the healing and soothing effect it has upon eyes. It is especially good for conjunctivitis — an inflammation of the conjunctival mucous membrane of the eye — which is a common symptom of measles. Eyebright is a parasitic plant, like mistletoe, that is used traditionally in lotions and washes for eye disorders. Eyebright is slightly astringent and can draw the inflamed tissues of the eye together, drying up discharges.

    1/2 ounce eyebright
    2 cups water
    Paper coffee filter
    Clean cotton washcloth

1. Combine the eyebright and water in a covered pot and simmer for 20 minutes.
2. Strain the herb very thoroughly through the sterile coffee filter and discard it. There should be no floating particles in the solution.
3. When the tea has cooled to tepid, comfortably warm for the eyes, it is ready to use. Refrigerate and reheat the remaining tea to a tepid temperature each time you use it. Discard any unused tea after 2 days.

APPLICATION: Make sure the infant is not hungry or tired before proceeding with the application. Hold the infant securely in your arms and place yourself in a comfortable position on the floor or on a bed. Put the washcloth into the pot of warm tea and place it close to you. Wring out the washcloth with one hand so that it is not dripping but is still quite moist. Gently lay the washcloth across the infant's eyes and hold it there with very minimal pressure. The infant will close his or her eyes. This is normal and the tea will still be of benefit. Leave the cloth in place over the eyes for 3 minutes, let the infant rest for 3 minutes, then rinse the cloth in the tea and repeat the process 2 more times. The infant will relax at first, then may try to remove the cloth. Keep replacing it gently until the skin around the eyes gets a little red. This is a good sign since it means that blood is circulating in the area. This process can be performed once or twice each day until the infant's eyes have returned to normal (about 1 week).

If the infant's eye disorder seems to cause severe discomfort, or if it persists or gets worse after 1 week of treatment, consult a physician.

Sage Bath
To relieve itching and tenderness of the skin during measles

Preparation Time: 20 minutes
Yield: 1 treatment
Children's Enjoyment: ☺

This bath is very good for infant measles. Sage washes are a traditional external remedy for disorders of the skin and scalp, slow healing wounds and ulcers, and chronic skin rashes such as eczema and psoriasis. As an internal medication, sage tea is used to dry up breast milk, rid the body of intestinal parasites, and calm the nerves.

> 4 ounces dried sage leaves
> 2 quarts water

1. Combine the sage and water in a covered pot, bring to a boil, and simmer for 5 minutes.
2. Remove the pot from the heat and steep the herb for 15 minutes.
3. Strain out the herb and discard it.
4. Pour the tea into the tub while the bathwater is running so that it will be well combined. Run the herbal bath as hot as you usually

run a bath for the infant, but make sure the water is not too hot after adding the brewed tea. The tea turns the bathwater a light gray-green color, with the pleasant scent of sage.

APPLICATION: Soak the infant for 20 minutes, and allow him or her to play in the water. Let the skin air-dry after the bath, but be sure the room is warm enough to prevent a chill. Repeat the bath once each day until the skin condition clears up, usually 3 days to 1 week.

If the skin condition does not respond or worsens after 1 week of treatment, consult a physician.

Willow Bark Tea
To reduce fever and discomfort during measles

Preparation Time: 20 minutes
Yield: 4 treatments
Children's Enjoyment: ☹

This tea is excellent for reducing fever and discomfort from measles. White willow bark has been used since the prehistoric times to kill pain, bring down fever, reduce inflammation, and reduce water retention. Willow bark contains salicin, which is converted in the body to salicylic acid, a substance that closely resembles aspirin. This versatile herb can be used in tea or tincture form and is available in health food and herb stores. There are several varieties of white willow bark tablets available that can be crushed up and mixed with juice for infants.

     1/2 ounce white willow bark pieces
     2 cups water

1. Combine the willow bark with the water in a covered pot, bring to a boil, and simmer for 20 minutes.
2. Strain out the herb and discard it. The tea is a dark burgundy color and has a slightly bitter, astringent taste. Do not sweeten.

191

3. Cool the tea to room temperature before serving. Store remaining tea in the refrigerator and reheat with each use. Discard any unused portion of the tea after 2 days.

APPLICATION: Administer 10 drops 3 times each day, by sterile dropper or teaspoon, until pain or fever disappears (1 to 3 days).

Do not use this tea if your infant has been diagnosed as aspirin allergic or sensitive. If pain becomes severe or fever rises above 103 degrees at any time, consult a physician.

CHILDREN

All children should receive measles and mumps vaccines by the time they are two years old. In many states, a child will not be allowed into kindergarten unless a record of vaccinations is presented to the school nurse. This is to prevent these highly contagious diseases from spreading and to enable statistical information to be gathered on the effectiveness of the vaccination throughout the population. Although rubella — or German measles — is not dangerous to infants, children, and adults, the danger of infecting a fetus is acute. If rubella affects a fetus in the first trimester of life, serious congenital malformations may occur. Parents should be responsible for seeing that their children are vaccinated in a timely manner so that these diseases are not spread.

Children with measles usually need only bed rest and fever-reducing herbal remedies. Your child may have no appetite for a few days, but this is not serious as long as there is adequate fluid intake. The disease is no longer contagious five days after the onset of the rash.

Chicken pox — or varicella — is a mild disease in children over the age of two. The most important thing for parents to do is keep their child from scratching the eruptions on the skin. Scar tissue is easily formed on chicken pox eruptions if the scab is repeatedly broken or if a minor infection sets in. Special care must be taken to keep a child from scratching the facial skin, since that is where the danger of scar tissue formation is highest and where scar tissue will be most visible. As soon as the eruptions have formed scabs, chicken pox is no longer contagious and your child may return to school.

A child with chicken pox will usually exhibit skin eruptions as the only symptom. A mild feeling of malaise may set in before the pox appear, but this is often mistaken for a poor night's sleep or indigestion. Once a child has chicken pox, you may have to keep him or her from running over to the neighbor's house to show off. Remember, this is a highly contagious disease, and care should be taken to keep exposure and infection to a minimum. Complications of chicken pox are rare in children who are basically healthy and strong. If your child has chicken pox, there are two herbal baths that will allay discomfort and speed the healing process. (See also WHEN TO SEE THE DOCTOR: COMPLICATIONS OF CHICKEN POX, page 204.)

CHICKEN POX

Skin Food Bath
To dry up the eruptions of chicken pox and measles

Preparation Time: 20 minutes
Yield: 1 treatment
Children's Enjoyment: 😊

This bath is very soothing to the itchy, inflamed eruptions of chicken pox and should speed the scab formation on the pox. Oats and barley are widely cultivated as edible grains, but cooked oats and barley can produce a soothing washing water that is healing to skin surfaces. This water is used to treat dermatitis, chicken pox, poison oak, poison ivy, eczema, and dry skin. A bath tea made from oats and barley makes the skin feel soft and tender, dries up excretions, and speeds skin regeneration.

     1/2 cup rolled oats
     1/2 cup pearled barley
     2 quarts water

1. Combine the oats, barley, and water in a large covered pot, bring to a boil, and simmer for 20 minutes.

2. Strain out the oats and barley. Either discard them or save in the refrigerator for breakfast or to use as a thickener for soups and stews.
3. Pour the tea into the tub while the water is running so it will be well combined. Make sure the temperature of the bathwater is not too hot after adding the brewed tea. The bathwater is milky and opaque, with a bland, grainlike smell, and feels soft and silky, as though bath oil were added.

APPLICATION: Bathe the child for 20 minutes once each day until the skin clears, which, depending on the condition, is usually 3 to 5 days. The skin will be soft and tender after bathing. Gently pat the skin with a washcloth; it is not necessary to wash with soap. Let the child air-dry after the bath, but be sure the room is warm enough to prevent a chill.

If the skin condition shows no improvement or gets worse after 5 days of treatment, consult a physician.

Slippery Elm and Comfrey Sprinkle
To form unscratchable scabs over chicken pox

Preparation Time: 5 minutes
Yield: 5 treatments
Children's Enjoyment: ☺

This procedure is good if the pox are still running and have not yet formed scabs. Comfrey root and slippery elm bark are skin-nourishing herbs that, when combined with water, form a hard, healing scab. They are good for treating chicken pox, poison ivy, poison oak, minor burns, or a fresh wound or blister that has not yet formed a protective scab. It is a good idea to keep these herbs on hand for such occasions. This herbal sprinkle relieves itching at the same time as it forms a scab and stops open sores from running. Powdered comfrey root was once used to coat wet bandages of splints for broken limbs. When the bandages dried, the comfrey powder formed a hard cast that supported the bone at the same time as it helped to knit the break.

> 1 ounce comfrey root
> 1 ounce powdered slippery elm bark

1. If you use these herbs in bulk form, use a coffee grinder to grind the herbs into a smooth, powdery consistency. There may some large pieces left in the powder, but these fall off when applied to the wound, leaving only the powder to form the scab.
2. Store the powder in a labeled, dated jar with a tight-fitting lid. Discard any powder after 6 months.

APPLICATION: Gently wash the child's wound or skin eruption to remove any debris and get clean blood to the wound surface. Sprinkle the powdered herb combination generously over the wound or pox. You may even want to pat the sprinkle on with the palm of your hand. The powder adheres immediately to the surface and stops any bleeding or running from the pox. It is not necessary to cover or bandage the wound or eruption. A child feels no pain when the herbs come in contact with the skin, and a hard, protective scab forms that is nearly impossible to scratch or pick off. The skin will appear pink and healthy looking when the scab finally falls off, which, depending on the size and depth of the abrasion, is usually 1 week. If there are many pox on the face, you may want to put Band-Aids over the worst-looking scabs to save your child some embarrassment.

This sprinkle should be used only on fresh sores or wounds. If a child's wound is deep or bleeding profusely, or if it is not healing well or is infected, consult a physician.

**MEASLES —
RUBELLA
AND
RUBEOLA**

If you think your child has measles, report it to a health professional so that diagnosis of rubella or rubeola can be confirmed. Rubella is characterized by a mild rash that lasts three days, a low fever, and occasional swollen lymph glands. Rubeola symptoms include loss of appetite, runny nose, mild conjunctivitis, fever, and a generalized rash on the body, including the inside of the mouth. Although rubeola causes much more discomfort to your child, it is not considered dangerous and complications are rare in healthy children.

The incubation period for rubella is fourteen to twenty-one days; for rubeola, ten to fifteen days. A child is contagious during the incubation period for both of these diseases. There are vaccines to protect against rubella and rubeola, and parents should work with a pediatrician to see that their children are properly immunized and records are kept up to date. These records will be very important later in your child's life if more immunizations are required because of a dog bite or puncture wound, or if your child is traveling to a foreign country.

If your child does contract measles and you have visited the doctor to have the diagnosis confirmed, there are several herbal remedies you can try to make your child more comfortable. (See also WHEN TO SEE THE DOCTOR: COMPLICATIONS OF MEASLES, page 204.)

Angostura Soda
To reduce the discomfort and fever of rubeola

Preparation Time: 5 minutes
Yield: 1 treatment
Children's Enjoyment: ☺

This is a good remedy for a child with rubeola. Since loss of appetite is one of the symptoms, this remedy will provide adequate fluid intake while it helps settle the stomach. It is also good for reducing a fever and making a child feel more comfortable. Since it is easy to make, I let my children prepare it to their own particular tastes. Angostura Soda is excellent for relieving both fever and diarrhea. Angostura Bitters is a popular flavoring and mixer in cocktails such as the old-fashioned and the Manhattan. The primary ingredient in Angostura Bitters is gentian root, which is known for its worm-killing, fever-reducing, stomach-strengthening, and liver-stimulating properties. It is also a topical and internal antiseptic, and is used in gentian violet, a topical medicine for canker sores, minor cuts, and scrapes. The soda is easy to make, has a pleasant taste, and is a good way to get extra fluids into a child. I let my children prepare it to their own tastes.

> 1 cup any brand sparkling water
> 5 to 10 drops Angostura Bitters
> Mint sprig (optional)

1. Fill a glass with sparkling water.
2. Let the child shake the Angostura Bitters drops into the soda and stir it. The soda is light pink in color. You can garnish it with a sprig of mint if you like.

APPLICATION: You can serve the soda plain or on the rocks. The soda has an aromatic, slightly sweet taste that children love. Give the child this soda once or twice each day between meals until the fever or diarrhea is gone. Store Angostura Bitters in the liquor cabinet or any place that is out of the reach of children.

In cases of very high fever (103 degrees and above), severe vomiting or gastrointestinal pain, or paleness and lassitude, consult with a physician.

Camomile Compress
To soothe swollen, inflamed eyes

Preparation Time: 15 minutes
Yield: 1 treatment
Children's Enjoyment: ☺

This compress is good for conjunctivitis, which often accompanies rubeola. The heat of this compress relaxes and relieves eye discomfort and speeds recovery. Camomile has mild painkilling and muscle-relaxing properties, which make it an excellent children's herb.

> 2 cups water
> 2 ounces dried camomile flowers
> Clean muslin dish towel

1. Put the water in a covered pot and bring to a boil.
2. Remove the pot from the heat and immerse the camomile flowers in the hot water.
3. Cover the pot and steep for 10 minutes.
4. Strain out the herb and set it aside. You may either discard the light green camomile tea or serve it as a digestive aid or as a mild calmative before bedtime.

APPLICATION: Fold the steaming herbs in a damp towel to form a 5-inch-wide strip with the herbs in the center. Cool the compress until it is warm, but not too hot to place on the child's eyes. When the compress has cooled sufficiently, explain to the child that it will feel a little hot. Have the child lie down and get comfortable. Place the compress over the closed eyes and press gently. The child will relax as soon as the compress is applied and will probably want to hold the compress in place unassisted. When the compress is cold, remove it and discard the herbs. Repeat this treatment twice each day until the conjunctivitis has disappeared (about 1 week).

If the conjunctivitis is extremely uncomfortable or severe, consult a physician.

Pennyroyal Bath

To cool a fever and open the pores of the skin

Preparation Time: 20 minutes
Yield: 1 treatment
Children's Enjoyment: ☺

This bath is soothing to children suffering from either rubella or rubeola. Pennyroyal will cool a fever and cause the pores of the skin to open and sweat out toxic wastes. Pennyroyal belongs to the mint family and has a peculiar, camphorous smell. You will probably recognize the smell immediately, since pennyroyal oil is a common ingredient in many commercial insect repellents. This herb is used in Europe and America to promote sweating at the onset of a cold. Pennyroyal also relaxes sore muscles and refreshes the skin when used in a bath.

> 2 ounces dried pennyroyal
> 2 quarts water

1. Combine the pennyroyal and water in a large, covered pot; bring to a boil and simmer slowly for 20 minutes.
2. Strain out and discard the herb.
3. Pour the tea into the bathtub while the water is running so that it will be well combined. Run the herbal bath as hot as you usually run a bath for the child, but make sure the temperature of the bath is not too hot after adding the brewed tea. The bathwater is light green and smells strongly of peppermint and camphor.

APPLICATION: Explain to the young child that this bath makes the skin feel slightly tingly. Let the child soak in the tub for 20 minutes. You can add some dried leaves of pennyroyal to the bathwater for the child to play with, but make sure you cover the drain of the bathtub with a strainer when you empty the tub. This bath can be repeated once each day in the early evening until the cold disappears (usually 1 week).

If a high fever (above 103 degrees), lassitude, or nausea are present, or if the cold persists or gets worse after 1 week, consult a physician.

MUMPS   Mumps — known medically as parotitis — is a painful swelling of the salivary glands. It is extremely contagious, although it is generally considered a mild disease with rare side effects in healthy children. There is no factual basis for the fear that mumps will result in sterility in male children. Swelling of the testicles may follow a bout with mumps, especially if the child is over ten years of age, but it will resolve spontaneously with no long-term effects.

Symptoms of mumps include mild headache, mild fever, muscular pain especially in the neck, and pain and swelling in one or both of the parotid glands located at the base of the jaw. Usually one gland swells before the other. The jaw line may be completely obliterated by the swelling, giving your child a peculiar, moon-faced look. Your child should be isolated until the swelling subsides. Although mumps can change your child's appearance drastically, it is not really a serious disease and its symptoms can be treated easily with herbal remedies. While many parents may remember having mumps as children, the chance of a child contracting mumps today has been significantly reduced by a mumps vaccine.

If you think your child has mumps, a visit to the doctor is in order to confirm the diagnosis and update the vaccination record. Treatment for mumps is entirely symptomatic. In other words, an effort is made to reduce any swelling and discomfort, but no antibiotics are administered unless there are complications. Mumps can be treated easily at home if your child is generally healthy, and there are several comforting herbal remedies you can administer to your child. (See also WHEN TO SEE THE DOCTOR: COMPLICATIONS OF MUMPS, page 204.)

Clove Oil Gum Rub

To reduce soreness of the gums during mumps

Preparation Time: 5 minutes
Yield: 8 treatments
Children's Enjoyment: 😖

Sore gums and difficulty in chewing are common complaints of children with mumps, and clove oil, which is a powerful topical anesthetic, can help reduce pain inside the mouth. Clove oil can be used to allay the pain of mumps and to soothe upset stomachs. Whole cloves can be sucked on to refresh the breath. They contain hot carminative oils that aid in digestion, which is why cloves are often combined with meats that are high in fat, such as ham. Clove oil is a powerful pain reliever when used in a dilute solution in the mouth or on the skin. Essential oil of cloves is a clear, amber color. The label on the bottle should state clearly that the oil is suitable for internal consumption, since some methods for extracting essential oil can involve harmful chemicals.

> 1/2 teaspoon essential oil of cloves
> 2 teaspoons fresh olive, corn, or other vegetable oil

1. Combine all the ingredients in a small dish or jar lid.
2. Stir with your index finger for 2 minutes to make sure the oils are thoroughly mixed and will not burn the skin.
3. When the oil makes your fingertip tingle mildly, it is ready to use.

APPLICATION: For a child with mumps, first explain that the gums will feel tingly, then a little numb. Rub the oil into the gums where the molars are. The child may apply the oil unassisted with clean hands. Make sure the child's hands are thoroughly washed afterward to keep clove oil out of the eyes. This treatment can be repeated as often as needed until the mumps run their course (1 week).

Children with mumps are rarely in danger of complications, and the oil should help to relieve pain while the child gets well. If a child complains of a painful toothache, consult a dentist before applying the oil.

Apple Juice and Clove Tea
To reduce pain upon swallowing and flush the lymphatic glands

Preparation Time: 15 minutes
Yield: 8 Treatments
Children's Enjoyment: ☺

Apple juice is a good lymphatic-system flush that helps the body rid itself of toxins. This makes apple juice particularly useful in treating swollen glands and mumps. The fresh juice of apples is alkaline and helps balance the body if too many acid-forming foods, such as red meat or sugar, are ingested. Cloves act as a topical painkiller and, when taken with the apple juice, help to reduce pain and discomfort from swallowing. Apple juice and cloves are available in any grocery store. Try to get fresh, unfiltered juice if possible. If you juice your own apples, use Granny Smith or McIntosh apples that have not been waxed.

8 whole cloves
1 quart fresh apple juice

1. Add the cloves to the juice and simmer slowly in a covered pot for 15 minutes.
2. Strain out the cloves and discard. The tea will look and smell like spiced apple juice and may have some essential oil of cloves floating on top.
3. Stir the tea to recombine the oil.
4. Cool the tea to room temperature before serving. Refrigerate any remaining tea and warm it to room temperature for each treatment. Discard any unused portion after 5 days.

APPLICATION: Have the child drink 1/2 cup of the tea twice each day, in the morning and afternoon, until the mumps are gone. This combination is pleasant to drink, but tell the child that the tea will taste strongly of cloves and that there will be a slight numbness in the mouth and throat afterwards.

If swollen glands persist beyond 1 week of treatment, if there is glandular swelling in other parts of the body, or if there is severe pain, consult a pediatrician.

Flannel Muffler Wrap
To reduce pain and swelling in the throat area

Preparation Time: 10 minutes
Yield: 1 treatment
Children's Enjoyment: ☺

Flannel mufflers are an old-time remedy for sore throats, swollen glands, and mumps. Warming the throat area can reduce swelling and encourage healing, especially when some eucalyptus oil is rubbed onto the throat beforehand. Any old flannel shirt will do for this process, but make sure it is clean.

> 1 application of Eucalyptus Oil Rub (page 38)
> 1 five-inch-wide strip flannel, long enough to comfortably tie
>   around the child's throat

APPLICATION: Perform this treatment just before bedtime. Apply a palmful of the Eucalyptus Oil Rub on the child's throat, starting at the point of the jaw slightly behind the ears and continuing down to the collarbone. Rub gently but vigorously. Encourage the child to tell you where it hurts as you rub so that you can apply the oil where it will do the most good. When the oil is applied and absorbed, warm the flannel muffler briefly in the oven and wrap it around the child's throat. Tie the muffler loosely in the back and make sure the child can sleep comfortably with it on. Leave the wrap on all night. In the morning, wash all the unabsorbed oil off the child's throat and rinse the flannel clean. Repeat the procedure once each night with the same clean piece of flannel until the sore throat or swollen glands have disappeared.

If the swollen neck glands persist after 1 week of treatment or are very painful, or if glandular swelling occurs anywhere else in the body, such as the armpit or groin, consult a physician.

WHEN TO SEE THE DOCTOR

✦ COMPLICATIONS OF CHICKEN POX: Infection of the eruptions on the skin may cause severe scarring, especially in facial tissue. Care should be taken to prevent your child from scratching and to keep fingers and fingernails clean. Other rare complications of chicken pox include pneumonia, encephalitis, hepatitis, and nephritis. Chicken pox may be fatal to children with immune deficiencies and those with leukemia or other malignant diseases, who are receiving steroids or antimetabolites. If your child has symptoms of any of these complications, or has a preexisting condition that causes vulnerability, a physician's examination and skill is required.

✦ COMPLICATIONS OF MEASLES: The major complications of rubeola, or ten-day measles, include middle ear infections, pneumonia, and encephalitis. Fever is a symptom of this disease, but if the fever rises higher than 103 degrees, professional medical care is indicated. For a child with rubella, precautions must be taken to keep the child from developing other acute infections such as middle ear infections, pneumonia, meningitis, or urinary tract infections, although these complications are rare in healthy children. If your child is already in poor health or exhibits symptoms of any of these disorders, a physician's care is required.

✚ COMPLICATIONS OF MUMPS: Complications of this disease are extremely rare in healthy children, and there is no factual basis for the fear that mumps will result in sterility in male children. Complications of mumps can include pancreatitis, nephritis, mastitis, deafness, arthritis, and meningoencephalitis, which is closely related to bacterial meningitis. Should they appear, a physician's examination is required to diagnose and treat these disorders.

CHAPTER NINE

TOOTH AND GUM DISORDERS

INFANTS

Thrush

Preventing Tooth Decay

CHILDREN

Preventing Tooth Decay

Toothaches

Losing Teeth

Wisdom Teeth

Bleeding Gums

Cold Sores

*t*ooth and gum disorders are a leading cause of poor health in children and young adults. Fortunately, these conditions are also the most easily diagnosed and corrected. Although tooth and gum disorders can be attributed in part to heredity, the primary causes are lack of preventive dental care and poor dental health practices. Diet greatly affects the formation and maintenance of teeth and gums, and should be the first consideration of any parent who wishes to preserve a child's dental health. Parents can set an example by taking good care of their own teeth and including their children in the daily process of eating well, brushing, and flossing.

INFANTS

If you are healthy and have had an uncomplicated pregnancy, your infant will generally enjoy good health, including good dental health. Prolonged illnesses in a child's prenatal, neonatal, and infancy periods, especially those for which antibiotics are necessary, can interfere with the development of tooth buds and primary teeth. This can result in a yellowed, striated appearance in the primary teeth. Mothers who take antibiotics during their pregnancies should be especially aware of pediatric dental hygiene and preventive-care techniques as their infants first teeth start to appear.

THRUSH Many infants develop little white spots in their mouths soon after birth. This condition, called thrush, is a common newborn malady — especially among infants who are bottlefed. Thrush is caused by a microorganism known as *Candida albicans*. Because an infant's protective bacteria may not yet be developed or may be out of balance owing to antibiotic therapy, *Candida albicans* can flourish. It appears as a white coating on the tongue, and white spots on the roof of the mouth and the insides of the cheeks. Parents should be careful not to mistake curdled milk on the tongue for thrush. Thrush usually clears up by itself, and an infant rarely experiences any discomfort, but some difficulty in feeding may occur. If your infant has a severe case, five drops of 3 percent hydrogen peroxide should be administered twice each day until the symptoms of thrush disappear. As you can imagine, this therapy tastes terrible. Be ready to feed and soothe your infant after leaving the hydrogen peroxide in the mouth for about a minute. The peroxide will bubble up, and your infant will drool most of it out; this is normal. If your infant has only a mild case of thrush, there is an effective and pleasant herbal wash that will help.

Bay Leaf Mouthwash
To relieve infant thrush

Preparation Time: 20 minutes
Yield: 10 treatments
Children's Enjoyment: ☺

Bay Leaf Mouthwash is an excellent remedy for infant thrush, canker sores, bad breath, and bleeding gums. Bay leaves are highly astringent and contain carminative oils that can soothe colic in infants and digestive problems in children and adults. Dried bay leaf is available in all grocery stores, but you'll get more for your money in herb or health food stores. Bay laurel grows in many parts of the country, and it's fun to harvest the leaves with your children. Gather leaves from trees that you know are not sprayed with insecticides. Wash the leaves thoroughly and use them fresh or dry them for later use.

> 5 fresh or dried whole bay leaves
> 2 cups water

1. Combine the bay leaves with the water in a covered pot and simmer for 20 minutes.
2. Strain out the bay leaves and discard them. The tea will be a light green in color and smell strongly of bay. It may have some essential oil floating on top, which should be stirred to combine.
3. Cool the tea to room temperature before using. Refrigerate any unused portion of the tea and warm it slightly for each treatment. Discard the remaining tea after 2 days.

APPLICATION: If you are using the tea as a mouthwash for thrush, put 10 drops in the infant's mouth by sterile dropper twice each day, between meals, until the thrush disappears. The infant may dislike this treatment but will probably not fuss much. Try to perform the treatment when the infant is not tired or hungry.

If the thrush is not gone after 1 week of treatment, discontinue administering the tea and give the infant 1/4 teaspoon of 3 percent hydrogen peroxide in the mouth twice each day until the thrush disappears. The infant will dislike this treatment, but it is very effective. If the thrush still persists, consult a pediatrician.

PREVENTING TOOTH DECAY

The prevention of tooth decay begins as soon as a child is born. Parents should not introduce sweets at an early age, which often happens if a pacifier is dipped into something sweet to get the infant to take it, or if baby formula is overconcentrated. Avoiding sugar in infancy will help keep your child from craving and demanding sweets later on.

If you breast-feed your infant, the chance of developing baby-bottle caries (cavities) is low. However, dental caries in primary teeth can occur when mothers consistently fall asleep with the baby still at the breast. A far more common cause of dental caries in primary teeth occurs when a child falls asleep with a full bottle resting in his or her mouth. Drowsy children will often take a sip of milk or juice from the bottle and then forget to swallow, leaving a pool of sugary milk or juice in their mouths. Bacteria multiply readily in this rich culture, and the acid created by these bacteria will etch the tooth enamel. If your child must have a bottle at night to fall asleep, fill it with warm water or offer a pacifier instead.

A child should visit the dentist as early as two years of age. Tooth decay usually begins at this age, and if caught in time, future problems with permanent teeth can be avoided. Tooth decay detected at an early stage makes visits to the dentist trauma-free, so the child will not develop a negative attitude toward dental care. If dental caries in primary teeth are left unattended — often because the parent assumes the tooth will fall out anyway — there is a danger of painful abscess in the gum and damage to the permanent tooth still developing in the gum tissue. (See also WHEN TO SEE THE DENTIST: DENTAL CARIES, page 219.)

CHILDREN

The most important decay-prevention techniques that parents should practice with their children are regular, sustained brushing and the avoidance of sweets in the child's diet. Children should begin brushing their teeth as soon as they have enough teeth to chew their food. Don't try to drill the up-and-down method of brushing into the head of a two-year-old; it won't work. Instead, let them brush back and forth, play with the toothbrush, experiment with the toothpaste tube, and learn to spit water out of their mouths somewhere in the vicinity of the bathroom sink. Try to make teeth-brushing fun, not a chore. The only thing a parent should do is make sure the child brushes every day, preferably after each meal. If it is not possible to brush after each meal, children should be taught to swish some water around in their mouths after each meal.

PREVENTING TOOTH DECAY

When children are weaned from the breast or bottle to a cup, get them used to juices that are not excessively sweet, such as raw unfiltered apple juice or fresh orange juice. Concentrated or frozen juices often have sugar added and should be avoided. As your child grows and spends more time away from you, he or she will be exposed to sweets such as ice cream, candy, soft drinks, cakes, cookies, and sweetened cold cereals. Obviously, parents can't prevent their children from eating these things, but some compromise should be made. Teach your child that these things are treats, *not food.* They should be told to brush their teeth after eating sweets, and if they are unable to brush, to swish some water in their mouths. If a parent sustains this routine and gives a good example for the child to follow, dental problems can be virtually eliminated throughout a child's life. (See also WHEN TO SEE THE DENTIST: DENTAL CARIES, page 219.)

TOOTH-ACHES

Toothaches can vary in severity and cause. A tingling sensation when something sweet or spicy is eaten is a symptom of the simplest type of toothache. The ache is caused by erosion of the tooth enamel, which exposes the dentin underneath. The dentin in a tooth contains nerve endings and will tingle or even jolt a child if the wrong food touches it. If your child is experiencing swelling, pain, or tenderness at the base of a tooth, it could be caused by gum infection resulting from an injury or uninhibited tooth decay. Toothaches can also be caused by permanent teeth attempting to erupt while primary teeth are still firmly rooted to the gum tissue. A child with a persistent toothache should be taken to the dentist promptly. The sooner the problem is dealt with, the less discomfort your child will experience. In the meantime, there is an herbal procedure that will help relieve the discomfort of toothache. (See also WHEN TO SEE THE DENTIST: DENTAL CARIES, page 219; and INJURIES TO THE TEETH, page 219.)

Clove and Peppermint Oil Toothache Remedy
To help relieve the pain of toothache

Preparation Time: 5 minutes
Yield: 5 treatments
Children's Enjoyment: ☹

Clove and peppermint oil are time-honored pain relievers, traditionally used for toothaches as well as for external pain. These two oils are extremely hot, so they must be diluted with peanut or olive oil before use. They do not taste very good, and your child will not enjoy having a lump of cotton packed into his or her mouth, but the pain relief is immediate and calming. Explain all the steps to your child first, and proceed slowly to ensure complete cooperation.

> 4 teaspoons peanut or olive oil
> 1/2 teaspoon clove oil
> 1/2 teaspoon peppermint oil
> 1 cotton ball

1. Combine the oils in a small dish or bowl.
2. Stir the oils with a wooden or stainless-steel spoon until they are thoroughly combined.

3. Dip the tip of your index finger (clean, of course) into the mixture to test for hotness. Your finger should tingle but not burn. When you have judged the strength of the oil to be correct, proceed.

APPLICATION: Take the cotton ball and soak it in the oil mixture. Have your child point to exactly where it hurts, and place the cotton ball next to the tooth between the cheek and the gum. Make sure the oils are not too hot by asking the child how it feels. If the mixture is too hot, dilute it by adding more vegetable oil until the child feels no discomfort. Have the child keep the cotton wool on the gum for as long as it offers pain relief. After 20 or so minutes, when the oils are all absorbed, remove the cotton ball, apply more oil to a fresh cotton ball, and replace it in the child's mouth. Discard the oil after 2 days and make a fresh batch if necessary.

Do not let the child use this treatment continuously for more than 3 hours, as it can result in an upset stomach. This treatment is strictly temporary and should be used only to relieve pain while waiting for a dentist's examination.

LOSING TEETH

Children will begin to lose their primary teeth as early as four years of age, although five or six years old is more common. Sometimes the primary teeth remain in place after the permanent teeth have erupted through the gum tissue. Usually the primary teeth will be pushed out and parents can wait as long as six weeks to let nature take its course. If the primary teeth show no signs of loosening after this time, or if your child is experiencing pain or bleeding, a visit to the dentist is necessary. The permanent teeth must have room in the gum tissue, since gum inflammation or crooked permanent teeth can result if the primary teeth are not pulled. Do not, under any circumstances, try to pull your child's teeth out by yourself.

If your child loses a primary tooth long before the permanent tooth is due to erupt, it may be necessary to bridge the space with a space maintainer. This device keeps the neighboring teeth from crowding together and maintains them in normal alignment so that permanent teeth have a chance to grow in straight. Children often have primary and permanent teeth right alongside each other in the gums for several years. Primary teeth can be retained until eleven or twelve years of age before they finally fall out. Usually, the permanent teeth fill the gaps very quickly. If your child has just lost a tooth and the gum is mildly tender and bleeding, the Myrrh Mouthwash, page 216, will relieve discomfort and condition the gum tissue for the arrival of the new tooth.

WISDOM
TEETH

By fifteen to seventeen years of age, all the permanent teeth should have come in. This includes an extra set of back molars called wisdom teeth, or third molars. It is a matter of opinion among dentists whether to remove the third molars as soon as they appear or to adopt a "wait and see" attitude. Occasionally, wisdom teeth are removed immediately if there is infection of the gum tissue or impaction. Another reason many dentists feel third molars should be routinely removed is the danger of malocclusion caused by pushing the teeth of the lower jaw forward. The roots of the third molars do not become fully formed until twenty-five to thirty years of age and the possibility of malocclusion, although reduced, remains until that time.

Your child should see an orthodontist or dentist as soon as the third molars appear. If there is great pain, swelling, or inflammation, treat the situation as an emergency and get help immediately. If there is only mild swelling and pain, similar to infant teething, set up an appointment at your convenience. You and your orthodontist or dentist can then determine if braces will be necessary to prevent malocclusion, or if there is any danger of infection or inflammation to the gums. If braces are recommended, be sure to get a second opinion. (See also WHEN TO SEE THE DENTIST: MALOCCLUSION (BRACES), page 220.)

BLEEDING
GUMS

It is normal for the gums to bleed around the base of a loose tooth or at the site of a newly erupting one. However, if your child's gums bleed during brushing or eating, or if they sometimes bleed spontaneously, it is indicative of poor dental hygiene and a lack of calcium in the diet. Plaque (a film of hardened mucous that harbors bacteria) that collects on the base of a tooth can irritate the gum tissue and cause it to bleed. If a child brushes regularly and correctly, and has regular dental checkups, plaque buildups can easily be prevented.

All children require calcium in their diets to ensure proper growth and cell regeneration. If a child's diet is calcium-poor, the gum tissue can become tender and spongy. Other areas of the body can be affected, too; for example, nosebleeds can result from weakened tissues in the lining of the nose, and bruised areas will be slow to heal. Include lots of green, leafy vegetables in your child's diet if bleeding gums are a problem. These contain easily assimilated calcium, vitamin C, and vitamin A, all of which contribute to healthy gum tissue. There are two herbal procedures that I have successfully used to relieve bleeding gums in children and adults.

Calcium Tea
To increase the strength of the gum tissue

Preparation Time: 20 minutes
Yield: 3 treatments
Children's Enjoyment: ☺

Calcium Tea is excellent for treating bleeding gums, recurring nosebleeds, and wounds that are slow to heal. The primary ingredient in this tea is oat straw, which is very high in calcium and valuable for strengthening and regenerating gum tissue. The tea can also be used as an external wash for flaky skin.

1/2 ounce dried oat straw
1/2 ounce dried horsetail
2 cups water

1. Place the herbs and water in a covered pot, bring to a boil, then turn off the heat and steep for 20 minutes.
2. Strain out the herbs and discard them. The tea will be dark yellow in color and smell like wet grass or hay.
3. Cool it to room temperature before serving. Refrigerate the remaining tea and reheat it to tepid with each use. Discard any unused tea after 2 days.

APPLICATION: A child with bleeding gums should drink 1/2 cup of the tea 3 times each day until the bleeding occurs less frequently or stops altogether (about 2 weeks). Do not sweeten. The tea has a grassy, mildly bitter taste, so the child may need a chaser of orange juice.

If the bleeding gums do not show any sign of improvement after 2 weeks, or if they become worse, consult a dentist or periodontist.

Myrrh Mouthwash
To revitalize and disinfect bleeding gums

Preparation Time: 10 minutes
Yield: 2 treatments
Children's Enjoyment: 😟

Myrrh mouthwash is excellent for tightening up loose and spongy gum tissue, healing sores in the mouth, and fighting bad breath. As a gargle, it relieves sore throats and tickly coughs from colds. This mouthwash tastes bitter and may not be sweetened, so be sure to explain this to the child, and have a good-tasting chaser on hand. Also, because this preparation is astringent, the inside of the mouth may feel slightly puckered. You can make puckered mouth faces at your kid while he or she is gargling to get them to forget the awful taste.

> 1 teaspoon powdered myrrh
> 2 cups water
> Paper coffee filter or cheesecloth

1. Combine the myrrh and water in a small covered pot, bring to a boil, and simmer for 5 minutes.
2. Strain out the powdered myrrh through a coffee filter or cotton cheesecloth and discard.
3. Allow the mouthwash to cool to a comfortably warm temperature and pour 1/2 cup into your child's favorite cup.

APPLICATION: Make sure your child has comfortable access to the kitchen or bathroom sink for spitting out the mouthwash. Instruct the child to swish the mouthwash around in the mouth and between the teeth for at least 3 minutes. Give your child the mouthwash every night for 5 nights just before he or she goes to bed. Make sure the mouthwash is used before brushing the teeth. If the bad taste creates a struggle, your child can use the mouthwash every other night until results are achieved.

If your child's gums are still bleeding or the bleeding worsens after 1 week of treatment, consult with a dentist or periodontist.

COLD SORES

There are two medical conditions that fit under the category of cold sores. The first one, herpes simplex gingivostomatitis, is extremely contagious in humans. The symptoms include lesions that swell and burst on and around the lips, gums, tongue, and cheeks. Herpes simplex is differentiated from herpes zoster (shingles) and herpes genitalis in that the lesions only appear above the waist, usually around the mouth. The other common condition that falls under the term "cold sore" is aphthous ulcers, or canker sores. The cause of canker sores is unknown, but they resemble herpes, occur in the mouth area, and, like herpes, often develop after stressful periods. Both conditions respond to the same treatments.

Children with canker sores or a herpes simplex infection should be kept from putting their hands in their mouths, which aggravates the condition and can help spread it to other family members. Other symptoms of herpes simplex include fever, increased salivation, bad breath, and loss of appetite. Parents should not try to force the child to eat because chewing and swallowing may be quite painful. The following recipe for Herbal Ice Cubes will help relieve the pain, nourish your child, and speed recovery. (See also WHEN TO SEE THE DENTIST: SEVERE HERPES SIMPLEX, page 220.)

Herbal Ice Cubes
A cooling mixture for relief of mouth pain and fever

Preparation Time: 1 hour
Yield: 12 treatments
Children's Enjoyment: ☺

These ice cubes are excellent for children with herpes simplex or canker sores. Cranapple juice is good tasting and has a mildly astringent action on the open sores. Peppermint will bring down any accompanying fever and will help relieve pain. Angostura Bitters is very tasty, helps relieve fever, and will settle an upset stomach. Children, especially very young children, love to suck on ice cubes, and this is a good way of getting fluids into a child who will not eat or drink.

> 1 peppermint tea bag
> 1 cup water
> 2 cups cranapple juice
> 1 teaspoon Angostura Bitters

1. Place the peppermint tea bag and water in a small pot and bring to a boil. Turn off the heat and allow the bag to simmer for 10 minutes.
2. Remove the tea bag and discard. Allow the tea to cool for 5 more minutes.
3. Add the remaining ingredients to the peppermint tea. Stir the mixture thoroughly.
4. Pour the mixture into a clean ice-cube tray. Place the tray in the freezer until the cubes are frozen solid.

APPLICATION: Remove an ice cube from the tray and place it in a cup. Let the child suck on it, rub it on his or her lips, or chew it until it is gone. The child can have 1 to 3 ice cubes every hour. The condition should clear up in about 1 week.

When giving the ice cubes to a child 2 years of age or younger, adult supervision is necessary to avoid the possibility of choking. If the child's fever reaches 103 degrees at any time, or if the condition persists past 1 week, consult a physician.

WHEN TO SEE THE DENTIST

✚ DENTAL CARIES: Caries, or cavities, begin with the demineralization of tooth enamel caused by the acids of fermented sugars and carbohydrates in the mouth. After the enamel has been demineralized, it can be invaded by bacteria that destroy the organic components of the tooth. This results in localized decay of the tooth enamel and dentin, which must be removed and filled. Caries can be greatly reduced by the use of fluoride, especially between the ages of four and eight, when the enamel of the permanent teeth is being formed. A child with a toothache or visible dark spot on a tooth should see a dentist promptly.

✚ INJURIES TO THE TEETH: Dental injuries are most common in toddlers and young children who fall. The front teeth are usually involved, although displacement of other teeth can occur. In young children who still have their primary teeth, the injured tooth is usually extracted and a space maintainer is inserted. Sometimes a fall can knock the tooth up into the gum. The usual procedure in this case is to let the tooth re-erupt over a period of three to four weeks. X-rays are necessary, however, to make sure there has been no damage to the jaw bone and permanent teeth. A permanent tooth that has been chipped will usually be left alone if the chip is not noticeable and if there is no pain. If the tooth is broken and unsightly or enough dentin has been exposed to cause pain, the tooth will be capped. If a child has lost a permanent tooth because of injury, reimplantation is often possible. Wrap the tooth in a wet cloth and go immediately to the nearest emergency room. The operation is usually not successful if more than an hour has elapsed after the injury.

+ TEETH GRINDING: Teeth grinding, or bruxism, is common among children who are mentally retarded or have had meningitis or other diseases that cause unconsciousness. It can also occur in normal children who are emotionally stressed. Bruxism has also been known to accompany iron-deficiency anemia in children. Side effects of bruxism include flattened tooth cusps, worn incisors, sore, tense jaw muscles, and headaches. If bruxism occurs in a normal child during sleep, the family situation should be examined for possible stress-causing factors.

+ MALOCCLUSION (BRACES); This term, used by dental professionals, indicates a condition in which teeth do not fit together properly for normal chewing and biting. Malocclusion can be caused by premature loss of primary teeth, heredity, thumb sucking that persists past the age of four, premature eruption of permanent teeth, or incorrect alignment of the mandibular and maxillary (jaw) bones. This last condition can cause popping and discomfort to the child while chewing. Generally, braces or other dental procedures are required.

+ SEVERE HERPES SIMPLEX: Herpes simplex can become severe if the child is undernourished or severely strained emotionally. Secondary infections in an open lesion can occur if the child is constantly touching it with dirty hands. The lesions can then become quite painful and slow to heal. Other serious problems associated with herpes include very high fevers, inability to eat for prolonged periods of time, swelling in the tongue and throat, and intense pain. Children who exhibit any of these symptoms should be taken immediately to an emergency room where antipyretic drugs, intravenous feeding, or pain-control medicines can be administered.

CHAPTER TEN

WEIGHT AND APPETITE DISORDERS

OVERWEIGHT CHILDREN

LOSS OF APPETITE

DIETARY GUIDELINES

Infant Diet

Toddler Diet

Diet for Children

there is nothing that worries parents more than what type, how often, and how much food their child is eating. Eating habits vary from culture to culture and generation to generation. Even geographic location and lifestyles can produce very different ways of eating. Your child's need for nutritious food, however, is basic and lifelong. Only the amount that is eaten should change as your child grows. During the first year of life and during adolescence "appetite peaks" will occur. These represent periods of rapid growth, when your child's need for nutrients is intensified.

Children require a balanced combination of carbohydrates, fats, proteins, water, vitamins, and minerals to grow properly and enjoy good health. In a society such as ours, this balance can be compromised by fast foods, highly processed foods, and changing responsibilities for food preparation within the family. Because of these influences, many children are exposed to an inappropriate or insufficient variety of foods, which can result in weight and appetite disorders.

If your child is overweight, underweight, or will only eat certain types of foods, a weight and appetite disorder is indicated. It is your responsibility to seek nutritional counseling for yourself, as a food provider, and for your child, who may need to start a special weight gain or loss diet. If you start early enough, you and your child can be "re-trained" away from low-nutrient, highly processed foods and unhealthy eating habits toward a balanced diet composed of all the necessary food groups.

OVERWEIGHT CHILDREN

Your child can be overweight if he or she is considered fat by peers, caretakers, and other adults involved in everyday care, and is more than 20 percent over the ideal weight for his or her height. A tendency toward overweight, or obesity, is often an inherited condition, and heredity alone accounts for most mild obesity. Another common cause is overeating and underexercising. Endocrine abnormalities account for only about 1 percent of all cases of obesity in children.

Mild obesity is not a health threat, but it can develop into one if preventive measures are not taken. Obesity can be harmful to health in a number of ways: Obese individuals suffer from accelerated deterioration of the joint surfaces, cardiovascular problems, and poor psychological adjustment. Overweight children are frequently teased by peers and discriminated against when there is selection for teams and other physical activities. A negative self-image can develop during adolescence when physical appearance becomes an important part of development. A young girl or boy can sometimes feel isolated, depressed, and rejected. These feelings often lead to inactivity and increased eating, which result in further weight gain.

In a fat-conscious society such as ours, it is possible to over-react to what may be nothing more than normal baby fat. A young child should not be put on a diet meant for obese adults. So that your child's normal growth is maintained while excess weight is lost, consult with a physician and/or nutritionist. Once your child's overweight condition is properly diagnosed, you can hasten weight loss by adding some of the following herbal recipes to the diet.

Weight-less Waldorf Salad
To supplement a child's weight loss diet

Preparation Time: 20 minutes
Yield: 4 servings
Child's Enjoyment: ☺

Apples and celery, both efficient weight-reducing foods, are combined in this delicious salad. Nutmeg and cinnamon are added to enhance the flavor of the salad and to stimulate the digestive system. Use only Granny Smith or Pippin apples, preferably organic, in this salad.

2 large Granny Smith or Pippin apples
2 large stalks celery
1/4 cup golden or regular seedless raisins
1 cup plain, low-fat yogurt
1/8 teaspoon ground cinnamon
1/8 teaspoon grated nutmeg

1. Clean and chop the apples and celery into bite-size pieces, then place in a medium-size bowl.
2. Add all the other ingredients and mix thoroughly with a wooden spoon.

APPLICATION: Give an overweight child 1 cup of the salad on a bed of lettuce or just straight twice each day until the desired weight is achieved. A serving approximately 30 minutes before lunch or dinner will decrease appetite and enhance weight loss. If a child craves between meal snacks, serve this salad instead. Refrigerate any leftover salad between servings. Discard leftovers after 2 days.

If your child does not lose weight or continues to gain after eating the salad for 3 weeks, consult a physician and/or nutritionist.

Watercress Salad
To stimulate the endocrine system and enhance weight loss

Preparation Time: 10-15 minutes
Yield: 1 serving
Children's Enjoyment: ☺

Watercress is rich in vitamins and minerals, especially vitamin C. It stimulates the endocrine system and is excellent for the relief of water retention, which can contribute to an overweight condition. Use fresh, organic watercress for this salad.

4 ounces fresh, young watercress
1 ripe tomato or red bell pepper
5 large leaves butter, Boston, or Romaine lettuce
Juice of 1/2 lemon
1 tablespoon virgin olive oil

1. Thoroughly wash the watercress, tomato, and lettuce leaves. Pat dry.
2. Chop the stems off the watercress.

3. Chop the tomato or pepper into bite-size pieces.
4. Combine the watercress, tomato, lemon juice, and olive oil in a small bowl and toss.
5. Arrange the lettuce leaves on a serving plate and place the watercress-tomato mixture in the middle.

APPLICATION: Serve the watercress salad to an overweight child 3 times each week, 30 minutes before dinner, for 3 weeks. The Watercress Salad can be served alternately with the Weight-less Waldorf Salad (page 223) to keep your child from getting bored. Always prepare the salad fresh with each serving.

If your child does not lose weight or continues to gain after eating the salad for 3 weeks, consult a physician and/or nutritionist.

Black Currant Soda
A special treat for a restricted diet

Preparation Time: 2 minutes
Yield: 1 soda
Children's Enjoyment: ☺

This soda is an excellent dessert or treat for an overweight child whose sweets are necessarily restricted. Black currants are stimulating to the digestive system and help the body digest food more quickly, before it has a chance to turn into excess calories. This soda also helps relieve water retention, which can contribute to an overweight condition. Black currant syrup is available in some gourmet food stores and most health food stores. There are many brands available, but I prefer those imported from Europe, especially Switzerland and West Germany, where preservatives are not commonly used in syrups.

     1 10-ounce bottle sparkling water
     1 tablespoon black currant syrup
     Mint sprig or dried rose petals (optional)

1. Pour a tumblerful of sparkling water. You can add ice or not depending on your child's preference.
3. Add black currant syrup and stir thoroughly.
4. Add a sprig of mint or some dried rose petals to enhance the flavor and make the soda more special for your child.

APPLICATION: Give an overweight child no more than 3 servings of the soda a week. Do not serve your child the soda just before bedtime. The soda can be served as a dessert or as a treat between meals. The syrup does not have to be refrigerated, but write the date it was opened on the label and store it in a childproof place. Discard the syrup 6 months after it has been opened.

If your child does not lose weight or continues to gain after maintaining a weight-loss diet for 3 weeks, consult with a physician and/or nutritionist.

LOSS OF APPETITE

Because newborns and very young babies seem to be constantly hungry, you may expect this appetite level to continue into toddlerhood and beyond. In fact, your child's need for food decreases markedly after he or she passes the one-year mark. This decrease in appetite frightens many parents, and they often over-react by trying to force-feed or trick a child into eating. Many unhealthy eating habits get their start when the dinner table is turned into a battleground.

Your child's appetite is controlled by the appetite center in the brain. It is impossible for a normal child to starve voluntarily; if your child is hungry, he or she will eat. Your job as a parent is to provide a healthy selection of foods. Often, far too much food is loaded onto a child's plate at mealtimes, and if the plate is not cleaned, a battle ensues. If you know you are not filling your child up with cookies and chips before mealtimes, relax. Your child is eating as much as he or she needs to maintain health and vitality.

If your child strongly dislikes a particular food, replace it with a nourishing food that he or she finds more palatable. Don't force your child to eat something that he or she finds repulsive. Your child may slip it to the dog, chew it for three hours, throw it up all over the dinner table, or hide it under a napkin, but it *won't* be eaten.

When your child acts fussy with food, it is important to keep control of yourself. Remember, eating habits are formed early and can have a large determining influence on the health your child will enjoy as an adult. Do not threaten your child with punishment if you think the proper amount of food has not been eaten. Do not withhold dessert if the plate is not cleaned. Do not wake your child up at night or interrupt playing to give him or her something to eat. And please don't try to force-feed your child by loading up a fork or spoon and tricking them into opening wide.

If you are concerned that your child is not getting the proper amounts of nutrients, supplement the diet with a good-tasting, chewable multivitamin. Keep in mind, however, that this will not increase your child's appetite. You should be concerned about your child's eating habits only if the following symptoms appear: weight loss, vomiting after large meals, or no weight gain in the past six months. A child who exhibits any of these symptoms should see a physician. If your child is healthy and you simply wish that he or she would eat more food or eat a greater variety of foods, there are two appetite-stimulating teas for you to try. (See also WHEN TO SEE THE DOCTOR: ANOREXIA NERVOSA, page 232; and BULIMIA, page 233.)

Angostura Soda
To increase a fussy eater's appetite

Preparation Time: 5 minutes
Yield: 1 treatment
Children's Enjoyment: ☺

Angostura Bitters will settle the stomach and stimulate appetite and digestion — excellent effects if you have a fussy or poor eater to feed. Angostura Bitters is available in any liquor store and in many grocery stores. The soda is easy to make and has a pleasant taste.

1 cup any brand sparkling water
5 to 10 drops Angostura Bitters
Mint sprig (optional)

1. Fill a glass with sparkling water.
2. Let the child shake the Angostura Bitters drops into the soda and stir it.
3. Garnish the soda with a sprig of mint, if you like.

APPLICATION: You can serve the soda plain or on the rocks. The soda has an aromatic, slightly sweet taste that children love. Give a child with a poor appetite 1 serving of the soda each day before dinner until the appetite improves. Store Angostura Bitters in the liquor cabinet or any place that is out of reach of children.

If your child's appetite does not improve or if there is weight loss after 3 weeks of administering the soda, consult a physician.

Anise Tea
A pleasant-tasting, appetite-stimulating tea

Preparation Time: 20 minutes
Yield: 2 treatments
Children's Enjoyment: ☺

Anise has been used for centuries to ease colic, increase appetite, and enhance the body's ability to absorb nutrients. This herb has a naturally sweet taste and is often added to other mixtures to make them more palatable. Your child should enjoy the taste of this tea.

1/2 ounce anise
2 cups water
Honey (optional)

1. Combine the anise and water in a covered pot and simmer for 20 minutes.

2. Strain out the herb and discard. The tea will be a light gray-green in color and smell sweet and aromatic.
3. Honey can be used to sweeten the tea, if you desire. Cool the tea to room temperature before serving.

APPLICATION: Give a child with a poor appetite 1 cup of the tea each afternoon, between lunch and dinner, for 3 weeks. Refrigerate leftover tea and reheat with each use. Discard any leftover tea after 2 days.

If your child's appetite does not improve or if there is weight loss after 3 weeks of administering the tea, consult a physician.

DIETARY GUIDELINES

The food a child eats has a direct effect on the quality of health that he or she will enjoy. Overly processed foods that are low in fiber and high in fat or sugar will bog down immature digestive systems and prevent them from eliminating wastes efficiently. The immune system is severely taxed as it tries to keep these residual wastes from causing infections and illnesses, and the body's attempts to rid itself of these toxins can result in skin rashes, allergies, indigestion, diarrhea, and recurring colds or sore throats.

In the course of raising three children, I found that the best way to keep them healthy and happy was to be open-minded and flexible about diet. As my children grew older and started attending birthday parties and school outings, they were given foods they had never had before, such as potato chips, ice cream, candy, cakes, and other highly processed foods. The high sugar, salt, and fat content of these foods made them taste wonderful and instantly satisfying, but the bellyache that resulted was a more effective lesson than any lecture I could have given. My kids found out for themselves that sugar, salt, fat, and spices were not good for them when eaten to excess.

Children are natural creatures who pay attention to the signals their bodies give them, and they *always* remember which foods make them feel bad. If their normal diet is healthy and high in nutrients, their bodies will react immediately and unforgettably every time they eat foods

229

that are devitalized, so very little parental supervision will be necessary. Children who develop an independent appreciation of good, wholesome food will continue to eat healthfully as adults, and will teach their own children good dietary habits in turn.

INFANT DIET   Birth to Ten Months — Most parents keep a close watch on infant diets to make sure their baby thrives. There are only a few options available for infant feeding (breast milk, formula, or goat's milk), so it is hard to go wrong. When an infant reaches about six months, solid food can be introduced into the diet. Parents should be aware that it is not absolutely necessary to start solid food at six months. Instead, they should watch their infant for signs that he or she is ready. Infants who still act hungry after a bottle-feeding, who stop taking naps regularly, or who suddenly become whiny and fretful are often telling a parent that they are ready for solid food. The eruption of teeth usually accompanies this desire for solid food and may contribute to the infant's irritability.

Good starting foods for infants are mashed bananas, mashed avocado, applesauce, pureed tofu, pureed potatoes or yams, and well-cooked and pulverized grains such as oats, rice, and barley. This food can supplement milk or formula, which should continue to be part of an infant's diet until eighteen months to two years of age. As more teeth come in and the infant is capable of chewing soft things, introduce pieces of apple or other fresh fruits and whole-grain crackers. If possible, all infant foods should be prepared fresh. Commercial baby food should be used only as a last resort when traveling or visiting. Most commercial baby foods contain high amounts of filler, often cornstarch, and are not very high in nutrients or fiber. Read the labels, they speak for themselves.

TODDLER DIET   Ten Months to Two-and-a-half Years — Between the ages of ten and eighteen months, children develop their back molars. Parents can now serve many of the same foods they consume themselves. They should chop it up first by hand or in a blender to make it a little easier to chew. Toddlers and very young children should not be given spicy, salty, or overly sweetened foods. At this age, they do not need much

230

variety in their diets. The more plain and unprocessed the food is, the healthier it will be for the child.

This is a good time to introduce mashed beans like lima and pinto, small amounts of cheese and yogurt, finely ground lean meats and fish, scrambled eggs, and fresh corn. It is important for parents to observe a child's bowel movement each time a new food is added to the diet to determine how efficiently it is digested. Parents may have to wait until their child is older to introduce new foods if the child has stools that are difficult to pass, are dark colored and hard, or contain undigested bits of the food they have eaten.

Two-and-a-half Years and Up — As a child gets older, parents exercise less and less control over diet. Kids can get fussy about certain vegetables, such as cabbage or squash, or become obsessive about some foods to the exclusion of all others. Parents must make sure that a balanced diet is presented to their children by keeping on hand healthy snacks, such as whole-grain crackers, fresh fruit and fruit juices, and finger vegetables like carrots and celery. Also, parents must make sure that an adequate amount of fiber is present in the diet. Foods rich in fiber are apples, whole-grain crackers and bread, high-fiber breakfast cereals, and cooked grains such as brown rice, barley, and whole-grain porridges.

DIET FOR CHILDREN

A good diet is a plain but complete mixture of fruits, green and yellow vegetables, meat, whole grains, tubers such as potatoes and yams, legumes (beans), seeds, and nuts. Some of these foods, meat and fruit in particular, should be given to a child no more than three times a week. Meat is high in fat and low in fiber, making it difficult to digest. Fruit, which contains a lot of vitamins, unfortunately also contains a lot of sugar, which converts to acid in the bloodstream. This can result in symptoms such as hyperactivity, sleeplessness, and indigestion. Other foods children should eat in moderation are cheese, whole milk as opposed to low-fat milk, and butter, since all are high in fat. Bread can be constipating if eaten too frequently and can aggravate pre-existing allergic conditions.

Vitamin supplements are not necessary if a child is eating a well-balanced diet free of processed foods. When a child is ill or traveling, vitamins can help the body maintain a nutritional balance. If parents want to regularly supplement their child's diet with added vitamins and minerals, a tablespoon of blackstrap molasses twice each week adds B vitamins and iron to the diet. Unfiltered black cherry juice and prune juice are also high in vitamins and minerals, and may have a more agreeable taste than molasses. Black currant syrup is a good-tasting supplement, but it is very sweet and could create cravings for sugar. Fresh vegetable juices, such as carrot and tomato juice, are very high in nutrients and are easily added to the diet between meals. All these supplements can be used individually or in combination to round out the diet and ensure your child's proper growth and resistance to illness.

WHEN TO SEE THE DOCTOR

✛ ANOREXIA NERVOSA: The symptoms of anorexia nervosa can include a morbid preoccupation with and desire to eat food, accompanied by an obsessive refusal to eat, resulting in drastic weight loss. In true anorexia, this weight loss can amount to as much as 25 percent of total body weight. Adolescent girls are affected almost one hundred times more than boys, and they may develop chronic amenorrhea (loss of monthly period) and other endocrine problems. This problem requires intensive medical and psychiatric care for the affected individual, and evaluation of the family environment.

✛ SEVERE OBESITY: Severe obesity in children and adults is usually caused either by an unusually high number of fat cells present in the body or by enlargement of normally occurring fat cells. Individuals who have been obese since childhood display a marked increase in fat cell number, while individuals who became obese after puberty usually have enlarged fat cells. Physical problems associated with obesity include cardiovascular problems, kidney problems, increased strain on the musculo-skeletal system, and poor psychological adjustment. Severe obesity is treated with specially formulated diets, exercise programs, and behavioral therapy.

232

✚ BULIMIA: Bulimia is defined as periodic food binging followed by self-induced vomiting. The food binge may also be followed by excessive intake of diuretics or laxatives to purge the body and prevent weight gain. Body weight is usually kept in the normal range, but vitamin and mineral levels are drastically reduced. Ninety percent of bulimics are adolescent girls and young women. Psychotherapy is required along with a strictly regulated diet to maintain vitamin, mineral, and cell salt levels.

CHAPTER ELEVEN

BEHAVIOR DISORDERS

INFANTS

Sleeping Disorders

Crying Fits

CHILDREN

Nightmares

Fear

Nervousness and Anxiety

Rage

Bed-Wetting

Hyperactivity

all parents want their children to grow into healthy, mature individuals who are capable of tempering their decisions with their own good judgment. This is the basic goal of parenting and, as with the attainment of any other life goal, there is bound to be a little anguish along the way. Raising children will test your mettle as nothing else can. By being tested, however, your own and your family's inner strength will grow.

If you want to reduce the number of behavioral problems that emerge when raising a child, treat your child as a guest in your home. Your child is actually on a very extended, yet temporary visit, with an unknown future. When you think about it, this attitude takes a lot of the pressure out of parenting. You know that someday your little guest will continue on his or her way, things will return to normal, and you can once again resume your own life. In the meantime, you can do your best to see to your guest's comfort and well-being, while simultaneously enjoying his or her presence.

With some obvious exceptions, your children deserve the same respect for their freedom, individuality, and judgment as you would offer a guest. It has been my experience that it's never too soon to regard your child as a rational individual, capable of discernment, prudence, logic, and foresight. If you can hold this attitude in mind, you and your child will gracefully weather even the worst days.

As with any loving parent, all your goals, dreams, and cherished visions of the future are focused in your sticky-fingered, dirty-faced, quarrelsome little ingrate. Remember, however, that they are *your* goals. Your child may have quite a different path in mind. Your job is to provide the car, the gas, and the roadmap. Try to remember, as often as possible, that nobody likes a backseat driver.

INFANTS

There are only a few behavior patterns in infants that can be classified as "abnormal." Infants have very basic requirements: nourishment, shelter, physical affection, and the opportunity for adequate sleep. If any of these needs is not sufficiently met, a behavior disorder will surface along with the infant's developmental skills. The best way to reduce fear and tension during the first year of your infant's life is to educate yourself about infant development. Happy, secure babies are usually the product of calm, loving parents. If your baby sleeps soundly and cries only when there is a good reason to, such as in pain or in fear, you have little to worry about.

It is important for infants to keep regular hours — awake during the day and asleep at night. Your own activity need not be curtailed during the day. Your little companion is very portable, and will sleep just about anywhere. I kept my infants as busy as possible during the day and was rewarded with unbroken sleep at night as early as three weeks with my youngest daughter.

SLEEPING DISORDERS

Between the ages of six months to one year your infant may become aware that your attention can be commanded at night by waking and crying. Discourage such behavior. Let your infant know you are displeased at being awakened at 3:00 A.M. by consistently putting him or her back to bed. Remain to pat the back or hum for two or three minutes, and then leave the room — permanently. If the infant continues to cry, ignore the crying as long as you can. If you must, return to the room with a businesslike look on your face and repeat the procedure. Nursing or bottle-feeding infants, playing with them or changing them, or appearing to be concerned only reinforces such behavior. In this way, your infant will wake up nightly for a week or so, then give it up.

Many parents make the mistake of creeping back to the room after all has been quiet for a few minutes. They are usually unpleasantly surprised to find the infant has been waiting and starts to cry again when they leave. Resist the temptation to check. Remember, it is essential for you to get your sleep so that you can be a healthy, even-tempered parent the next day.

No matter how firm or consistent you are, there are some infants who just won't break the 3:00 A.M. habit once it has started. For these nightowls, there are some effective, sleep-inducing bedtime herbal procedures.

Infant's Calming Herbal Bath
To calm a tense or wakeful infant

Preparation Time: 20 minutes
Yield: 1 treatment
Children's Enjoyment: ☺

A hot bath is an effective sleep aid that works well for people of all ages. Lavender and camomile are an ideal herbal combination for calming and soothing an infant. Both herbs have mild sedative effects and lend a wonderful fresh scent to bathwater. Most infants enjoy this bath very much and come to associate its scent with relaxation and sleep time.

> 1 quart water
> 1 ounce dried lavender buds
> 1 ounce dried camomile flowers

1. Bring the water to a boil in a covered pot.
2. Remove the pot from the heat and add the herbs; cover the pot again. Remove the herbs from the heat and let them steep in the hot water for 20 minutes.
3. Strain the tea and discard the herbs. The bath tea will be dark yellow and smell pleasantly of lavender.
4. Pour the tea into an infant bathtub and add enough warm water to fill it. The herbal bath should be as warm as a normal bath for the infant.

APPLICATION: Make certain the room is warm before the bath. Place the infant in the bathwater and hold him or her reassuringly, humming and crooning all the while. Soak the infant in the bath for at least 10 minutes. Do not try to wash the infant during an herbal bath. Gently pour the water over the belly and legs, and just let the infant play and splash. If the child is old enough to sit up, let him or her play with tub toys. Use this bath as often as you like.

If the infant still wakes up at night after administering this bath, try the following Camomile Tea, after the bath.

Camomile Tea
To soothe a restless infant and induce sleep

Preparation Time: 20 minutes
Yield: 3 treatments
Children's Enjoyment: ☺

Because it is a mild tranquilizer, Camomile Tea is good for a restless, wakeful infant. Camomile has a mildly sweet, pleasant taste and your infant should enjoy a bottle or cup of the tea before bedtime. For maximum drowsiness, this tea may be taken during or immediately after a warm herbal bath.

> 1/2 ounce dried camomile flowers
> 2 cups water

1. Combine the camomile and water in a covered pot and simmer for 20 minutes.
2. Strain out the herb and discard it. The tea will be a beautiful golden color and smell mildly sweet.
3. Cool the tea to room temperature before serving.

APPLICATION: For a wakeful, restless infant, administer 6 tablespoons of tea at bedtime. If the infant will not take a bottle, use a teaspoon to spoon the tepid tea into the mouth. Remember to hold the infant in a comfortable, secure position to receive the tea. In this way, he or she will get used to the routine, and there will be less resistance. You can leave the tea-bottle in the bed with an older infant, but be sure the tea is unsweetened.

If the infant still wakes up at night after administering the tea, combine this treatment with the Infant's Calming Herbal Bath, page 238.

CRYING
FITS

All infants cry. They cry when they are hungry, cold, afraid, tired, or in need of a diaper change. They also cry when they have experienced physical pain. Parents who have the training and experience to foresee the needs of their infant will have little crying to deal with. However, it is impossible to predict that an infant will be accidentally hurt or frightened. All infants burst out crying on such occasions, and require attention from the parent to become calm again. It is important for a parent to know how to calm an infant so that crying incessantly over minor problems does not occur.

A newborn infant will not cry to excess. Newborns are creatures of instinct; they cry to satisfy a need and stop crying when that need is met. Excessive crying or crying fits usually begin when a child is able to recognize the pattern of cause and effect generated by crying. This can occur as early as six to eight months. Here is an example:

Baby Nicholas burns his finger on a birthday candle, and cries out in pain. His parent's reaction at this time will determine whether he stops crying in a minute or two, or if the crying will go on for half an hour. If Nicky's parent gasps, drops the phone receiver and leaves it dangling, rushes over and grabs him, while wearing a look of near-hysteria, he will be frightened and cry all the harder. Nicky will quickly become used to this reaction, and recognize it as an opportunity to become the center of attention. If his parent continues to over-react to his everyday trials and tribulations, the attention-getting pattern will be very difficult to break. Nicky will have a crying fit every time he is not immediately gratified. In effect, he has discovered a useful way of controlling the world and has, thus, become a tiny dictator.

Now, let's replay the scene mentioned above, with Baby Alex, who mildly burns her finger and starts to cry. Her parent calmly establishes eye contact with Alex, then explains to whomever is on the phone that Alex has been burned and requires attention. Alex's parent walks un-hurriedly over, kneels before her, but does not immediately grab or hug; instead, the parent asks where it hurts. (I have found that an infant no more than five months old can be calmed simply by being asked what has happened.) Alex's parent wears a sympathetic but not frightened look, and gently takes the hand and kisses it, saying over and over that it's really all right. Alex re-examines the burnt finger and realizes that it is indeed all right. At this time, a quick reassuring hug may be administered. Her parent's face wears a bright, confident smile, and Alex stops crying and forgets all about it. Her parent gets up and does something else, as though everything were completely normal. If this pattern of behavior is repeated every time Alex starts to cry, she will gain self-control over her upsets.

There are, unfortunately, no herbal procedures or medicines that guarantee a healthy parent-child relationship. Many parents "grow up" with their children, and no matter how many books they read (including this one), they will always learn best from the actual experience of parenting. They quickly learn when their child really has something to cry about and when he or she is manipulating them. By establishing a healthy, consistent pattern as early as possible, you can help to make parenting a joyful experience for both you and your child.

CHILDREN

Children are not born with a full arsenal of social skills. Behavior must be taught to them, and the parent's job is to reinforce good behavior. Children learn how to talk and act around other people, and learn how to understand themselves. As a child grows older, school-teachers, peers, and others will all participate in the teaching and learning process.

There are many kinds of reinforcers, just as there are many kinds of punishment. My favorite reinforcement is "social" reinforcement — giving your child a supportive hug, listening intently to your child's story, or offering praise for a job well done. Other reinforcers are "tangible," such as money, treats, or gold stars. "Activity" reinforcers include staying up late to watch TV, having a story read, or being taken to the movies.

Punishment for unacceptable behavior can be just as varied as the reinforcers. The suitable punishment depends on your child's age. When your child is a toddler, a baleful look of disapproval, or the word "no" firmly spoken is the best way to react to misbehavior. At this age, however, your child must be taught what is unsafe. If he or she runs into the street or leans out of a three-story window after being clearly told not to, more severe punishment may be required, including yelling or a light spank on the bottom. At no time should you pick up and shake a child, or hit a child with an object. (See also WHEN TO SEE THE DOCTOR: CHILD ABUSE, page 258.)

As your child grows, different forms of discipline will be needed. Your child should always understand why he or she is being punished, and punishment should always occur immediately following the offense. I have found that sending a child away from the group, to a bedroom or other place where he or she can be alone, is a good way to correct misbehavior. Healthy children have an innate sense of dignity and a deep desire to do the right thing. Try to show respect for and encourage these traits in your children by using discipline to teach, not humiliate or hurt them. Your child feels trust and security when you react in a predictable, rational way to misbehavior. If you raise your child in this kind of environment, he or she will naturally want to behave well. Fear, aggression, and anxiety, though naturally experienced by every child at some point, will be controlled and minimized.

NIGHT-MARES

Children between the ages of one and five experience nightmares frequently. At this age, children can become frightened by strangers, unusual objects, frightening programs on TV, and other things that occur in daily life. Children two years old and younger cannot readily distinguish between reality and dreams, and may become reluctant to go to bed if they are afraid of the characters appearing in their dreams. If you ask your two- to three-year old to describe a bad dream, you will probably hear a fanciful tale of ghosts, monsters, or fierce animals. You may have to convince your child that there really is no goblin at the end of the bed waiting to pop up as soon as the light is out.

No matter how happy and stress-free their home environments are, all children will occasionally experience nightmares. Children have vivid imaginations and will attribute strange powers to many different objects or situations. The most common nightmares involve fear of animals, being chased by strangers, or feeling helpless and abandoned in a strange place. Try to get your child to tell you why he or she thinks this dream occurred. You will probably be quite surprised to hear your child's interpretation of a bad dream.

If you are awakened by your child's bad dream, the best thing to do is walk your child back to bed and ask him or her to explain the dream. Be sympathetic, but don't act frightened or overly concerned. Stroke your child's back or head while he or she is explaining, and don't let the explanation go on for too long. I've found approximately ten minutes from the time I'm awakened to the time I'm back in bed is sufficient for even the scariest nightmare. It is very important not to ridicule or belittle a child's nighttime fears. They *can* be truly terrifying. If your child is starting to have regular nightmares, it may be because of the arrival of a new sibling, a new event such as starting school, or perhaps some other frightening experience. It is important to encourage the child to talk about it. The best therapy for nighttime fears is your obvious concern, but here is a delightful herbal pillow that will help guard your child's sleep. (See also WHEN TO SEE THE DOCTOR: NIGHT TERRORS, page 256.)

Herbal Pillow
To discourage a child's nighttime fears

Preparation Time: 1 hour
Yield: 1 to 2 months of effectiveness
Children's Enjoyment: 😋

Herbal pillows have been used for centuries to cure depression, nightmares, and insomnia. Some herbal pillows were formulated to provide the user with visionary dreams or clairvoyant abilities. They can also be used simply to fill the bedroom with a nice scent. This Herbal Pillow can become a transitional object if your child's sleep is disturbed, the same way a teddy bear or favorite blanket is used.

1 ounce dried thyme
1 ounce dried rose buds
1 ounce dried rosemary
1 ounce dried lavender
Piece of fine-weave cotton muslin, 14 inches long
and 12 inches wide
Piece of thick cotton flannel, 15 inches long
and 13 inches wide
10-inch piece of Velcro, approximately 1 inch wide

1. Combine the herbs in a stainless-steel bowl and mix them thoroughly with your hands or with a wooden spoon.
2. Fold the muslin in half lengthwise. Sew up the two 7-inch sides to form a pouch with an opening at the top. Turn the pouch inside out, trim the seam allowances, and press flat.
3. Fill the muslin pouch with the herbs. Push the herbs to the bottom of the pouch. Fold over 1 inch of the top edges to the inside. Press the edges to the inside and sew the pouch closed.
4. Make a pouch of the cotton flannel following the same procedure in step 2. Fold down the top edges of the flannel pouch to the inside, press, and sew, but do not sew the pouch closed.
5. Pin the Velcro into place on the inside edges of the flannel pouch. Make sure the Velcro meets and holds properly before sewing it into place. Once it has been sewn in, the Velcro should securely hold the muslin pouch inside.

APPLICATION: You now have a reusable flannel herbal pillow case and a fresh muslin pouch of herbs to put inside it. The pillow case will stay closed and hold the herb-filled pouch securely, and the child can have fun plumping and pummeling the pillow to whatever shape he or she likes to sleep with. I do not recommend letting the child sleep directly on the pillow; just let them hold it or sleep with it nearby. The outer case can be washed regularly, and a new muslin pouch with fresh herbs can be inserted every few months or so.

If your child suffers frequently from nightmares and disturbed sleep, consult a family therapist.

A child's fear can vary from butterflies in the stomach to outright **FEAR**
panic. A one-year-old will be frightened by strange objects or sudden
movement and noise. A two-year-old will be frightened by flushing
toilets, dogs, or darkness. Three- to four-year-olds are frightened by
imaginary bogeymen, shadows at night, and sirens or thunder.

Children have different ways of expressing fear, depending on their
age. An infant will scream and cry, shuddering and stiffening up with
fright. Two- to four-year-olds will cry, run away, and hide in a corner
or under the covers, usually with their hands over their ears and their
eyes tightly shut. By the time a child reaches the age of five or six, his
or her fears are based on more concrete things, such as falling from a
height or walking past a barking dog. These fears are easier to explain
away.

Children must learn to distinguish between what is frightening and
dangerous and what is simply new. If your child has been frightened
by someone or something that is new and unfamiliar, calmly and reassuringly demonstrate that the fear is not based in reality. Do not tell
your child in a casual way that there is nothing to be afraid of, because
as far as he or she is concerned, there most certainly is. Discuss with
your child the characteristics and circumstances of the object or person
that he or she fears. This will create a more rational focus. Do not,
under any circumstances, try to force your child to touch, acknowl-
edge, or participate in a situation in which he or she is still obviously
afraid. Do not taunt your child or mock his or her fearfulness. This
will only make matters worse for both of you.

The best way to deal with your child's fear is to let him or her watch
you or siblings deal with the frightening object, person, or situation. It
will become obvious to your child that there is really nothing to be
afraid of. You must try very hard not to be impatient, and older
siblings must be prevented from teasing and taunting. If a rational and
predictable procedure is followed every time your child becomes
frightened, he or she will soon develop the confidence and security to
deal with the situation independently.

If your child has had a very frightening experience or is having trouble forgetting a situation that was frightening to him or her, here is an
herbal bath that will have a soothing and calming effect.

Jasmine Bath
To soothe and relax a frightened child

Preparation Time: 20 minutes
Yield: 1 treatment
Children's Enjoyment: 😊

Jasmine has been used for centuries as a calmative. It has an intoxicating scent and is extremely pleasurable and relaxing in a bath. Jasmine oil added to the bath is even better, but this oil is expensive and hard to find. If you can't find dried jasmine, you can use a prepared bath oil or crystals by following the directions on the package.

4 ounces dried jasmine
2 quarts water

1. Combine the jasmine and water in a large, covered pot, bring to a boil and simmer slowly for 20 minutes.
2. Strain out and discard the herb.
3. Pour the tea into the bathtub while the water is running so that it will be well combined. Run the herbal bath as warm as you usually run a bath for the child or infant, but make sure the temperature of the bath is not too hot after adding the brewed tea. The bathwater may have a light sheen of jasmine oil and will smell strongly of jasmine.

APPLICATION: Let the child bathe and play for at least 20 minutes. There is no need for the child to wash during the bath. You can add some dried jasmine flowers to the bathwater for the child to play with, but make sure you cover the drain of the bathtub with a strainer when you empty the tub. This bath can be repeated whenever your child needs to be calmed and soothed. A light massage following the bath will greatly enhance its effect.

If you child is frequently fearful or anxious, consult with a family therapist.

Nervousness and anxiety are caused by situations or patterns of behavior your child has trouble coping with. Anxiety-causing situations include a change in home life caused by one or both parents taking a job or going back to school, divorce, unsatisfactory day-care arrangements, unrealistic parental expectations, or the death of a beloved pet. Extreme nervousness and anxiety can be caused by alcoholism in one or both parents, child abuse, or the death of a sibling, parent, or other important loved one in the family.

NERVOUS-NESS AND ANXIETY

If you are unable to assist your child through difficult times because of your own emotional upheaval, a good therapist can be very helpful. The advice and support of a professional can help you and your family through the rough times with a minimum of confusion and fear. Children have a tendency to blame themselves for all the bad things that happen as they are growing up. It is important to reassure your child that whatever happened, it was not because he or she spilled the milk or broke an expensive vase.

Children who are suffering from nervousness and anxiety will do poorly in school and may have difficulty making and keeping friends. Schoolteachers are an invaluable source of information, since they are probably spending as much time with your child as you are, and they have the advantage of observing your child's behavior in a group. If you know your child is having difficulty, a parent-teacher conference is helpful.

Physical signs of anxiety in a child include teeth-grinding at night, facial tics, insomnia, and aggression. If your child is experiencing any of these symptoms, consult with a professional family therapist. If you would like to calm your child while going through a rough time that you know will be temporary, such as divorce or some other upsetting change in lifestyle, the following herbal treatments may help. (See also WHEN TO SEE THE DOCTOR: TICS, page 256; and CHILD ABUSE, page 258.)

Valerian Root Tincture
To calm a fearful, nervous, or anxious child

Preparation Time: 14 days
Yield: 6 months' worth of tincture
Children's Enjoyment: ☺

Valerian root is excellent for relief of tension, anxiety, insomnia, and hysteria. Its calmative powers have long been recognized, and a chemical synthesis of the properties present in valerian root have resulted in the popular sedative Valium. Nervous children are soothed and comforted by this formula, and valerian root has the added advantage of having a beneficial effect on the digestive system. The root has an unpleasant odor, which is why it is administered as a tincture.

> 2 cups high quality vodka
> 1 ounce dried valerian root pieces

1. Pour the vodka into a spotlessly clean quart-size jar with a tight-fitting lid.
2. Add the valerian root. Screw on the lid and shake the jar vigorously for 5 minutes.
3. Label the jar with the date and name of the tincture, put it in a dark closet, and be sure to shake the jar for 5 minutes each day for the next 2 weeks.
4. Decant the tincture by straining out the valerian root through fine-weave cheesecloth. Discard the herb and return the strained mixture to the labeled jar.

APPLICATION: Administer 5 drops under the tongue with a medicine dropper whenever nervousness and anxiety are a problem. Do not do this more than 3 times a day or for longer than 1 month. This tincture is especially good at bedtime to help an anxious child sleep.

If your child's anxiety does not disappear after 1 month of using the tincture, or if it is becoming a serious problem, consult with a family therapist or physician.

Calcium Tea
To help a child remain calm

Preparation Time: 20 minutes
Yield: 3 treatments
Children's Enjoyment: ☺

Calcium is an important mineral for a healthy nervous system. When a child is experiencing stress for any reason, the calcium in the blood is quickly depleted. This makes it harder for the body to achieve and maintain a calm, balanced nervous system. This tea is also excellent to help safeguard a child's immune system, which can be compromised by stress.

> 1/2 ounce dried oat straw
> 1/2 ounce dried horsetail
> 2 cups water

1. Place the herbs and water in a covered pot, bring to a boil, and simmer for 20 minutes.
2. Strain out the herbs and discard them. The tea will be dark yellow in color and smell like wet grass or hay.
3. Cool the tea to room temperature before serving. Refrigerate the remaining tea and reheat it to tepid with each use. Discard any unused tea after 1 week.

APPLICATION: Give the child 1/2 cup of the tea 3 times each day until the child seems calmer and more relaxed. Do not sweeten. The tea has a grassy, mildly bitter taste, so the child may need some kind of chaser, such as orange juice.

If your child's nervousness does not disappear or becomes worse after 2 weeks of drinking the tea, consult with a family therapist or physician.

RAGE A child's uncontrolled anger may be due to fear, anxiety, dread, jealousy, frustration, or victimization. Children have little control over these emotions until they reach an age at which they are able to reason with themselves and those around them. You must reassure your child and teach him or her acceptable ways of expressing anger.

Children can learn to manipulate their parents and the environment around them by unleashing their rage. These children will be quite resistant to parental training, especially if it is harsh or inconsistent. Neglected children use tantrums as a way of getting attention, though the attention they receive is usually negative. If a child is the victim of the parent's own anger and frustration (as some children are), he or she learns to release anger by throwing fits, smashing toys, or verbally or physically abusing a younger sibling or pet.

Children between the ages of one and three are capable of the most outrageous behavior. This behavior ranges from saying no to everything, no matter how nicely you put it; engaging in breath-holding spells; or screaming at the top of their lungs in public places. Many parents over-react by giving in to the child's demands or by screaming back and creating a scene. Either way, the child is not learning how to control anger.

Here is a good way to handle your own and your child's anger in a public situation: Quickly exit the restaurant, theater, or your boss's living room with your child in tow. Find a place where you and your child are alone together, and deliver a blistering lecture on proper social conduct. Even if your child is only two years old or younger, a strong show of parental disapproval will make a lasting impression. Anger should be shown with your eyes, posture, and tone of voice — not by spanking or hitting. Do not promise punishment at a later date or try to frighten your child into good behavior with threats. A healthy child will stop misbehaving and start seeking your forgiveness, which should be shown immediately with a hug and quiet, warm tones of voice. This pattern should be repeated consistently every time your child misbehaves in this extreme way. Remember, your child loves and needs you, and really doesn't like being in the doghouse.

Older children will have more control over themselves, but they are still subject to fits of anger, often caused by teasing from siblings or peers, or by some other form of intolerable frustration. It is extremely important for a parent to teach children to direct their anger without causing harm to themselves or others.

Children, like adults, don't like to discuss something that's bothering them. They will attract attention to their discomfort by slamming a door or bursting into tears over a trifling annoyance. Although you may not want them to do this in front of the in-laws, it is okay to have a yelling match within the privacy of your own home. You should not be frightened by, or try to suppress your child's display of anger. Instead, you should act as a referee. I have found that, more often than not, anger turns to hilarity. Once your child has blown off a little steam, it's a good time to sit down and have a talk (or a good laugh).

If your child's anger seems uncontrollable and extreme, seek professional help. A child's anger should be temporary and infrequent, tapering off dramatically with mental and emotional growth. A family therapist can help bring out and relieve the cause of a child's anger and re-establish the stability of the whole family. (See also WHEN TO SEE THE DOCTOR: BEHAVIORAL PROBLEMS AT SCHOOL, page 257; BREATH-HOLDING SPELLS, page 257; and CHILD ABUSE, page 258.)

BED-WETTING

Bed-wetting, or enuresis, is an involuntary loss of urine occurring at an age when bladder control has usually been acquired, that is, at approximately age four. Children around this age may be completely trained for months, relapse temporarily, and then regain bladder control. This is normal in the course of potty training and you should try not to over-react. Even after good control has been achieved, children still wet their pants when they are excited, frightened, stressed, or deeply involved in playing. This should not be considered enuresis.

Primary enuresis is a condition in which bladder control has never been achieved. Children affected by primary enuresis may have an unusually small bladder capacity. This problem can be corrected by a bladder-training program. Your child should be encouraged to drink as much fluid as possible during the day and to hold the urine as long as he or she can. This will increase the bladder's capacity and strengthen the bladder sphincter muscles. Bladder-training programs have helped many children, but they work best when you do not over-react to the many accidents that occur in the beginning. You must also determine whether or not your child is constantly dribbling a flow of urine, or remains dry for a few hours at a time and then wets. A constant flow of urine can indicate a structural problem in your child's urinary tract.

Secondary enuresis occurs in children who had complete bladder control and subsequently have lost it. Secondary enuresis can be caused by obstructions in the urinary tract, urinary tract infections, diabetes, and epilepsy. Psychological factors causing secondary enuresis can include regression on the part of the child in an effort to receive more attention, fear, anxiety, and resentment, in which bed-wetting becomes a way of "getting even."

If your child has secondary enuresis, you can correct this problem by keeping your child from drinking fluids for three to four hours before bedtime and making sure he or she urinates before going to bed. Wake your child after the first three hours of sleep to urinate again. Give your child rewards for "dry" days, but don't react with anger or disgust on the days he or she wakes up in a wet bed. This will only reinforce the problem. There are some commercial alarm systems for bed wetters that are sensitive to moisture and will wake your child when he or she starts to urinate. If this problem persists into adolescence, these devices may be very helpful, but in children six years and younger, they may be extreme. It is better for a young child to be wakened by you.

If your child's bed-wetting problem persists, in spite of your best efforts to control it, take a close look at your family environment. High stress and anxiety levels in a child's life may cause a loss of bladder control. Family therapy and a change in your attitude toward the problem and your child can improve the situation. In the meantime, here is a tea that will help strengthen your child's bladder and kidneys.

Comfrey Root and Corn Silk Tea
To help relieve a child's bed-wetting

Preparation Time: 20 minutes
Yield: 8 treatments
Children's Enjoyment: ☺

Corn silk has been used for generations to relieve bed-wetting and incontinence. The combination of corn silk and comfrey in this tea will help to relieve irritation in and strengthen the tone of the bladder. Children who experience bed-wetting as a problem should also be encouraged to eat fresh corn silk whenever corn-on-the-cob is served. Use only organically grown corn for this purpose.

> 1 1/2 ounces corn silk
> 1/2 ounce comfrey root
> 1 quart water

1. Combine the herbs with the water in a covered pot, bring to a boil, and simmer for 5 minutes.
2. Remove the pot from the heat and steep for 15 minutes.
3. Strain out the herbs and discard them. The tea will be light, tawny brown in color and smell slightly sweet.
4. Cool the tea to room temperature before using. Store the leftover tea in the refrigerator between servings and warm it slightly for each use. Discard any unused portion after 2 days.

APPLICATION: Give your child 1/2 cup of the tea, twice a day in the morning and afternoon for 6 days, rest for a day, and then resume the tea schedule for another 6 days. Do not sweeten the tea and do not give it to your child before bedtime. This tea works best when combined with a bladder training program or other routine. Results should be apparent within 2 weeks.

If your child has a severe problem with enuresis, or if you suspect a structural problem within the urinary tract, consult a physician.

HYPER-
ACTIVITY

Hyperactivity, also known as Attention Deficit Disorder, or ADD, is not easy to define or diagnose. Simply put, hyperactivity is motor activity that is greater than normal for the age of the child. Obviously, parents, teachers, psychologists, and physicians will all have a different idea of what is "normal." A child is often considered hyperactive just because he or she is livelier than classmates or friends.

Causes of hyperactivity include ingestion of food additives, anatomic defects, birth injuries, prenatal conditions, diseases of the central nervous system, and poor parenting. Many physicians feel that hyperactive children improve with the onset of adolescence. Medical treatment for hyperactivity includes initiation of a behavioral program for mild cases and medications for children who are severely affected. Therapy and support are also important for parents of hyperactive children.

If you feel your child has been correctly diagnosed as hyperactive, start him or her on a diet that is free of additives (such as artificial coloring, flavoring, and preservatives). Foods that are high in vitamin C and B-complex are excellent for hyperactivity. These include tubers, citrus fruits, grains, nuts, fish, and small amounts of meat. Read the labels carefully on any packaged foods you serve your child. Startling results have been achieved by changes in diet alone, but these can be supplemented by the following teas.

Red Clover and Lemon Grass Tea
A cleansing tea for hyperactivity

Preparation Time: 20 minutes
Yield: 4 treatments
Children's Enjoyment: ☺

This tea is an effective blood cleanser that rids the body of food additives and environmental pollutants. It is good for hyperactive children, whose nervous systems are especially sensitive to synthetic chemicals. This tea has a mild, lemony taste and smell, and is very pleasant to drink.

1/2 ounce red clover
1/2 ounce lemon grass
2 cups of water

1. Combine the herbs with the water in a covered pot, bring to a boil, and simmer for 5 minutes.
2. Remove the pot from the heat and steep the herbs for 15 minutes.
3. Strain out the herbs and discard them. The tea will be tawny yellow in color and smell sweet and lemony.
4. Cool the tea to room temperature before using. Store the leftover tea in the refrigerator between servings and warm it slightly for each use. Discard any unused portion after 2 days.

APPLICATION: Give a hyperactive child 1/2 cup of tea 3 times each day, between meals, for 2 weeks. This tea may not be sweetened, so keep a chaser such as golden raisins on hand.

If your child is severely hyperactive, seek the help of a physician, child psychologist, or family therapist.

Camomile Tea
To soothe a hyperactive child

Preparation Time: 20 minutes
Yield: 5 treatments
Children's Enjoyment: ☺

Camomile Tea is beneficial for a hyperactive child because it acts as a mild tranquilizer. Camomile is also a blood purifier that hastens the process of toxin excretion through the skin. It is excellent for the digestive tract and has a pleasant taste and color. This tea can be used in combination with the Red Clover and Lemon Grass Tea (page 254).

1 ounce dried camomile flowers
2 cups water

1. Combine the camomile and water in a covered pot and simmer for 20 minutes.
2. Strain out the herb and discard it. The tea will be a beautiful golden color and smell mildly sweet.
3. Cool the tea to room temperature before serving.

APPLICATION: Give a hyperactive child 1/2 cup of tea 3 times each day, between meals, for 2 weeks. This tea may not be sweetened, but it has a naturally sweet taste your child should enjoy.

If your child is severely hyperactive, seek the help of a physician, child psychologist, or family therapist.

WHEN TO SEE THE DOCTOR

✚ NIGHT TERRORS: Night terrors occur most frequently in children one to four years of age. The child is actually not awake but sits abruptly upright and starts to scream in terror. The eyes are not open or may be partially open. Night terrors occur during sudden arousal from non-REM sleep and are never remembered by the child the next morning. During the attack, the child is difficult to console and may not be aware of your presence. The attacks usually last from ten to fifteen minutes, after which the child falls back to sleep. The cause of night terrors is unknown, but the attacks are usually infrequent. If your child has frequent attacks, he or she should be examined by a physician. Drugs such as Valium are used in cases of frequent attacks, and psychotherapy may be indicated for children suffering from severe night terrors.

✚ TICS: Tics are movements of muscle groups anywhere on the body that are not associated with any disease of the neurological or musculoskeletal system. These movements include frequent eye blinking, rolling of the head, wrinkling of the forehead, twitching of the shoulders, throat-clearing, coughing, or twisting of the mouth. These movements can occur in different degrees of severity. Tics usually develop in children at approximately six or seven years of age, and they may be aggravated by anxiety, tension, excitation, or underlying emotional problems. Tics may disappear with adolescence and adulthood, but your child may need to have professional help from a family therapist. Psychotherapy or medical evaluation is indicated in children with severe affliction.

✦ BEHAVIOR PROBLEMS AT SCHOOL: Behavior problems at school can be widely varied and are often incorrectly diagnosed. Many children are not properly socialized in the home environment before entering school and have immature social interactional skills. These children will be anxious at the beginning of the school year, but will improve rapidly as they adjust. Monitoring by parents and teachers is the only therapy required. Some children, however, do have problems that need attention from parents, physicians, and school psychologists, preferably with all three parties working as a team. These problems include self-initiated isolated play, frequent violent physical and verbal interactions with other children, avoidance by classmates, daydreaming and inattention to tasks, and inappropriate responses such as rage, depression, or listlessness to normal stimuli. Treatment involves therapeutic management of the child's behavior to teach proper interactional skills, evaluation of the family situation, and in more severe cases, transferal to a special education class.

✦ BREATH-HOLDING SPELLS: Breath-holding spells are often preceded by crying and temper tantrums, and may actually be considered a form of temper tantrum. During a breath-holding spell, the child holds his or her breath for anywhere from a few seconds to one minute. The spell may be accompanied by bluish facial pallor, loss of consciousness, and convulsions. Breath-holding can begin as early as eighteen months of age, with the highest frequency of attacks occurring between the ages of one and four. Attacks may be caused by pain, fear, anger, or strain at school; and the child may not have control over them. Breath-holding spells have been found to be hereditary, and can be a symptom of epilepsy. Treatment consists of eliminating provocative situations in a child's life, with care given to keeping the child from using the attacks as a manipulative tool. Tests for epilepsy should be performed on children who experience frequent breath-holding spells, especially when they cause unconsciousness and convulsions.

✦ CHILD ABUSE: Child abuse is considered a generational problem that generally begins with a grandparent who abuses the parent who, in turn, abuses the child. There may be many other factors that contribute to the problem, including mental disorders, alcoholism, teenage marriages, unwanted pregnancies, social isolation and loneliness, and financial or other stresses. Most parents are married and living together at the time the abuse occurs. The most common instruments of abuse are hairbrushes, belts, hot irons, and fists. Abused children usually exhibit unusual fearfulness, inappropriate stoicism, or aggressive and destructive behavior. Physicians suspecting child abuse perform radiologic skeletal surveys of the long bones for signs of previously healed calcifications as well as check for scars, burns, and bruises. Many hospitals and clinics have developed programs to help abusive parents and their children, and the success rates of these and other organizations such as Parents Anonymous are quite high. If you feel you might be capable of child abuse or you are already abusing your child, seek help immediately by joining one of the above organizations or by calling a local child-abuse hotline.

THE
INGREDIENTS

NAME	DESCRIPTION	PRIMARY USES	SECONDARY USES
AGAR *Gelidium amansii*	Agar is a derivative of red algae (of the *Gelidium* genus) and is gathered by hand or with rakes along the seashore.	Agar is used industrially as a sterile medium for pills, suppositories, and lotions. Medicinally, agar can be used for chronic constipation.	Agar is used as a gelatin substitute.
ALMOND *Prunus amygdalus*	Almonds are cultivated as food in California, the Mediterranean, and southern Europe. Almond oil is high in vitamin E.	Sweet almond oil is used as a skin oil and can be taken internally to soothe gastritis. Bitter almond oil is used in cough preparations and is a mild sedative.	Ground almonds make an excellent facial scrub and almond butter is a delicious alternative to peanut butter.
ANISE *Pimpinella dulcis*	Anise is an ancient herb. It was employed medicinally by the Egyptians and was grown on the imperial German herb farms of Charlemagne.	Anise helps increase the body's ability to absorb nutrients. It has a soothing effect on ulcers, kidney and urinary-tract inflammations, and infant colic.	Anise tea can be used to increase the flow of milk in nursing mothers. It can also be added to many brews to impart a pleasant flavor.
BARLEY *Hordeum vulgare*	Barley is a grain used in soups and stews to provide a thick, nourishing broth. When its tough, outer hull is removed, barley is known as "pearled barley."	Barley water (or tea) can be taken to soothe throat, stomach, and intestinal irritations. Externally, barley water is an excellent demulcent wash for skin irritations.	Barley water taken internally acts as a mild diuretic and helps relieve high blood pressure.
BASIL *Ocimum basilicum*	Basil grows wild in tropical and subtropical parts of the world and is widely cultivated as a kitchen herb.	Basil tea can soothe stomach cramps, aid digestion, and cleanse the lower intestine of mucus.	In the past, basil was widely used as an antispasmodic. Basil tea is also good for helping to promote breast-milk production.

APPEARANCE	FORMS AVAILABLE	WHERE TO FIND IT	RECIPES
Agar is a processed substance that appears as a white powder, flakes, or pressed into short sticks.	Agar can be found packaged in dried powder, stick, or flake form.	Health Food Store Grocery Store	Black Cherry Agar Gelatin
Almonds are approximately 1 inch long and oval shape, with a rough, brown skin. Almond oil is usually clear or light yellow, with a mild, sweet smell.	Almonds are available fresh or as an oil extract.	Health Food Store Grocery Store Pharmacy (oil only)	Almond Oil Rub Diaper Rash Skin Ointment
Anise grows up to 6 feet in height, producing clusters of white flowers. The light green, oval seeds are about 1/4 inch long. Anise prefers fields and damp places.	Anise seeds are available dried, in bulk.	Health Food Store Grocery Store (seeds for flavoring, some anise oil) Grows wild	Anise Tea
Pearled barley grains are oval-shape, approximately 1/4 inch long, and have a whitish, "pearly" appearance.	Barley can be found in chopped, rolled, unhulled, or pearled forms.	Health Food Store Grocery Store (nonorganic)	Skin Food Bath
The basil plant grows in bushy stems from 1 to 2 feet high. The leaves are broad and flat and are greenish purple in color. Dried basil retains the dark green color.	Basil can be found fresh or dried.	Health Food Store Grocery Store Grows wild	Sweet Basil Tea

NAME	DESCRIPTION	PRIMARY USES	SECONDARY USES
BAY LEAF *Laurus nobilis*	Bay leaves, a symbol of the gods of ancient Greece and Rome, are an indispensable kitchen herb. Bay laurel grows wild in California and the Mediterranean region.	Bay leaf tea is good for soothing and cleansing the digestive tract. As a wash, bay is astringent and can be used on the skin to heal boils and eruptions.	Bay oil, pressed from the leaves and berries, is used in salves for bruises and muscle aches. Bay leaf poultice can be applied to the chest for colds.
BEESWAX	Beeswax is used as a medium for ointments and salves, as well as in home canning and candlemaking.	Beeswax makes a good solidifier for herbal ointments and salves and has minor protective qualities for the skin.	Beeswax can be used as a base in scented pomanders and candles.
BLACK CURRANT *Ribes nigrum*	Black currants are used to make liqueur, jam, jelly, and syrup. Black currant is a popular garden herb that also grows wild in temperate zones.	Black currant syrup is a good-tasting vitamin supplemenp, high in vitamin C and iron, it. Mixed with cold water or soda, it reduces fever and helps relieve water retention.	Black currant juice or tea can be used as a mouthwash for bleeding or inflamed gums.
BORAGE *Borago officinalis*	Borage is easy to grow and produces beautiful blue flowers, making it a popular garden herb. Borage is also known as bugloss.	Borage tea is used to reduce fever by promoting a sweat. It can be used in tonic formulas to restore strength after a long illness.	Borage can be used to help stimulate the flow of milk in a nursing mother. It was once used in anti-inflammatory and calmative herbal mixtures.
BURDOCK *Arctium lappa*	Burdock is a common roadside weed that derives its name from the stiff burrs found at the top of the stems.	Burdock root is used in a blood-purifying tonic high in trace minerals and iron. Fresh burdock leaves make a good dressing for burns and wash for skin irritations.	Fresh burdock root can be grated raw into salad or cooked and eaten as you would any root vegetable. Burdock root is known as *gobo* in Japanese cuisine.

APPEARANCE	FORMS AVAILABLE	WHERE TO FIND IT	RECIPES
Bay is a small evergreen bush or tree that rarely exceeds 50 feet in height. Bay leaves are leathery, silvery-green, pointed at both ends, and highly aromatic.	Bay leaf can be found fresh or dried.	Health Food Store Grocery Store	Bay Leaf Mouthwash
Raw beeswax is usually deep, golden brown in color. If the beeswax is part of a honeycomb, it will be made up of many evenly spaced cylinders.	Beeswax can be in the form of raw honeycomb or it can be found in jars or formed into blocks for use in candlemaking and home canning.	Health Food Store Pharmacy	Diaper Rash Skin Ointment
Black currant bushes can reach a height of 4 feet. The berries hang down in clusters and are black in color. Dried currants resemble small, round raisins.	Black currants are available dried or as jam, jelly, juice, or syrup.	Health Food Store (dried fruit, syrup) Grocery Store (dried fruit, syrup) Grows wild	Black Currant Syrup
Borage can grow 2 feet high. The leaves are bristly and the flowers are a bright blue. Dried borage is dull gray-green and fuzzy.	Borage can easily be grown in the garden and used fresh, or it is available chopped and dried.	Health Food Store	Borage and Wintergreen Tea
Wild burdock looks like nettles. The fresh root is 1 to 2 inches in diameter and dark brown with a white center. Dried burdock leaves are fuzzy and gray-green in color.	Burdock is available in the wild, as a fresh or dried root, or as dried leaves.	Health Food Store (fresh or dried root, dried leaves) Grocery Store (fresh root) Grows wild	Peppermint and Burdock Bath Sage and Burdock Bath

263

NAME	DESCRIPTION	PRIMARY USES	SECONDARY USES
CAMOMILE *Matricaria chamomilla*	Camomile is cultivated in gardens for its delicate white and yellow flowers. Camomile grows wild in many parts of Europe and the Mediterranean region.	Camomile tea promotes calmness, settles the stomach, and is a mild laxative. As a compress, it reduces inflammation of skin and mucous tissue.	Camomile flowers make a soothing and delicious beverage tea and can be brewed into a bath formula for hemorrhoids or to repair the perineum following childbirth.
CARROT *Daucus carota*	Carrots are cultivated for their root, which can be cooked, juiced, or consumed raw. Wild carrot, or Queen Anne's Lace, grows in empty lots and along roadsides.	Carrots juiced, raw, or cooked can relieve mucous congestion of the gastrointestinal tract. Grated carrot makes a good poultice for ulcers and slow-healing wounds.	Wild carrot seeds are brewed as a remedy for flatulence. Carrots also contain carotene, which the body utilizes in vitamin A production.
CASTOR OIL Derived from the bean of the Castor Bean Plant, *Ricinus communis*	Castor bean plants are cultivated in Mexico. They have a poisonous substance that remains in the seed after the oil is carefully extracted.	Castor oil is used as a strong laxative.	Warmed castor oil can be rubbed on the abdomen to help relieve colic, constipation, and liver congestion.
CATNIP *Nepeta cataria*	Catnip is a member of the mint family and is a longtime home remedy in Europe and North America.	Catnip produces a mild sweat, making it a good fever remedy for children. It is also slightly calmative, and will soothe an upset stomach and relieve intestinal gas.	Catnip tea can be used to reduce acid buildup in the bloodstream and a strong decoction can be used to calm a hysterical child.
CHICKWEED *Stellaria media*	Chickweed is considered a nuisance by gardeners, but it can be used as a delicious salad green and is high in calcium.	Chickweed is useful in ointments for the skin and it can be applied as a fresh poultice for burns and scalds, bug bites, and minor skin irritations.	A strong tea of chickweed is a good laxative for children. In adults, the tea is good for helping to expel mucus from the lungs and sinuses.

APPEARANCE	FORMS AVAILABLE	WHERE TO FIND IT	RECIPES
Camomile grows to 2 feet in height, with spiny, sparse leaves and 1/2-inch diameter white and gold flowers. Dried camomile flowers are a vivid gold color.	Camomile flower buds are available in whole, dried form.	Health Food Store Grocery Store	Camomile Compress Camomile Tea Infant's Calming Herbal Bath
Carrot root is bright yellowish orange, usually reaching a foot in length. Wild carrots have a white, lacy, umbrellalike flower and a thick, inedible, white root.	Carrots are widely available as a fresh root vegetable. Fresh carrot juice is commonly available in specialty stores.	Health Food Store Grocery Store	Carrot Juice
Castor oil is colorless, with a thick, viscous consistency.	Castor oil is available as a prepackaged medicine.	Health Food Store Pharmacy	Hot Castor Oil Rub
Catnip plants grow from 3 to 5 feet high, with fuzzy, dark gray-green leaves and white, purple-spotted flowers. Dried catnip resembles dried oregano.	Catnip is available as a dried herb.	Health Food Store (not pet store)	Catnip Tea
Chickweed is a bright green creeping plant with small white flowers. It grows along roadsides and in empty lots. Dried chickweed looks like dried oregano.	Chickweed is available fresh or dried.	Health Food Store Grows wild	Chickweed and Elecampane Tea Chickweed Ointment Diaper Rash Skin Ointment

NAME	DESCRIPTION	PRIMARY USES	SECONDARY USES
CINNAMON *Cinnamonum zeylanicum*	This delightful herb is used medicinally throughout the world and as a popular flavoring agent for cordials, syrups, and candy.	Cinnamon is a popular remedy for intestinal gas and digestive disorders. It can be used to warm the lungs and intestinal tract after a chill or during a cold.	Cinnamon can be cooked into vegetable oil and applied as a rub to sore muscles. Essential oil of cinnamon can be used as a topical anesthetic.
CLEAVERS *Galium aparine*	Cleavers, known as bedstraw, cheese rent, and gravel grass, was used as a stuffing for mattresses, a curdling agent for milk, and a tea for kidney and gallstones.	Cleavers tea makes an excellent wash for skin irritations of all kinds. In a bath–tea formula, cleavers will help reduce a fever.	Cleavers tea is good for kidney disorders, including kidney stones. It can also be consumed raw in a salad.
CLOVE *Caryophyllus aromaticus*	Cloves are a popular culinary herb used in desserts and for seasoning meat. Cloves were once eaten to restore sexual vigor.	Clove tea helps relieve a sore throat, indigestion, and nausea. Clove oil is a popular painkiller, used mostly in dentistry.	Cloves are frequently used in sachets and pomanders for their highly aromatic scent. Chewing dried cloves can refresh the breath.
COCOA BUTTER Oil extract of the bean of the cacao tree, *Theobroma cacao*	Cocoa butter is a natural vegetable fat from the bean of the cacao tree. After the oil is extracted, the bean is ground into cocoa powder to make chocolate.	Cocoa butter makes an excellent base for herbal ointments and salves, and it has minor demulcent properties.	Cocoa butter is an ingredient in suntan lotions, cosmetics, and lip balms. It is mixed with cocoa powder, chocolate liquor, and sugar to make chocolate bars.
COFFEE *Coffea arabica*	Coffee is a popular herbal beverage consumed throughout the world. Coffee flavoring is used in many confections and desserts.	Coffee promotes the flow of bile into the intestines and is a fast-acting laxative. It contains large amounts of caffeine, which makes it an effective stimulant.	Coffee can stimulate the kidneys and help pass kidney stones. A mild brew of coffee can help relieve intestinal gas and settle the stomach.

APPEARANCE	FORMS AVAILABLE	WHERE TO FIND IT	RECIPES
Cinnamon is an evergreen shrub with dark green leaves, dark red berries, and yellowish white flowers. The inner bark is the medicinal part of the plant.	Cinnamon bark is available in curled sticks, chopped into pieces, and powdered in bulk.	Health Food Store	Hot Toddy
Cleavers is a small, grasslike weed that likes moist places such as stream beds and swamps. Dried cleavers are dark green and usually chopped into small pieces.	Cleavers are available dried and chopped.	Health Food Store	Peppermint and Cleavers Bath
The clove tree is an evergreen, native to the Philippines and the West Indies. Dried cloves, dark brown and about 1/2 inch long, are the tree's dried flower buds.	Dried cloves are available whole or ground.	Health Food Store Grocery Store Pharmacy (clove oil)	Antiseptic Skin Wash Apple Juice and Clove Tea Clove and Peppermint Toothache Remedy Clove Oil Gum Rub
Cocoa butter is golden yellow in color, with a distinctive chocolate smell.	Cocoa butter is available in jars or shaped into bars or sticks. It is sometimes white and odorless, depending on how much it has been processed.	Health Food Store Grocery Store Pharmacy	Diaper Rash Skin Ointment
The coffee plant's bean is 1/2 inch long, oval-shape, and green when fresh, then dark brown and slightly oily in appearance after roasting.	Coffee beans are available dried and roasted, after which they are left whole or ground to a coarse powder for brewing.	Health Food Store Grocery Store	Coffee Sips

THE INGREDIENTS

NAME	DESCRIPTION	PRIMARY USES	SECONDARY USES
COMFREY *Symphytum officinale*	Comfrey grows wild in moist places in the U.S. and Europe. The whole plant can be used — the root for medicine and the leaves for tea or as a fresh salad green.	Comfrey root is used to heal burns, severe rashes, skin eruptions cuts and scrapes. It also helps to heal damaged tendons, broken bones, and severe bruises.	A decoction of comfrey root soothes a sore throat, stops internal bleeding, heals stomach ulcers, and normalizes excessive menstrual flow.
CORN SILK *Zea mays*	Corn silk must be stored in an airtight, lightproof container since many of its properties are volatile. Corn silk contains allantoin, a beneficial substance.	Corn silk is a mild stimulant and diuretic good for treating cystitis, urethritis, and prostatitis. It is also a good herb to use for children's renal disorders.	Fresh squeezed corn oil combats dandruff, cornmeal is a good poultice for skin problems, and cornstarch is an antidote to iodine poisoning.
ELDER FLOWER *Sambucus canadensis*	At least four varieties of elder are used medicinally: sweet elder, black elder, red elder, and dwarf elder. The flower, root, leaves, leaf buds, fruit, and bark are used.	A tea made from the flowers can induce sweating, and it can also be taken to relieve headache and discomfort from colds.	Elder berries are used in jams and pies. Leaf-bud tea is a strong purgative. A wash or ointment made from the bark is good for burns and skin problems.
ELECAMPANE *Inula helenium*	Elecampane grows in the northeastern United States. Its medicinal quality was discovered by Indians and early settlers who noticed their horses seeking it out.	Elecampane tea helps expectorate mucus from the lungs. It also helps reduce inflammation of mucous-lined organs such as the intestines and the urinary tract.	A strong decoction of elecampane will expel worms, and an elecampane skin wash can be used for scabies (microscopic skin parasites).
EPHEDRA *Ephedra nevadensis*	Ephedra is also known as Mormon tea and Brigham weed, because it was used as a cure-all by the pioneer Mormons on their way west.	Ephedra is useful as a decongestant in cases of asthma, and relieves spasmodic coughing. It is also a strong stimulant	Ephedra tea has been used in the past to relieve migraine headaches and to stimulate the liver and kidneys.

APPEARANCE	FORMS AVAILABLE	WHERE TO FIND IT	RECIPES
Comfrey leaves are thick, fleshy, and fuzzy-feeling when touched. The fresh root is dark brown on the outside and stark white on the inside.	Dried comfrey root is available chopped into small pieces or ground into a powder. It can be found in tablet form or as capsules.	Health Food Store Grows wild	Comfrey and Eucalyptus Poultice Comfrey Rinse Diaper Rash Skin Ointment Peppermint and Comfrey Bath
This species of corn is somewhat shorter and stockier than commercial corn, with more variegated kernels. Dried corn silk is dark gold in color.	Corn silk is available dried in bulk.	Health Food Store	Comfrey Root and Corn Silk Tea
Elder trees grow from 5 to 12 feet high. The stems are filled with a light, porous pitch, and the bark is scabby. Elder flowers are white, with a heavy, shrubby odor.	Dried elder flower buds are available in bulk.	Health Food Store Grows wild	Elder Flower and Mint Tea
Elecampane has a thick stem and large yellow flowers. It grows to a height of 5 feet. The dried root is dark brown and usually chopped into small pieces.	Elecampane root is available dried and chopped. It can be found in tablet form and is also powdered and put into capsules.	Health Food Store Grows wild	Chickweed and Elecampane Tea
Ephedra is a small bush with stiff stems and branches. Dried ephedra is hay colored and looks like small, shriveled sticks.	Ephedra is available dried and chopped into 2-inch–long sticks, or it can be found powdered in capsules or formed into tablets.	Health Food Store Grows wild	Ephedra Tea

269

NAME	DESCRIPTION	PRIMARY USES	SECONDARY USES
EUCALYPTUS *Eucalyptus globulus*	Eucalyptus is native to Australia and Tasmania. Eucalyptus trees make a sizable windbreak, and their long, strong roots hold windblown soil together.	Eucalyptus leaves yield a yellowish oil used to combat lung congestion, colds, and sore throats. It is a healthful inhalant for asthma and other respiratory ailments.	A wash made from eucalyptus pods can be used on slow-healing sores, and a tea made from the leaves is good for reducing fever.
EYEBRIGHT *Euphrasia officinalis*	Eyebright is a parasitic plant that grows in deeply shaded woods. It is best used fresh, but is also effective as a tea brewed from the chopped, dried herb.	Eyebright is used to produce a soothing wash for inflamed or running eyes.	None
FENNEL *Foeniculum vulgare*	Fennel is a member of the parsley family and is cultivated in Europe for its sweet-smelling flowers and aromatic seeds. The seeds are a popular culinary herb.	Fennel arouses the appetite, dispels intestinal gas, and relieves abdominal cramps. It is a good colic remedy and used to mask the taste of bitter herbs in teas.	Fennel seeds boiled with barley water make an excellent tea for promoting the flow of breast milk. Fennel syrup is soothing to a sore throat.
GARLIC *Allium sativum*	Garlic is a popular kitchen herb for flavoring soups, sauces, and salad dressings. It is an antibacterial agent and helps lower blood cholesterol levels.	Garlic helps relieve mucus buildup in the respiratory and gastrointestinal systems. It has a beneficial effect on blood circulation and high blood pressure.	Garlic powder is an antiseptic on open wounds. Garlic poultices help expel toxins from the body through the skin. Garlic tincture can eliminate pinworms.
GENTIAN *Gentiana lutea*	Gentian is used to make Angostura Bitters, which lends an aromatic and pungent taste to cocktails. It is also the main ingredient in gentian violet.	Gentian can be used to promote the appetite, relieve indigestion, and reduce fever.	Tincture of gentian is a mild antiseptic, good for canker sores, bleeding gums, and minor cuts and scrapes.

APPEARANCE	FORMS AVAILABLE	WHERE TO FIND IT	RECIPES
The eucalyptus tree is a tall evergreen that can grow to 300 feet or more. The long, spiny leaves are highly aromatic. The tree is covered with peeling, papery bark.	Eucalyptus leaves are available fresh, dried and chopped, or as an oil extract.	Health Food Store Pharmacy (oil) Grows wild	Comfrey and Eucalyptus Poultice Eucalyptus and Wintergreen Bath Eucalyptus Oil Rub Flannel Muffler Wrap Head Lice Hair Oil
Eyebright is a waxy yellow, parasitic plant that grows on decaying wood and vegetable matter. Dried eyebright is yellow and has a crisp texture.	Eyebright is available chopped and dried. It can also be found as a tincture.	Health Food Store	Eyebright Eyewash
Fennel is a brushy, light green plant that grows 4 to 6 feet high. Its stem looks like bamboo. Fennel seeds are gray-green and approximately 1/4 inch long.	Fennel seeds are available in bulk. Fennel root is also used medicinally and can be found chopped and dried.	Health Food Store Grows wild	Fennel and Orange Peel Tea
Garlic is a white bulb, or head, consisting of individual cloves. Garlic bulbs can vary in size, usually from 3 to as big as 8 inches in diameter.	Garlic can be found fresh, dried in flakes or pieces, powdered in capsules or in bulk, or pressed into tablets. Garlic oil can be found in bulk or in gelatin capsules.	Health Food Store Grocery Store	Garlic Oil Ear Drops Garlic Syrup
Gentian grows well at high altitudes; it has gray-green, oval leaves and yellow or violet, star-shaped flowers. Dried gentian root is dark brown.	Gentian root is available as a tincture, dried, or powdered.	Health Food Store Pharmacy (tincture)	Angostura Soda Herbal Ice Cubes

NAME	DESCRIPTION	PRIMARY USES	SECONDARY USES
GINGER *Zingiber officinale*	Ginger has been cultivated for centuries. It came originally from China and India, and is a popular medicinal and culinary herb.	Ginger is a mild stimulant that warms the lungs and gastrointestinal tract. It dispels intestinal gas and brings on a sweat when eaten in large quantities.	Ginger tea can be drunk to promote suppressed menstruation. When raw ginger root is chewed, it can soothe a sore throat.
GOLDENSEAL *Hydrastis canadensis*	Goldenseal root, along with corn and tobacco, was among the first gifts given to the Pilgrims by Native Americans of the northeastern United States.	Goldenseal tea is an antiseptic wash for skin irritations. It relieves stomach ailments and sinus and lung congestion. It is also considered a liver stimulant.	Goldenseal can be used as a snuff to relieve a running nose and, taken in small doses, can allay nausea during pregnancy.
HORSETAIL *Equisetum arvense*	Horsetail forms crystals of silica on the cell walls of the stems and branches as they dry. Horsetail was also known as scouring rush and was used to scrub pewter.	Horsetail is excellent for healing wounds and skin conditions. In tea or tablet form, it is soothing and regenerating to the kidneys and bladder.	Horsetail tea can be drunk to relieve chilling and poor circulation in the hands and feet.
JASMINE *Jasminum officinale*	Jasmine flowers are an attractive and delightful-smelling addition to potpourris. Jasmine is native to India and Asia, and is cultivated in parts of United States.	Jasmine flowers have a strong, sweet scent that calms the nerves when inhaled. The scent relieves insomnia and has been used to facilitate childbirth.	Jasmine flowers are used to produce jasmine oil, which is often combined with olive or peanut oil for massage oil. In India, they are used in snakebite treatments.
LAVENDER *Lavendula officinalis*	Lavender is a very popular garden herb. It is cultivated in the United States and Europe for its highly scented flowers, which are used in perfumery.	Lavender oil or tea can be used as a sedative, to help relieve migraine headaches, indigestion, and stomach and liver problems.	Lavender tea makes a mildly antiseptic skin wash when used in a bath. Lavender flowers can be used in herbal pillows to facilitate sleep.

APPEARANCE	FORMS AVAILABLE	WHERE TO FIND IT	RECIPES
The ginger plant has narrow, lance-shape leaves and purple flowers with yellow spots. Dried ginger root is tan in color, with a thick, gnarly texture.	Ginger is available as a fresh or dried root, chopped root pieces, or powdered in bulk.	Health Food Store Grocery Store (fresh root)	Hot Toddy
Goldenseal is a small plant with 5-pointed leaves; a knobby, red flower; and a thick, yellow root. The dried, powdered root is deep golden-yellow in color.	Goldenseal is available powdered in bulk, in capsules, and in tablet form.	Health Food Store	Diaper Rash Skin Ointment Goldenseal and White Rice Porridge
Horsetail looks fernlike, with a brushy, horsetail shape to the whole plant. The plant is light gray-green and produces no flowers.	Horsetail is available chopped and dried.	Health Food Store Grows wild	Calcium Tea
Jasmine is a vinelike plant with dark green, lance-shape leaves and lovely, sweet-smelling white flowers. Dried jasmine flowers are faded white in color.	Whole, dried jasmine flowers are available in bulk.	Health Food Store (whole flowers and natural bath salts)	Jasmine Bath
Lavender has gray-green leaves and lilac-colored flowers, and grows to 2 feet in height. Dried lavender buds are the size of barley grains, with a dark purple color.	Lavender flower buds are available dried or as an oil extract.	Health Food Store	Antiseptic Skin Wash Herbal Pillow Infant's Calming Herbal Bath

NAME	DESCRIPTION	PRIMARY USES	SECONDARY USES
LEMON GRASS *Cymbopogon citratus*	Lemon grass originated in India and makes a delightful lemon-flavored tea.	Lemon grass is a good additive to almost any herbal tea because of its sweet lemony taste. It is used cosmetically in facial preparations and hair rinses.	Lemon grass is frequently used in Southeast Asian cuisine. Lemon grass yields an essential oil, citral, which is used in scents and perfumes.
LICORICE *Glycyrrhiza glabra*	Licorice root was a popular cure-all in ancient Egypt and China. It is sweeter than sugarcane and can be mixed with herbal remedies to make them more palatable.	Licorice tea is good for mucus congestion of the lungs and sinuses. It helps hoarse throats, gastric ulcers, bladder inflammation, and kidney ailments.	Licorice can be used to regulate the menstrual cycle and relieve inflammation of the prostate gland. Licorice tea is a good-tasting, mild laxative for children.
MARIGOLD *Calendula officinalis*	Marigold is a common garden plant with brilliant orange-gold flower petals. Some varieties have a sweet scent, while others smell distinctly unpleasant.	Marigold flowers are used in ointments, washes, and salves as an antiseptic ingredient. Marigold tea reduces fever and helps the body fight infection in wounds.	Marigold ointment can also be used for sprains and pulled muscles. Marigold hair rinse brings out golden highlights in blondes.
MARSHMALLOW *Althaea officinalis*	The marshmallow plant derives its name from its favorite habitats, which are moist, swampy lowlands, marshes, and roadside ditches.	Marshmallow, high in calcium, relieves sore throats and urinary tract inflammations. As a wash, marshmallow tea soothes itching skin.	Marshmallow tea increases the flow of milk in nursing mothers. A rinse of marshmallow rubbed into the scalp was once believed to reduce hair loss.
MYRRH *Commiphora myrrha*	Myrrh was once vigorously traded in the Middle East. When Dias discovered the Cape of Good Hope in 1486, myrrh was transported to the Western world.	Myrrh, found in some incense and perfumes, is used to treat external wounds, to strengthen bleeding gums, and to relieve coughs, asthma, and other chest problems.	Myrrh powder can be rubbed into sores and wounds as a disinfectant. Myrrh in solution can be used as a douche.

APPEARANCE	FORMS AVAILABLE	WHERE TO FIND IT	RECIPES
Lemon grass resembles rushes, and grows in hot, moist climates. Dried lemon grass looks like cut, flat grass stalks and is usually a silvery-yellow color.	Lemon grass is available chopped and dried.	Health Food Store	Red Clover and Lemon Grass Tea
Licorice is a woody plant with dark green, oval-shape leaves. Its flowers vary from purple to yellow. Dried licorice root resembles small, straight sticks.	Dried licorice root is available in sticklike pieces or chopped.	Health Food Store	Licorice Lollipops Licorice Tea
Marigolds have fuzzy, stiff stems and long, slightly limp leaves. The flower has many small orange-gold petals.	Marigold can be found as a dried flower bud.	Health Food Store Grows wild (gardens)	Rosemary and Marigold Wash
Marshmallow can grow to 3 feet in height, with wide, dark green leaves and a beautiful white, five-petal flower. Dried marshmallow is dark green.	Marshmallow leaves and stems are available chopped and dried.	Health Food Store	Diaper Rash Skin Ointment Marshmallow Tea
Myrrh can be packaged as a powder, in irregular shaped chunks, or in tear-shape pieces. It varies in color from light yellow to dark reddish brown.	Myrrh is available as a powder or dried in chunks and tear-shape pieces.	Health Food Store	Myrrh Mouthwash

NAME	DESCRIPTION	PRIMARY USES	SECONDARY USES
NUTMEG *Myristica fragrans*	Nutmeg is grown as a culinary herb and an ingredient in perfumes and potpourris. The membrane surrounding the nutmeg kernel is ground to produce the spice mace.	Nutmeg tea can settle an upset stomach and improve appetite. This tea can also improve the body's ability to absorb nutrients.	Cooking ground nutmeg in oil produces a soothing rub for rheumatism and arthritis.
OAK BARK *Quercus alba*	Oak bark, specifically white oak bark, comes from a native North American oak tree that grows along the eastern seaboard and inland as far west as Texas.	Oak bark tea makes an astringent wash that reduces swelling of hemorrhoids and varicose veins. Taken internally, the tea helps relieve diarrhea and reduce fever.	Oak bark can be ground to a powder and snuffed into the nose to relieve mucous congestion and nosebleeds.
OAT BERRIES *Avena sativa*	Oats have been an important food for centuries. Oatmeal is a favorite dish in Scotland, and, because it is easily digested, it is a nutritional food for convalescents.	Oat berries can be made into a cereal to treat gastroenteritis and dyspepsia. A wash made from the brewed berries is good for skin diseases and dry, flaky skin.	Oat berry extract and tincture were once used as a tonic for nervous conditions.
OAT STRAW *Avena sativa*	Oat straw is a healthful by-product of oat berry processing, along with oat flowers, which are used in a homeopathic remedy.	Oat straw tea is indicated for broken bones or other musculo-skeletal damage, since it is very high in calcium. It is also used to treat kidney disorders.	Oat straw tea bath helps relieve muscle tension and fatigue, and is rejuvenating for the skin.
ONION *Allium cepa*	Onions are high in vitamin C and are a valuable food crop. There are a number of varieties of onion, and many of them are found in the wild.	Onions make an excellent cough syrup, since they help expel mucus from the body. They will also draw out infection from the ear or a wound.	Raw onion consumed in small amounts relieves indigestion, heartburn, and flatulence.

APPEARANCE	FORMS AVAILABLE	WHERE TO FIND IT	RECIPES
Nutmeg is a tropical evergreen whose fruit is the nutmeg kernel. Whole nutmegs are oval-shape, dark brown, and look veiny. Ground nutmeg is brownish yellow.	Nutmeg is available whole or ground.	Health Food Store Grocery Store	Nutmeg Milk
Oak trees can grow to 150 feet in height, with large, lobed leaves. The oak seed, or acorn, can be leached, ground, and used as food. Dried oak bark is dull yellow.	Oak bark is available chopped into pieces or powdered in bulk or in capsules.	Health Food Store Grows wild	Oak Bark Snuff
The oat plant is a grass that grows from 2 to 4 feet high. Oat berries are its long and narrow fruit. Dried oat berries are dark golden-brown in color.	Dried oat berries are available unhulled, rolled, chopped into small pieces, or ground to a powder.	Health Food Store Grocery Store Pharmacy (powder)	Skin Food Bath
The oat plant is a grass with a hollow stem, which grows from 2 to 4 feet high. Dried oat grass is pale yellow and resembles straw, hence the name, oat straw.	Oat straw is available chopped and dried.	Health Food Store	Calcium Tea
The most common varieties of onion are white or yellow, round, squat bulbs consisting of layers. The bulbs can reach 8 inches in diameter.	Onions are available fresh, dried and flaked, or ground to a powder.	Health Food Store Grocery Store Grows wild	Colic Tea Onion Syrup

NAME	DESCRIPTION	PRIMARY USES	SECONDARY USES
ORANGE PEEL *Citrus aurantium*	Sweet oranges are the delicious fruits made into juice or eaten straight. The oil of bitter, or Seville, orange flowers is a strong sedative when inhaled.	Sweet orange peel tea is helpful for expelling intestinal gas and settling the stomach.	Sweet orange blossoms can be used to scent potpourris and sachets. A tea made from the blossoms is a mild stimulant.
PENNYROYAL *Hedeoma pulegioides*	Pennyroyal, also known as squaw mint and squaw balm, was used by Native Americans for women's complaints. Pennyroyal oil is a potent insecticide.	Pennyroyal leaf tea is excellent for bringing out a cold by inducing a sweat. It also helps regulate the menstrual cycle and relieve menstrual cramps.	Pennyroyal tea can be used as a wash on itchy or inflamed skin. Oil of pennyroyal is useful for ridding the hair of lice and fleas.
PEPPERMINT *Mentha piperita*	Peppermint is a popular flavor for gum, toothpaste, and cordials. It is used as a culinary herb in hot countries because of its cooling effect on the body.	Peppermint tea helps relieve gas pain, upset stomach, and nausea. A strong brew of peppermint tea reduces fever and relieves mild headaches.	Peppermint oil is used in herbal inhalants to clear blocked sinuses. Diluted and rubbed on the body, it relieves joint pain and itching skin.
PLANTAIN *Plantago lanceolata* and *Plantago major*	Two common varieties of plantain, lance-leaf (*Plantago lanceolata*) and broad-leaf (*Plantago major*), grow in temperate climates. Both have similar uses.	Plantain poultice or wash is used to treat burns and skin irritations. Plantain tea relieves gastrointestinal problems and lung and sinus congestion.	Plantain, soothing to mucous-lined surfaces, is a good ingredient in douche formulas. Juice from fresh leaves can be used to rid the body of intestinal parasites.
POTATO *Solanum tuberosum*	Potatoes are high in nutrients such as potassium and phosphorus. They are found in both humble and grand kitchens throughout the Western Hemisphere.	Potatoes are a healthful food, especially when the peel is consumed. A poultice of raw potato is good for ridding the skin of warts.	Potato juice taken internally will help alkalize the blood. The juice can also be washed on the face to combat acne.

278

APPEARANCE	FORMS AVAILABLE	WHERE TO FIND IT	RECIPES
Orange trees are evergreens that can reach a height of 30 feet and have very fragrant white flowers. Dried orange peel is dull yellowish orange in color.	Sweet orange peel is available fresh, or chopped and dried.	Health Food Store Grocery Store (not recommended for herbal use)	Fennel and Orange Peel Tea
Pennyroyal has small, numerous leaves and purple flowers. The whole plant has an aromatic smell. Dried pennyroyal is light green in color, with a strong, minty smell.	Pennyroyal is available chopped and dried or as an oil extract.	Health Food Store Pharmacy (oil)	Head Congestion Facial Head Lice Hair Oil Pennyroyal Bath Pennyroyal Tea
Peppermint is a creeping plant with dark green, sharply pointed, serrated leaves. Its dried leaves are light green in color, with a strong mint odor.	Peppermint is available dried, fresh, or as an oil extract.	Health Food Store Grocery Store Pharmacy (oil) Grows wild	Antiseptic Skin Wash Elder Flower and Mint Tea Herbal Ice Cubes Peppermint and Red Raspberry Syrup Rosemary and Mint Bath
Plantain is a common roadside weed that has a spiky blossom stalk with greenish white flowers at the tip. Dried plantain is dark green, with a mild, musty smell.	Plantain is available fresh or dried.	Health Food Store Grows wild	Plantain Poultice Plantain Syrup Plaintain Wash
Potatoes are knobby, oval-shaped, earth-colored tubers, approximately 5 inches in length. Their interior is creamy white.	Potatoes are available fresh.	Health Food Store Grocery Store Pharmacy Grows wild	Potato Poultice

NAME	DESCRIPTION	PRIMARY USES	SECONDARY USES
RASPBERRY *Rubus idaeus*	Raspberries are a tasty treat growing along roadsides and fields. The leaves and berries are easy to harvest as long as you watch out for thorns, poison oak, and poison ivy.	Red raspberry leaf tea relieves diarrhea and mild nausea. Pregnant women use it to relieve morning sickness and lessen discomfort during labor.	Red raspberries are delicious to eat and act as a mild laxative.
RED CLOVER *Trifolium pratense*	Red clover grows commonly in meadows throughout the United States and Europe. It is cultivated extensively in this country as a forage crop.	Red clover is used as an ingredient in many different blood-purifying formulas. Its action is mild, making it an excellent herb for children.	Red clover drunk as a tea or used as a poultice relieves childhood eczema and psoriasis. The poultice can also be used to relieve athlete's foot.
ROSE Rosa spp.	There are over 100 varieties of rose throughout the Northern Hemisphere. Red roses that are Hybrid Perpetuals are considered the best to use medicinally.	Roses are a good astringent ingredient in washes, oils, and ointments. Rosehips make a sour tea that stimulates appetite and allays nausea in pregnancy.	The flower petals of the rose plant can be made into a conserve and then eaten to allay colds, cough, lung problems, and inflammations of the bladder.
ROSEMARY *Rosmarinus officinalis*	The rosemary plant contains volatile oils that are used pharmaceutically. The leaves of young shoots are a popular herb for soups, stews, and sauces.	Rosemary tea relieves fatigue, indigestion, and nervous disorders and normalizes low blood pressure. As a wash or bath, it is astringent and helps relax the muscles.	Rosemary oil is used as an inhalant for head and lung congestion and as an ingredient in insect repellents.
SAGE *Salvia officinalis*	Sage is a popular kitchen herb. The strong flavor of sage leaves was used historically to mask the smell and taste of tainted meat.	Sage leaves prepared as a wash can relieve itching skin and excessive perspiration. Sage tea can relieve mild diarrhea and upset stomach.	Sage tea can be consumed by nursing mothers who wish to stop the flow of milk when weaning a child.

APPEARANCE	FORMS AVAILABLE	WHERE TO FIND IT	RECIPES
Red raspberry bushes usually form a thicket. The fruit is bright red when ripe and the leaves are small and silvery-green in color. Dried raspberry leaves are a dull gray-green.	Raspberry leaves are available fresh, dried, or powdered. Red raspberries are available fresh in season.	Health Food Store Grows wild	Peppermint and Red Raspberry Syrup Red Raspberry Leaf Tea
Red clover can grow to 2 feet in height. The leaves are usually a solid dark green, but can have white spots. The flowers vary in color from magenta to nearly white.	Red clover is available dried in bulk. It is also a popular ingredient in many herbal beverage tea products.	Health Food Store	Red Clover and Lemon Grass Tea
Wild roses are smaller and thornier than garden varieties, with yellow anthers in the center of the flower. Dried rose buds and petals are red or pink and withered looking.	Dried rose petals and buds are available in bulk.	Health Food Store Grows wild	Almond Oil Rub Herbal Pillow
Rosemary is a woody, evergreen shrub that can grow to 6 feet tall in hot climates. Its leaves are dark green and pointed. Rosemary has a camphorlike smell.	Rosemary can be found fresh, dried, or as an essential oil extract.	Health Food Store Grocery Store Grows wild	Head Congestion Facial Head Lice Hair Oil Rosemary and Peppermint Bath Rosemary and Wintergreen Oil Rub Rosemary Tea
Sage is a common garden plant with silver-green leaves covered with downy fuzz. Dried sage leaves are dark gray-green and very aromatic.	Sage is available fresh, chopped and dried, or powdered.	Health Food Store Grocery Store Grows wild	Sage and Burdock Bath Sage Bath

NAME	DESCRIPTION	PRIMARY USES	SECONDARY USES
SARSAPARILLA *Smilax officinalis*	Sarsaparilla tea was a favorite tonic and beverage of the Old West. Sarsaparilla has a plant hormone called sarsapogenin that is used to produce synthetic steroids.	Sarsaparilla root tea relieves the fever and congestion from colds. A strong decoction of sarsaparilla is a good blood detoxifier and induces a mild sweat.	Sarsaparilla root was the main ingredient in root beer until synthetic flavoring was developed. Sarsaparilla should be used only intermittently.
SLIPPERY ELM *Ulmus fulva*	Slippery elm is the dried and powdered inner bark of young elm trees. When it is boiled, it releases mucilage, making a slippery, gellike pablum.	Slippery elm is easy to digest, soothes the gastrointestinal tract, and relieves diarrhea. As a powder or paste applied to rashes and minor wounds, it promotes healing.	Slippery elm tea makes a good gargle for sore throats.
THYME *Thymus vulgaris*	Thyme is cultivated throughout the United States and Europe as a culinary herb. Its glossy leaves and spicy odor make it a delightful addition to your garden.	Thyme is used in ointments and salves for chest congestion and infected wounds. As a tea, it relieves coughs, sore throats, laryngitis, and digestive problems.	Diluted thyme tea can be used to relieve diarrhea in children. The aroma of thyme leaves has been used, upon inhalation, to relieve melancholy and depression.
TOBACCO *Nicotiana tabacum*	Tobacco is a small, leafy shrub, native to America. Native Americans smoked its leaves as a ritual of friendly alliance between neighboring tribes and settlers.	A tobacco poultice draws out boils and venom from snake and insect bites, and promote the healing of bedsores.	When smoked infrequently, tobacco can relieve fatigue and calm the nerves.
VALERIAN *Valeriana officinalis*	Valerian root contains a rich supply of the volatile healing oil, which is why it must never be boiled. It is used in tinctures or in powder form.	Valerian calms nervousness and anxiety, soothes chronic stomach and intestinal upsets, and is especially useful for calming people with heart conditions.	Valerian root is excellent for relieving menstrual cramps and for promoting delayed menses.

APPEARANCE	FORMS AVAILABLE	WHERE TO FIND IT	RECIPES
Sarsaparilla is a climbing vine with heart-shape, shiny leaves and small red berries. Dried sarsaparilla root is dull yellow, with a strong, sweet smell.	Sarsaparilla root is available dried and chopped.	Health Food Store	Sarsaparilla Syrup
Elm trees can grow to 50 feet or more. Their outer bark is dark brown and their inner bark is white. Powdered slippery elm bark is beige-pink in color.	Slippery elm bark is available in whole pieces, powdered, or shaped into tablets.	Health Food Store Grows wild	Slippery Elm and Comfrey Sprinkle Slippery Elm and White Rice Pablum Slippery Elm Ointment Slippery Elm Paste
Thyme is a small, shrubby plant with many down-covered stems. It grows from 6 to 12 in height and produces small, clustered bluish purple flowers.	Thyme is available fresh or chopped and dried.	Health Food Store (fresh in season or dried — organic) Grocery Store (fresh in season or dried — commercial)	Herbal Pillow
Tobacco plants grow to about 2 feet in height, with long, broad, dark green leaves. Cured tobacco is a dark, rusty-brown color, with a pleasant, bittersweet smell.	Tobacco is available cured, dried, and chopped in pouches, or rolled as cigarettes or cigars. It is also powdered and sold as snuff or dried into plugs for chewing.	Grocery Store Pharmacy	Tobacco Poultice
Valerian grows to 4 feet in height, with many small, pointed leaves and white or pink clusters of flowers. Powdered valerian root is a yellowish-gray color.	Valerian root is available in tablets, powdered into capsules, or in bulk.	Health Food Store Grows wild	Valerian Root Tincture

283

NAME	DESCRIPTION	PRIMARY USES	SECONDARY USES
WATERCRESS *Nasturtium officinale*	Watercress is a delightful aquatic plant that was introduced into the United States from Europe. It has a zippy, pungent flavor.	Watercress contains important nutrients. It is a tonic and mild alterative. Taken as a tea, it is a mild diuretic and may help break up kidney and bladder stones.	Watercress juice applied directly to the skin can rid the body of some types of fungus.
WHITE WILLOW BARK *Salix alba*	Willow bark has been used to reduce pain and inflammation for over 2000 years. Willow trees were planted in the Old West for decoration and shade.	Willow bark taken as a tea reduces the pain and swelling of rheumatism and arthritis, relieves headache, reduces fever, and helps slow internal bleeding.	Willow bark used as a wash relieves the soreness of burns and minor wounds and reduces the swelling of hemorrhoids. It makes a good foot bath for swollen feet.
WINTERGREEN *Gaultheria procumbens*	This hardy shrub grows as far north as Manitoba and Newfoundland, giving wintergreen one of its folk names, Canada tea.	Wintergreen tea relieves headches, arthritis pain, and gastrointestinal disorders. It can also be used as a gargle for sore throat and as a douche.	Diluted wintergreen oil rubbed on strained muscles or inflamed joints relieves pain and swelling. Wintergreen leaf poultices soothe and heal irritated skin.
WITCH HAZEL *Hamamelis viginiana*	Young hazel shoots were traditionally used as divining rods for finding underground water supplies, which is why this hazel is called "witch."	Witch hazel bark tea relieves diarrhea. As a wash, it stops insect bite, poison oak, and poison ivy itch; soothes sunburn; and relieves the pain and swelling of bruises.	Witch hazel bark wash is good for relieving eye inflammation. When used in a sitz bath, it reduces hemorrhoidal swelling and itching.
WORMWOOD *Artemesia absinthium*	Wormwood tea was once consumed as an aid for interpreting dreams. Oil of wormwood, anise oil, and alcohol were combined to produce absinthe.	Wormwood tea is used to increase the appetite; stimulate the liver, gallbladder, and pancreas; expel intestinal worms; and calm the nerves.	Dried and chopped wormwood can be stuffed into a pet's pillow or bed cushion to keep it free of fleas.

APPEARANCE	FORMS AVAILABLE	WHERE TO FIND IT	RECIPES
Watercress grows wherever clear, cold water flows — ditches, streams, and small rivers. Its fleshy, oblong leaves and small, white flowers grow above the water.	Young watercress shoots are seasonally available fresh.	Health Food Store (organic) Grocery Store (commercial) Grows wild	Watercress Salad
Willow trees can grow to a height of 75 feet, with long, pointy, silvery-green leaves and flexible branches that hang down. Dried willow bark is dark brown and odorless.	Willow bark is available dried and chopped into pieces, powdered in bulk or in capsules, or in tablet form.	Health Food Store Pharmacy (tablet form) Grows wild	Willow Bark Tea
Wintergreen is a creeping shrub with leathery, dark green leaves, white flowers, and red berries. Dried wintergreen is brownish green in color.	Wintergreen is available chopped and dried or as an oil extract.	Health Food Store Pharmacy (oil)	Comfrey and Wintergreen Poultice Eucalyptus and Wintergreen Bath Head Congestion Facial Wintergreen Tea
Witch hazel is a small, gnarly tree that yields edible nuts. Dried witch hazel bark is dark brown in color.	Witch hazel bark is available chopped and dried.	Health Food Store Pharmacy (fluid extract)	Antiseptic Skin Wash Witch Hazel Fomentation
Wormwood is a small, weedlike plant with silky, fine, gray-green leaves and stems. Dried wormwood looks like cut, dried grass and has a pungent smell.	Wormwood is available dried and chopped.	Health Food Store	Wormwood Tea

INDEX